Transnational Multi-Stakeholder Standardization

Transnational Multi-Stakeholder Standardization

Organizing Fragile Non-State Authority

Kristina Tamm Hallström

Associate Professor in Management, Stockholm Centre for Organizational Research and Lecturer, Stockholm School of Economics, Sweden

Magnus Boström

Associate Professor in Sociology and Environmental Lecturer, Department of Life Sciences, Södertörn University College, Sweden

Edward Elgar

Cheltenham, UK • Northampton, MA, USA

Published by
Edward Elgar Publishing Limited
The Lypiatts
15 Lansdown Road
Cheltenham
Glos GL50 2JA
UK

Edward Elgar Publishing, Inc.
William Pratt House
9 Dewey Court
Northampton
Massachusetts 01060
USA

A catalogue record for this book
is available from the British Library

Library of Congress Control Number: 2009937751

ISBN 978 1 84542 904 1

Printed and bound by MPG Books Group Ltd, UK

Contents

Acknowledgements

The topic of this book intrigues us. While we have been examining and discussing transnational governance in the making, our interest continues to increase. We are grateful that we have had the opportunity to (hopefully) shed some light on a few important aspects of a rapidly changing global order. The good cooperation and complementary thinking between us two authors have indeed constituted a driving force for our thinking and writing. We have different disciplinary backgrounds: management and sociology. However, such labels are just labels. Good theory has no disciplinary limits, and consequently we share a strong interest in the topic of power, legitimacy, multi-stakeholder work, and organizational processes. We are also convinced that good research follows a genuine interest in the actual phenomenon scrutinized.

We have been highly inspired by our case studies and the large number of practitioners involved in the FSC, MSC and ISO, who generously accepted to be interviewed and observed for our purposes. Of course, this research would not have been possible without the three years of funding from the Swedish Research Council for our joint project *Organizing private authority – hidden power struggles in standard setting*. The Swedish Research Council has also provided financial support for the language editing of this book, conducted by language editor Nina Colwill who did a tremendous job in making our arguments both understandable and sharper.

The multidisciplinary research environment of the Stockholm Centre for Organizational Research (Score) has been particularly stimulating and fruitful, as the group of management scholars (F-section) affiliated to Score. Several scholars from Södertörn University, where one of the authors has been researching and teaching the last couple of years, has also contributed with good perspectives and stimulating discussions.

There are a number of individuals to whom we wish to give special thanks for their critical and highly constructive comments on earlier versions of the manscript, in alphabetical order: Andrea Mennicken, Bengt Jacobsson, Catrin Andersson, Ebba Sjögren, Göran Ahrne, Göran Sundström, John Meyer, Linda Soneryd, Liv Fries, Matilda Dahl, Nils Brunsson, Sebastian Botzem, Susanna Alexius, Winton Higgins, and Yvette Taminiau. With a grant from the Bank of Sweden Tercentenary Foundation, in 2008, we were able to organize a small workshop in Rönninge, Sweden, on the topic of transnational governance. With the help of the knowledgeable and generous workshop participants – Andrea, Winton, Matilda, Bengt, Sebastian, Yvette, and Göran A – we considerably advanced our analysis of the legitimacy challenges and power struggles within the FSC, MSC and ISO. Furthermore, we wish to thank Coline Ruwet who at an early stage directed our attention to the problematics of stakeholder categorizations, and Christina Garsten for inviting one of us to a field trip to New York in 2007 within the project *Social affairs,* funded by the Bank of Sweden Tercentenary Foundation. The *Missing Pillar* research project, funded by the Swedish Research Council for Environment, Agriculatural Sciences, and Spatial Planning, covered the costs of some of the FSC interviews and analyses. A special thanks to research assistants Ida Seing and Sara Söderström for conducting most of the MSC and FSC interviews, and for their constructive feedback. We are also grateful to Ann Loftsjö at Score for the help with accounting and reporting.

Finally, we wish to thank our families for endless support and inspiration, including Daniel's invaluable formatting work. And special thoughts go to our children: Celine, Marvin, Dennis, Isak, Ivar, and Arvid.

Kristina Tamm Hallström and Magnus Boström
Stockholm, October 2009

Tables

Abbreviations

ANSI	American National Standards Institute
ASI	Accreditation Services International
BSI	British Standards Institution
CI	Consumers International
COPOLCO	Consumer Policy Committee
CSR	Corporate Social Responsibility
DC	Developed Country
EC	European Commission
FAO	Food and Agricultural Organization of the United Nations
FLO	Fairtrade Labelling Organizations International
FoE	Friends of the Earth
FSC	Forest Stewardship Council
GRI	Global Reporting Initiative
ICC	International Chamber of Commerce
ICSF	International Collective in Support of Fishworkers
IFOAM	International Federation of Organic Agriculture Movements
IGO	International Governmental Organization
ILO	International Labour Organization
IMF	International Monetary Fund
INGO	International Nongovernmental Organization
IO	International Organization
IOE	International Organization of Employers
ISEAL	Alliance International Social and Environmental Accrediting and Labelling Alliance
ISO	International Organization for Standardization
ISO 65	ISO standard on general requirements for bodies operating product certification systems
ISO 9000	The ISO standard series on quality assurance and quality management
ISO 14000	The ISO standard series on environmental management
ISO 14001	Certification standard of the ISO 14000 series on environmental management
ISO 26000	The (future) ISO standard on social responsibility
ITTO	International Tropical Timber Organization

ITUC	International Trade Union Confederation
IUCN	World Conservation Union
MAC	Marine Aquarium Council
MoU	Memorandum of Understanding
MSC	Marine Stewardship Council
NGO	Nongovernmental Organization
NSB	National Standards Body
OECD	Organisation for Economic Co-operation and Development
OHS	Occupational Health and Safety
PEFC	Programme for the Endorsement of Forest Certification schemes
SAI	Social Accountability International
SIDA	Swedish International Development Agency Swedish Standards Institute (SIS)
SLIMF	Small and Low Intensity Management Forest
SMO	Social Movement Organization
SR	Social Responsibility
SSRO	The stakeholder group Service, Support, Research and Others
TNC	Transnational Corporation
UN	United Nations
UNSCC	United Nations Standards Coordinating Committee
WHO	World Health Organization
WTO	World Trade Organization
WWF	World Wide Fund for Nature (In North America: World Wildlife Fund)

1. Organizing Transnational Multi-Stakeholder Standard Setting

TRANSNATIONAL NON-STATE AUTHORITY AS A SOLUTION

A new concern is increasingly penetrating many aspects of our lives. When going to a favourite shop to buy an attractive shirt, it has always been reasonable to think about price, durability, fashion, and fit. Until recently, those were our only concerns. It is increasingly difficult, however, to ignore the suspicion that a ten-year-old Vietnamese girl may have sewn the shirt.

There are numerous examples of our newfound reflection upon situations occurring at great distances. We see a documentary about the sweatshop conditions facing a large number of factory workers in a poor country or about Pakistani children producing hand-made carpets. We hear a reporter commenting on a mobile phone video clip of a rainforest landscape about to be destroyed – an eye-opener to new perspectives and new concerns. Do the employers of these workers comply with the United Nations (UN) Declaration of Human Rights? Do the companies follow the requirements of the International Labour Organization's (ILO) core labour standards for these workers? Have the managers considered if their practices can be justified under the principles of sustainable development?

These concerns are signs of the economic, political, and cultural globalization that constitutes an essential background to the topic we discuss in this book. We live in a context of *economic globalization*, in which the economic power, actions, and impact of transnational corporations drastically increase worldwide as they gradually become disentangled from the borders and regulatory frameworks of the nation state. *Political globalization* responds to economic globalization, but not in the form of world government. Rather, we note the emergence of a large variety of political mobilizations and activities initiated by such intergovernmental organizations as the UN Global Compact or by such lifestyle- and consumer-oriented transnational social movements as the Friends of the Earth. *Cultural globalization* provides common frames, understandings, and identities. Most people in most countries are learning to frame problems in terms of human rights,

1

sustainable development, or environmental justice. Although it is wise to acknowledge that such concerns do not appear everywhere in the world – there is certainly a Northern-Western bias – some would argue that the development of a rationalized culture of natural and moral law, originating in the West, has been globalized to an astonishing degree in the period following World War II:

> [A] surprising feature of the modern system is how completely the Western models dominate world discourse about the rights of individuals, the responsibilities and sovereignty of the state, and the nature of preferred organizational forms (Meyer and Jepperson, 2000, p. 106).

We are particularly interested in the consequences of these economic, political and cultural developments for rule-setting activities. Many commentators would argue that the type of sustainability concerns discussed here especially call for the establishment of political and regulatory frameworks that stretch beyond the territorial, national-state order of things. In his book, *Power in the Global Age*, Ulrich Beck (2005) argues that globalization has introduced a new space and framework for politics:

> Politics is no longer subject to the same boundaries as before, and it is no longer tied solely to state actors and institutions, the result being that additional players, new roles, new resources, unfamiliar rules and new contradictions and conflicts appear on the scene (pp. 3–4).

Although formulated at a general level, this quotation elegantly covers the essence of the topic of our book: *efforts to establish non-state authority for standards for socially and environmentally responsible organizational conduct*. The supply of such standards is fuelled by a perceived need for novel problem solving and institution building at the transnational level. By the term 'transnational', we refer to a nonterritorial policy- and rule-making space across national boundaries – a multilevel phenomenon that includes more than merely state actors (cf. Rosenau, 2003; Mason, 2005; Djelic and Sahlin-Andersson, 2006; Boström and Garsten, 2008).

We were particularly interested in investigating the establishment of rule-setting authority at the transnational level, as the lack of a world state has stimulated initiatives from a number of partly competing state and non-state rule setters. They all strive to establish authority and meet the increasing demand for coordinating and regulating mechanisms at the global level. One regulatory form that has grown strong at the transnational level – constituting the specific focus of our research interest – is what we call the *multi-stakeholder organization*. This type of organization builds on the idea of assembling actors from diverse societal spheres into one rule-setting process, thereby combining their competences and experiences. These processes can also be regarded as a way of letting competing interests participate in and struggle for different concerns in the same multi-stakeholder process. There could be environmental nongovernmental organizations (NGOs) fighting for better and stricter rules than those offered by existing regulatory frameworks, mainly to prevent corporations from *greenwashing*.[1] And there could be CSR-sensitive multinational corporations that will need to follow these standards and would rather push for standards that are more feasible and useful from their points of view – corporations that see standard setting as a way of preventing governments from developing stricter regulations. Representatives of small and medium-sized companies and representatives of governments in developing countries may be drawn to multi-stakeholder processes to ensure that these standards will not be impossible for their constituencies to follow and that they will not turn into trade barriers. Yet others will be there to push for universal conventions and agreements to be incorporated into the standard, as they believe that all parts of the world should follow the same requirements for human and labour rights. Given such controversies among possible stakeholders, how do multi-stakeholder rule setters convince others of the goodness and usefulness of their standards and of the legitimacy of their status as rule setters? Because we consider these to be pressing questions, especially at the transnational level, we return to them throughout this book. We discuss this topic – *how non-state authority is established, maintained, and challenged* – in terms of *struggles over authority, power, and legitimacy* within transnational regulatory space. Given the breadth of interests involved, then, our central assumption has been that we cannot take the authority of these non-state authorities for granted. How is it even possible that they can sustain themselves over time and not be ruled out by competing authorities?

The standard-setting processes used to illustrate our reasoning are briefly introduced at the end of this chapter. They are organized as multi-stakeholder processes: ongoing standard-setting processes hosted by the International Organization for Standardization (ISO) on the subject of social responsibility (SR) and the standard-setting activities of the Forest Stewardship Council (FSC) and the Marine Stewardship Council (MSC).

TRANSNATIONAL REGULATORY SPACE

In order to consider the competition, power, and friction embedded in and surrounding the standard-setting activities that we examine, we find Hancher and Moran's (1989) concept of *regulatory space* to be heuristically useful.

They see regulatory space as an analytical construct denoting the range of regulatory issues subject to public decision. We may speak of a general regulatory space in a given community (local, national, global) as well as specific ones in individual sectors. More specifically, regulatory space is available for occupation by organizations engaged in regulatory activities for various reasons and in various ways. Representatives of diverse interests or stakeholder groups may choose to participate in a regulatory space in debates over regulatory issues, to try to influence a regulatory issue in a desired direction by framing problems and solutions linked to the issue (Young, 1994). A problem, as defined by one stakeholder, could be a lack of practical guidance for implementing existing universal conventions – not a lack of substantial regulation, but procedural rules and guidance to facilitate implementation. A solution to such a problem could be a management system standard that provides a model for implementation. Debates over such a solution could include a discussion of the ISO management system approach or the Global Reporting Initiative (GRI). Or the debate could address the extent to which certification and labeling standards defining prescriptive criteria for 'fair trade', 'organic', or 'sustainable forestry' may serve as the optimal solution for pushing business toward more responsible conduct – or if there is a need for a completely new approach. Like Young, we argue that this type of dynamic, typically characterizing regulatory space, is crucial to uncover, for it has been largely neglected in the study of rule-making processes.

By acknowledging the impact of a variety of interdependent organizations at different levels and locations relating to a rule-making activity, the concept of regulatory space points to a spatial and relational dimension. As Djelic and Sahlin-Andersson (2006) have argued in their analysis of transnational governance and regulation, in which they reintroduce the concept of 'organizational fields', it is also critical to add a meaning dimension. Whereas Djelic and Sahlin-Andersson acknowledge the significance of studying 'transnational governance in the making', however, by following a traditional neoinstitutional analysis, they tend to give too much causal power to general external institutional forces such as scientification and moral rationalization, while minimizing the effect of the constructive actions of actors. This stance is apparent in their statement: 'Institutional forces frame and constitute organizations and individuals – their interests, values, structures, contents and meaning, activities and the nature and form of their interactions' (2006, p. 384). If the meaning dimension should be taken seriously, we must acknowledge how the actors themselves, creatively and in interaction, develop motives and strategies and construct meaning and framings in rule-setting activities (cf. Boström and Klintman, 2008).

Problems with the concept of regulatory space include a strong emphasis on the space dimension that serves to render the analysis static. It is also valuable to account for time and process. In the process of establishing authority, we therefore argue that it is necessary to add a time (process) dimension. We discuss this issue in terms of combining an organizational process approach with the contextual approach (i.e. regulatory space). Our research focuses, therefore, on the history and organizing processes as well – on the way multi-stakeholder standard-setting practices evolve and change over time and how the way of organizing an activity has an impact on its outcome.

AN ORGANIZATIONAL PROCESS APPROACH TO STANDARDIZATION

As we discuss in Chapter 2, authority can be defined as legitimate power. Because legitimacy is a central concept for the analysis of authority, we have chosen to focus on processes of legitimizing standard-setting activities. More specifically, the book deals with the practices of organizing and legitimizing activities in standard-setting arenas. There is a relationship, albeit ambiguous, between organizing and legitimizing. On the one hand, as the neoinstitutional school informs us, a standard-setting activity may be legitimized through specific ways of organizing the activity. Such words as 'partnership' and 'multi-stakeholder' are used for legitimizing aspirations among transnational rule-setting organizations. On the other hand, an activity may be organized to obtain a maximum of efficiency, which may run counter to what is legitimate according to some measures. It would probably be relatively easy and efficient, for instance, to reach consensus on a standard if only a small group of people were involved in that decision – preferably people who held similar views. If a decision-making process is opened to a large number of organizations, on the other hand, as it is in multi-stakeholder processes, debates and controversies will likely render the process less efficient and more time-consuming. Some issue areas are typically regarded as 'technical' and thereby suitable for smaller groups of people ('experts' in the field): telecommunication, optical equipment, airbags, and nuts and bolts, for example. Other issues are perceived as being more 'political', because they concern the public, and require a more representative rule-setting process. What is legitimate for one issue area may not be legitimate for another. Yet it is difficult to classify regulatory issues as either 'technical' or 'political'. One could argue that everything tends to be political in one sense or another? And what can be said to be purely technical? Experts with definitional power may make such strategic distinctions, which, in itself, could be seen as a political act. One way to politicize an issue is to try to open the black box of corporate technological and economic decision making to a public audience – an issue that Beck (e.g. 1992) has discussed extensively in his writings on the risk society.

The standard-setting processes that have captured our interest – social and environmental responsibility and sustainability – tend to be regarded as politically controversial and suitable for multi-stakeholder standard-setting processes that direct attention to the organizing process as a legitimizing tool. The topics they address have already been politicized. Groups with diverse interests and experiences are explicitly organized into the process, and it is critical, the argument goes, to ensure that all voices are heard and that due process is followed. Both practitioners and normative scholars argue that the multi-stakeholder feature of debates and decision-making processes provides a legitimate process for broad representation or deliberative democracy *and* the substantial benefits, including efficiency gains that transpire when a greater number of organizations with a range of expertise and experience can participate. We take a more critical stand, arguing that the values of efficiency and legitimacy may not easily be combined, although the establishment of authority likely requires both. We also argue that multi-stakeholder processes typically involve problems that are raised in creating a proper balance between efficient and legitimate processes. At the end of the day, such problems render cumbersome any efforts at establishing and maintaining authority.

Neoinstitutional organizational analysis is the theoretical approach that highlights the link between legitimacy and organization. According to this approach, much organizational behaviour can be explained by adjustments to the 'rules of the game' – institutionalized rules about organizational structures and behaviour that constitute the environment of organization. Such rules – or institutions – can be coercive, normative, or cognitive (Powell and DiMaggio, 1991). From this perspective, the structuring and organizing of an activity has a critical legitimacy value for organizations and their long-run survival, and organizational actors expend great effort in creating a legitimate organization. In this way, organizations seek to establish and maintain legitimacy by adapting to norms and cultural frames that are perceived as appropriate; they follow the logic of appropriateness, in other words, rather than rational choice.

The standard criticism of analyses conducted through an institutional perspective is that researchers who adhere to that view assume a passive view of actors. Although we acknowledge that organizations must respond and adjust to a variety of external pressures, we share this criticism, and argue that, to a greater or lesser extent, actors are active, constructive, strategic, and powerful when they orient themselves toward the environment and engage in organizational activities. In line with our constructivist perspective, we argue that ignorance of an actor's interests, motives, and power, as used in a rule-setting process, results in an ignorance of the real conflicts and friction embedded in global politics. In accordance with the institutional perspective, we acknowledge the role of organizing activities as crucial for legitimacy reasons. We also emphasize the role of actors and power in the social construction of legitimizing structures and procedures. According to our organizational process approach, we understand organizing activities not only as a way of adjusting to given institutions in the environment, but also as a means of exercising power.

One relevant aspect of organizing and legitimizing processes is the central role played by the *new actor categories* that must be created in order to distinguish among the various types of stakeholders participating in transnational multi-stakeholder processes. Some scholars of global governance and of emerging types of authority pay attention to the new roles and responsibilities (Pattberg, 2007). Motives and strategies that were defined in previous international relations, and stabilized through well-known national actor categories, need to be rethought and revised. Given the irrelevance of the 'national outlook', Beck (2005) strongly emphasizes the necessity for new categories to be invented and constructed. He argues that opportunities for exercising power on the global political scene can be generated only through a critique of the nation-state orthodoxy and through categories that point the way to what he calls a 'cosmopolitan outlook'. The new politics in the transnational context is, according to Beck, the politics of 'plural boundaries'. Organizing processes drive globalization, and organizations are the actors that create distinctions and identities that ignore national boundaries – the distinction between members and nonmembers, for example (Ahrne and Brunsson, 2008).

Beck uses the term 'meta-game', by which he means that the 'old world politics, which worked by applying the rules, and the new world politics, which works by changing the rules, are fully intermeshed with one another: they cannot be separated out whether in terms of specific actors, strategies or alliances' (Beck, 2005, p. 2). In this meta-game, the actors are not a given. They are created as actors (players) by virtue of the category in which they are placed. They must 'constitute and organize themselves politically *within* the game, *as part of* the game' (p. 14), and are expected to speak in one voice. As part of the rule-changing meta-politics, new transnational boundaries must be constructed, raising new problems around decision making. The new rules – the standards – cannot merely be negotiated among the stakeholders, because the stakeholders must negotiate who should be regarded *as a stakeholder*. In this book, we share our interest in categorization as part of the organizing and legitimizing work of a standard-setting activity as well as a source of power. We argue that it is necessary to consider how actors are created and shaped into players within a specific organizational (standard-setting) arrangement – how organizations are categorized as actors; the roles, responsibilities, and identities they are believed to assume; and who they are supposed to represent. In Chapter 2, we continue along this vein with a theoretical discussion of categorizations, followed, in Chapter 8, by an analysis of the consequences that follow and the power that may be embedded in a chosen categorization.

Although we have argued to this point for an organizational process approach, stressing the impact of organizing, we do not want to de-emphasize the more structural dimension of *organization*. It is also relevant to analyze standard-setting activities by focusing on formal organization and concrete organizational arrangements, including their 'bureaucratic authority' that has developed over time (Barnett and Finnemore, 2004), as transnational standard setting is a permanent activity that requires resources, administration, and enduring, rule-based interaction among stakeholders. Establishing a formal organization can in itself be helpful in carving out a permanent position in competition with other possible rule setters.

Through our questions about the organizing and legitimizing of standard-setting activities, we focus primarily on the perspective of the standard-setting organization, but in line with our definition of authority as legitimate power, the analysis includes a power perspective that attends to interactions and struggles among stakeholders. Changing power structures resulting from the growth and impact of non-state authority have attracted increased scholarly attention (Cutler, Haufler, and Porter 1999; Hall and Biersteker, 2002; Djelic and Sahlin-Andersson, 2006; Pattberg, 2007). Yet this research lacks the analytical tools to explain how authority is created through the establishment and maintenance of authoritative positions, the exercise of influence in these processes, and the development of power struggles and disagreements among the stakeholders – all central topics for the research presented in this book.

THE PROBLEM OF TRANSNATIONAL MULTI-STAKEHOLDER STANDARDIZATION

During the past two or three decades, we have witnessed a remarkable increase in rules for social and environmental responsibility and novel organizational arrangements created for the development of these rules. Fransen and Kolk (2007) distinguish between 'multi-stakeholder standards' and 'other collaborative standards'. We briefly elaborate upon this distinction in order to pinpoint the intriguing character of and the urgent need to address our research topic. 'Collaborative standards' are those issued by organizations with members of the same organizational type – international governmental organization (IGO) standards such as the Code of Conduct for Responsible Fisheries devised by the Food and Agriculture Organization of the UN (FAO) or those issued by business associations such as Responsible Care (run by the International Council of Chemical Associations) or such NGOs as the World Wide Fund for Nature (WWF; called World Wildlife Fund in North America), which issued a Code of Conduct for Arctic Tourism.[2] As discussed in Chapter 2, some scholars view non-state standardization as the exercise of 'private' authority, but they primarily narrow their discussion to such collaborative standards as the self-regulations developed by industry in such forms as networks, joint ventures, partnerships, and private regimes. There are other scholars of international relations, including those who work with regime theory, that restrict their analysis to the collaborative standards in state-centric solutions in such organizations as the UN and the Organisation for Economic Co-operation and Development (OECD).

The other type of standard mentioned by Fransen and Kolk (2007) – multi-stakeholder standards – are those issued by an assembly of organizations, including actors from diverse societal spheres. In essence, the authority of multi-stakeholder standards stems from multiple sources. They are hybrid arrangements that constitute a strength that may be lacking in a collaborative industry standard (consortia standard) or an individual corporate standard (propriety standard), for example. The strength of multi-stakeholder processes may lie in the fact that they can combine 'moral authority' and 'market authority' (cf. Hall and Biersteker, 2002). We believe that this sort of analysis is key, but that it requires greater refinement. We have tried to meet that goal in this book, by critically examining the practices of multi-stakeholder processes and by using existing knowledge about broad inclusion. An increasing number of scholarly works addresses the broad inclusion of actors in policymaking, governance, regulation, and management. There are numerous terms used to denote this topic around multi-stakeholder interaction: partnership (Bendell, 2000; Bäckstrand, 2006; Glasbergen, Biermann, and Mol, 2007), participatory governance (Lovan, Murray, and Shaffer, 2004), inclusiveness (Boström, 2006a), and hybrid organization (Cooney, 2006) to mention a few. Naturally, the increasing scholarly attention to such hybrid polycentric arrangements reflects their rapid growth in real political life. The concept of 'partnership', for instance, is embraced by the current UN discourse on sustainable development (Bäckstrand, 2006; Glasbergen et al., 2007).

One problem in the literature is a profoundly optimistic view of multi-stakeholder work. Scholars tend to assume that a number of positive synergies, including increased social and environmental responsibility, will necessarily follow the inclusion of actors representing different sectors or societal subsystems. Multi-stakeholder interaction and dialogue are claimed to be good for both democratic (legitimacy) and instrumental/practical reasons (combining ideas, knowledge, and other resources). In the environmental policymaking literature, for example, several scholars stress the benefits of including many knowledgeable actors to deal with complex and uncertain problems (e.g. Lafferty and Meadowcroft, 1996; Mol, Lauber, and Liefferink 2000; van Tatenhove, Arts, and Leroy, 2000; Pellizzoni, 2004, Glasbergen et al., 2007). These scholars argue that groups with diverse concerns, knowledge, and experiences may be able to shed light on various aspects of the problem and stimulate dialogue and reflection, while taking responsible measures. And they may develop mutual trust and learning, as well as being empowered and receiving a sense of ownership of the policymaking process.

We find these analyses and arguments relevant and useful. Yet there is an underemphasis on the obstacles involved in permanently organizing multi-stakeholder interaction on a transnational scene. Facilitating broad collaboration in temporary projects may be easier, or at least different, than establishing enduring multi-stakeholder governance arrangements. Our time dimension, emphasized in our organizational process approach, therefore becomes a key factor for examining the conditions of multi-stakeholder standard-setting work.

Multi-stakeholder standard-setting organizations are meta-organizations – organizations that have organizations rather than individuals as their members (Ahrne and Brunsson, 2008). There are typically several types of stakeholder organizations involved as members that tend to be relatively autonomous in relation to the meta-organization. Ahrne and Brunsson also note the difficulty in finding common points of interest and agreement among all members, making it necessary for the rules and decisions in meta-organizations to be relatively soft and flexible.

The meta-organizations we investigate in this book have a multi-stakeholder membership. Because the members rarely interact with each other in other circumstances, great challenges are created for the organizing process. There may even be mutual mistrust among these organizations, based upon previous antagonist relationships (Boström and Klintman, 2008), and firms may lack experience in collaborating with NGOs. The positions, tasks, responsibilities, and roles of any member are more ambiguous in a multi-stakeholder (meta-) organization than it would be in an individual-based organization, such as a private firm or an NGO.

There has been a dearth of analysis of multi-stakeholder authority at the transnational level, yet the conditions for establishing authority, including organizing and legitimizing activities may differ significantly between the transnational and the local scale. Furthermore, we believe that power struggles and power asymmetries have been underemphasized in the multi-stakeholder literature, as have the repercussions of these factors on the authority, decision making, power balance, and further development of the collaboration in the multi-stakeholder organization. Indeed, there appear to be few analyses of *long-term multi-stakeholder standardization arrangements at the transnational level.* In this book we aim to shed new light on this intriguing topic.

THREE EMPIRICAL EXAMPLES

Empirically, the book focuses on and compares standard-setting practices and processes of three transnational standard setters that follow a multi-stakeholder approach: the standard-setting activities conducted by the Forest Stewardship Council (FSC) and the Marine Stewardship Council (MSC) and the process of writing the ISO 26000 standard on SR hosted by ISO. The FSC and MSC cases are about sector-specific certification standards for sustainable forestry (FSC) and marine life (MSC) that have been up and running since the 1990s. The FSC was founded in 1993 and the MSC in 1997, and both restricted their standard-setting activities to their respective sectors. The ISO case, on the other hand, is about a standard aimed at all types of organizations, and one that is still in the making as this book is being written. ISO was established in 1946, and is currently developing standards in more than 200 technical areas, the area of SR being just one of many of its projects. The specific working group tasked to develop the ISO 26000 standard was not established until 2004. As demonstrated in this book, the differences among these three cases (see overview in Table 1.1) provide fascinating subjects of analysis.

The challenges involved in these standard-setting processes are, to some extent, similar. But they are also diverse, partly because of the scope of the standards (broad/generic versus narrow/sector specific) and the length of time during which the standards have been used, and, therefore, their degree of institutionalization. Whereas the FSC and the MSC share a number of key attributes, they are not totally equal, but present some key differences that must be accounted for in our comparative analyses. In Appendix 1, we discuss the material (interviews, various texts, participant observation) we collected, which formed the basis of our analysis of the three cases.

*Table 1.1 Overview of empirical examples and differences among the
FSC, MSC, and ISO 26000 committee*

Standard setter	ISO 26000 committee	FSC & MSC
Founded	2004	FSC in 1993 MSC in 1997
Organizational setting	New organizational unit and procedures established in 2004 within existing organization (ISO founded in 1946, standards in more than 200 areas)	New organizations established for one specific task/sector
Scope of standards	Broad/generic (all types of organizations)	Narrow, sector-specific for forest (FSC) or marine life (MSC)
Phase of development	Still in the making	Used, revised and further developed since 1990s

OUTLINE OF THE BOOK

In Chapter 2, we elaborate upon our formula, 'authority as legitimate power', and on the concepts of authority, power, and legitimacy. Then we begin our examination of the ISO 26000 committee (Chapter 3), the FSC (Chapter 4), and the MSC (Chapter 5), by analyzing the context of the initial and later phases of these organizations, as they were discussed and framed before their establishment and during further developments. Accounts from all three standard-setting activities examined in this book are not restricted to three chapters, however. We return to illustrations from the practices investigated throughout the analysis in our discussion of analytical themes that relate to the topic of this book. In Chapter 6 we provide a map of actors that are typically involved in transnational standard-setting activities, including their capacities as commonly discussed in the literature. Transnational corporations (TNCs) are typical examples of such actors or organizations, as are IGOs and NGOs. Given the variation in resources and motives for participation, this type of mixed membership complicates the organizing and legitimizing efforts of the standard setter. In Chapter 7, we narrow our focus by examining people and organizations as they participate in multi-stakeholder standardization, and discuss a number of strategies of participation that we observe in our material, including the work of the inner circle and the secretariat of the standard setter hosting the process. We also discuss the dynamic formation of preferences and strategies in Chapter 7, in order to provide a more elaborate picture of the complexities involved in transnational multi-stakeholder standardization. In Chapter 8, we continue our discussion by analyzing organizational structures that are established and used by a multi-stakeholder standard setter to categorize stakeholders. We examine the various functions and consequences of these structures for the legitimacy and efficiency of standard-setting activities and for the stakeholders' power and opportunity to perform collective action within these activities. In Chapter 9 we elaborate on the relational and dynamic character of legitimacy – how legitimacy is created and challenged during the course of events and in response to actions taken by stakeholders. We depart from the distinction among the terms *input legitimacy*, *procedural legitimacy*, and *output legitimacy*, to discuss how standard setters often use a number of legitimizing sources or strategies simultaneously, with new combinations of strategies. Finally, in Chapter 10, we synthesize our key findings and draw general conclusions about the fragility of the authority established and the problematic nature of the long-term transnational multi-stakeholder work upon which this authority is based. We present five aspects regarding the problematic establishment and maintenance of legitimacy and five aspects that relate to the challenge of maintaining a power balance within the multi-stakeholder organization. Although we focus on destabilizing tendencies, the chapter also addresses the glue that holds the organization together, and which consequently contributes to reaffirming its legitimate power.

NOTES

1. Greenwashing refers to the practice of advertising one's product as environmentally friendly when the claim is unjustified.
2. See also Pattberg (2007, chpt. 4) for an empirical overview about different types of standards.

2.   Authority as Legitimate Power

As discussed in Chapter 1, the purpose of this book is to examine the establishment of non-state authority as it applies to standards for socially and environmentally responsible organizational conduct. Specifically, we examine the practices of organizing and legitimizing transnational multi-stakeholder standard-setting activities. In order to fulfil these tasks, we develop and combine perspectives from organization theory, policy analysis, and political sociology. We argue that it is useful to understand authority as *legitimate power*, which leads us to combine the concepts of authority, power, and legitimacy in order to develop the analytical tools that we apply to the organization and activities of transnational multi-stakeholder standard setters.

AUTHORITY

For a rule setter to make others follow its rules, it must establish and maintain authority. There are notions of authority embedded in the individual roles of parent, teacher, and priest, and in all types of public and private organizations. The private authority literature takes as its starting point a picture of the world dominated by economic globalization and the decline of state regulation. It attends to new structures and sources of international political and rule-making authority. Hence, authority need not necessarily be associated with government institutions. Authority exists, according to Cutler, Haufler, and Porter (1999), 'when an individual or organization has decision-making power over a particular issue and is regarded as exercising that power legitimately' (p. 5). This definition of authority is similar to that of Weber (1948), who considers authority to be 'the probability that specific (or other) orders are followed by a certain group of people' (p. 144) and that 'a certain minimum of the will to obey, i.e. interest (outer or inner) to obey is part of every genuine relationship of authority' (p. 144).

Scholars active in the area of private authority focus particularly on international cooperation among mutually dependent firms, some of which are competitors. They examine the way this international cooperation takes shape, how its resources are assembled, and how it establishes common rules and durable government-like organizations. They study the repeated interaction among collaborating partners, and how it creates learning processes and common expectations for appropriate behaviour. Cutler et al. (1999) focus on inter-firm relationships in their search for explanations for the structure of market situations, narrowing their discussion to various forms of business self-regulation (networks, joint ventures, partnerships, private regimes). A state-centric perspective on international relations (including regime theory) is therefore complemented by a business-centric theory of authority.

Hall and Biersteker (2002) expand this issue of private authority by distinguishing among *market authority* (inter-firm collaboration), *moral authority* (exercised by NGOs), and *illicit authority* (organized violence), thereby providing further analytical tools to address hybrid types of private authority. They tend to see these three forms as independent, however, and fail to provide a systematic analysis of the way market and moral authority may be combined and blended within the same system, as it has been in some CSR-standard or sustainability-certification systems.

Higgott, Underhill, and Bieler (2000) have observed that power and authority have spread into non-state arenas, and address firms, international nongovernmental organizations (INGOs), and nongovernmental organizations (NGOs), as well as the interaction among such organizations. Yet they, too, fail to address the topic of durable hybrid arrangements, as does Rosenau (2003) who distinguishes between moral (e.g. NGOs), knowledge (e.g. epistemic communities), reputational (e.g. credit rating agencies), issue-specific (e.g. NGOs), and affiliative (e.g. cultural, religious organizations) authority. Although his notion of 'spheres of authority' correctly draws attention to the multiple sources and unclear boundaries of new authorities in an increasingly multicentric world, we suggest that more attention needs to be paid to permanently organized hybrid arrangements.

The private authority literature is indeed welcome, because it introduces the notion of political and regulatory authority as a feature in non-state arenas as well, and introduces a number of relevant analytical concepts. It acknowledges the public features of private authority, and addresses the challenge of establishing legitimacy that is inherent in the making of global governance in a multicentric world. Yet although the relationship between authority and legitimacy has been addressed, more attention needs to be paid to concrete organizational attempts, including the challenges involved in the establishment of legitimacy. The private authority literature tends to have a static and taken-for-granted view of established authority. By combining the notions of *regulatory space* and *organizational process* (see Chapter 1), we can focus greater attention on the constructive – and fragile – nature of the authority that is established, maintained, and challenged. The notion of an 'authority crises' (Rosenau 2003) may not apply only to the 'old' authorities in world politics.

The role of organization has been poorly addressed as well. Cutler et al. (1999) maintain that authority 'lies between negotiation, where action is shaped by the payoffs produced by particular bargains, and coercion, where compliance results from fear rather than respect or faith' (p. 334). Achieving cooperation beyond mere negotiation requires some level of organization. The meta-organization, in particular, is often appropriate for achieving soft regulation that is authoritative yet not coercive (Ahrne and Brunsson, 2008).

Barnett and Finnemore's (2004) analysis of authority and bureaucratic power in intergovernmental organizations offers another useful perspective for understanding aspects of authority in transnational multi-stakeholder organizations. They focus on the power, autonomy, and expertise of the international secretariats of IGOs, which has been a poorly addressed topic in studies of international relations. Scholars of international relations generally focus only on relationships among states within IGOs, and fail to consider the interest and role of the international secretariats. We expect that it is equally important to focus on the secretariat *as a particular type of stakeholder* with a key position in establishing bureaucratic authority within transnational multi-stakeholder organizations.

POWER

Because authority is partially composed of power, the rule setter must mobilize power. And it is only from among the stakeholders that the rule setter can mobilize power – that it can borrow and combine power. This is a delicate issue, because stakeholders may not be fully willing to 'lend' power to the rule setter, or may use their power to advance their own positions and address their own side interests and concerns. As we analyze organizations in which stakeholders have diverse interests and capacities, the situation clearly becomes delicate.

Accordingly, we refer to the notion of power in two interrelated ways: 1) power that the standard setter mobilizes in order to build up its own action capacity (power) and authority and 2) power struggles among the stakeholders and among stakeholders and the standard setter. Both these dimensions of power affect the conducting of a multi-stakeholder process, the type of standards that emerge, and the authority of the standard setter.

We argue that a focus on power necessarily involves a focus on power *relations* (cf. Clegg, Courpesson, and Phillips, 2006). Power is a relational concept. It is not a property that someone possesses, independent of social relations. Possessing certain properties, however, may be a way to utilize power. There is, of course, a huge body of literature on the concept of power. Although it is beyond the task at hand to elaborate on all its usages, there are several aspects and dimensions of power that must be acknowledged (cf. Lukes, 1974/2005). According to our view, it is necessary consider both visual and hidden expressions of power. We could speak of power in terms of socioeconomic resources and the ability to control an agenda, to shape debates and discourses, to create or reinforce barriers to the public airing of policy conflicts, to organize some issues into politics and others out of politics. We argue, therefore, that a power perspective should include the analysis of formal positions and the capacity to act, as well as things that happen backstage – behind the (rhetorical) scene. It is also critical to be sensitive to 'institutionalized power' – 'power coded into structural designs and bolstered by widely shared cultural norms and ideologies', thus less visible power structures that do not necessarily lead to open conflicts or resistance and that are, thereby, typically difficult to detect (McAdam and Scott, 2005, p. 10).

Considering all these aspects in our analysis of power relations, we distinguish among 1) formal positions in the standard-setting organizations; 2) the power resources of individual stakeholders – material, symbolic, expertise/cognitive, and social; and 3) power strategies, including rhetoric, framing, and shaping of organizational structures. In the following subsections, we elaborate upon these three types of power.

Formal Positions

Formal position refers, in part, to structural location in society or to the general transnational regulatory space. Having the status of a nation state, for example, has certain advantages and disadvantages (see Beck 2005 for an analysis of structural power among key actors in global politics). Formal position also refers to the tasks, formal decision-making power, and ascribed roles among various types of actors within and surrounding the organizational arrangements. It is critical, therefore, to consider the allocation of tasks and responsibilities, which affect a stakeholder's opportunity to raise concerns and push arguments. Some actors may have 'structurally privileged positions' (Cutler et al., 1999, p. 347), such as control over information and communication structures. Barnett and Finnemore (2004) argue that a body having a position *in authority* (having a delegated mandate to conduct a specific activity, for instance) can, by its very mandate, obtain considerable space for action that in turn leads this unit to develop eventually into *an authority* (which derives from such factors as demonstrated expertise, training, experience, and credentials). As mentioned, however, it is important to include the power struggles between stakeholders in the analysis, as the arrangements are established. Beck (2005) uses the notion of *meta-politics* to analyze such activities, emphasizing the role of meta-politics, as the organizational and procedural arrangements that are decided upon in such political processes may have considerable impact on the opportunities and maneuverability of various actors. Here, the standard-setting organizations, or rather their key units (e.g. the secretariats) and special task forces created to handle procedural issues should be (and are, in this book) key targets for scrutiny. Furthermore, we discuss the potential power of groups appearing as *outsiders* (not formally participating or being members in the standard-setting activity).

Power Resources

Stewart Clegg and colleagues notice that the concept of power is often used in a negative fashion: 'When words such as manipulation, violence, and domination are so often associated with power, it is not surprising that power is often seen as something bad, something ignoble, ... something corrupting' (Clegg et al., 2006 p. 2). It is important to note, however, that power should be seen not only in such negative ways, but also as a useful concept for understanding social change, resistance, the way in which groups can make a difference, and weak groups can empower themselves: 'power is not necessarily constraining, negative or antagonistic. Power can be creative, empowering and positive' (p. 2). Clegg and other scholars argue that the traditional understanding of power as *power over* should be supplemented by a more productive understanding of power as *power to*. This is not new thinking of course. Thoughts on the positive dimension of power can be found among such strikingly different social thinkers as Foucault and structural functionalist Talcott Parsons (see the Clegg et al., 2006 review, chpt. 7). In the more recent literature, we notice an argument in versions of governance theory (the strength of states [if it is still possible to speak of 'strong states'] is increasingly seen in relation to *power to* rather than *power over*; cf. Pierre and Peters, 2000).

To push this 'power to' notion of power further, we believe that it is fruitful to employ a 'power resource' perspective, which is found in a variety of literatures, including social theory (e.g. Bourdieu's notion of different forms of 'capital'), regime theory, political sociology, organization theory, and such social movement theorizing as the resource mobilization perspective. From this viewpoint, power is to be understood partly as stored-in resources. Organizations mobilize, accumulate, control, and use collective resources; and such collective resources may be used in power struggles. But again, power is more than that. It is not obvious that organizations are powerful merely because they possess resources. Resources can be misused. Following the relational view on power, it is not merely a property to be held by an actor and used as wanted (Clegg et al. 2006). And an actor may exercise power without using its resources, because it often suffices merely to threaten to use one's resources in a conflict in order to achieve the desired outcome. 'Making threats credible without having to go into full action is the most rational way of using power' (Ahrne, 1994, p. 120). Actors that are uncertain about the extent of others' power resources are more likely to refrain from participating in open conflict. Power resources that are not consumed with use may also be easier for the standard-setting organization to mobilize.

Given this recognition of the need to consider the power resources that stakeholders may acquire, and which the standard setter wants to mobilize, we believe that it is useful to distinguish broadly among four types of power resources: material, symbolic, cognitive, and social.

Material power resources include financial resources and (paid or voluntary) labour. We assume that material power resources are critical in transnational standard-setting processes, even more than they are in regulations at the national level. It has to do with stakeholders' capacity to provide donations to the standard setter, to participate regularly in standard-setting activities in various parts of the world, and to have the working capacity to make any type of preparation. As seen in previous studies of standard-setting work, participants, because of their unequal access to financial resources, do not have equal opportunities to participate (Schmidt and Werle, 1998; Cochoy, 2004; Tamm Hallström, 2004; Werle and Iversen, 2006). Likewise, in her study of transnational social movements, Jackie Smith found that '[t]ransnational organizing requires substantially greater resources than does more locally organized oriented action' (2005, p. 235; see also Smith, 2008).

Symbolic power resources include assets such as the name and logo associated with a particular organization. Everybody recognizes names such as WWF, Amnesty International, and Red Cross. The participation of generally appreciated NGOs, including environmental groups, animal-rights groups, labour unions, and human-rights NGOs can bring the necessary credibility to the rule setting because of their 'moral authority' (Hall and Biersteker, 2002; Rosenau 2003). It would be extremely difficult if standard-setting activities such as those conducted by the FSC, MSC, and ISO excluded this type of group completely, as these organizations reflect collectively shared values, voluntarism, and consumer power (cf. Boli and Thomas, 1999; Beck, 2005). But it should be mentioned that business players such as IKEA and IGOs such as the UN may possess a great deal of symbolic capital.

Cognitive power resources include language skills; sensitivity to different cultural traditions; the ability to provide technical expertise on subjects for standard setting; and the capacity to provide alternative framings, arguments, and viewpoints. Specific expert knowledge can be seen as a type of power resource that organizations can acquire. Unlike material and symbolic resources such as a protected name and logo, it is difficult to control knowledge as an exclusive resource and prevent others from exploiting it. Yet because actors have different histories and locations in society, they have different experiences and abilities to provide specific knowledge.

Social power resources include what scholars generally associate with 'social capital': access to networks. With social power resources, we wish to emphasize the ability of actors to establish or link into existing formal or informal cooperations and alliances. In the transnational settings we investigate, it becomes crucial to be able to mobilize coalitions in a way that facilitates broad, cross-cultural communication while managing diversity and coordinating joint action around a shared agenda. These demands differ sharply from those required of most national-level movement organizations (Smith, 2008). Certain NGOs may be extraordinarily well-versed in establishing links or alliances among groups on a global scale (Kekk and Sikkink, 1998). Another type of social capital relates to economic activities. In a market-based governance system, it is essential for a standard setter to include business actors with structural power (Clapp, 2005) – with central network positions that can address powerful demands along the entire chain of production and distribution (Green, Morton, and New, 2000; Cashore, Auld, and Newsom, 2004; Tamm Hallström, 2004; Boström and Klintman, 2008). We may also speak of organizational power resources. We think it is valuable to emphasize this dimension of *collective power resources* when analyzing the various capabilities of stakeholders. Large and small producers, retailers, labour unions, consumer groups, environmental NGOs, indigenous peoples groups, local community groups, certification bodies, state agencies, IGOs, and numerous other experts and stakeholders differ greatly in the amount and type of resources they possess. And it could matter considerably to which part of the globe these groups belong.

Any actor may possess any type of power resource – material, symbolic, cognitive, or social – but the access to and amount of a particular resource varies from one *type* of actor to another – TNCs versus NGOs, for example. Compared to large corporations, NGOs may be strong in symbolic resources but weak in financial resources. In Chapter 6, we further analyze the diversity of capacities among various types of organizations. And throughout the book, we analyze the ambiguous roles played by power resources. Each individual stakeholder may use its own power resources to argue and push for its own concerns, and thereby threaten the authority of the standard setter. The ambiguity derives from the fact that the authority of the multi-stakeholder organization depends on the sum and combination of these dispersed power resources.

Power Behind the Scenes

As we argued previously, it is important to emphasize that a power perspective cannot merely include a focus on formal positions and power resources. The analyst must also interpret what happens behind the scene, how power is exercised in the process (Clegg et al., 2006). Nondecisions (Bachrach and Baratz, 1970), unspoken agendas, implicit norms, expectations, and power embedded in organizational structures are as important to consider as manifest resources are. Such factors can reproduce power positions among elite groups and marginalize other groups. Here, power is also about persuasion, rhetoric, argumentative framings, and even manipulation.

Discourses, frames, and rationalities may affect the way issues are shaped. Although we want to stress the fact that organizations and people should not be seen as passive victims of hegemonic meaning systems or 'institutionalized forces' (cf. Djelic and Sahlin-Andersson, 2006, p. 23), we cannot ignore the fact that discourses and frames can easily be taken for granted and blind organizational actors to reality. The talk of such factors as consensus, voluntariness, and expertise could be seen as an act of power, as such rhetoric could be used for concealing and marginalizing disagreeing claim-makers. Scholars dealing with frame analysis have also investigated how intricate policy issues are simplified and packaged, and how certain aspects are selected or omitted (Fischer, 2003). Frames and framing simplify the complex and uncertain reality in order to make parts of reality more understandable or to push an agenda (Boström and Klintman, 2008). For our purposes, it is relevant to focus on power in the sense of ability, to set and control an agenda, or to have the capacity to shape debates and discourses through frames. Barnett and Finnemore (2004) draw attention to the way international organizations such as the International Monetary Fund (IMF) exercise 'bureaucratic power', through its regulative and constitutive effects. By the latter notion, they refer to the way such organizations define, classify, label, map, and categorize social reality. It is essential to note that power embedded within participatory processes need not necessarily reveal itself through exclusion; it can also be manifested in forms of inclusion. We therefore need a critical examination of the participatory processes and the negotiation of converging and conflicting interests.

Over time, as a standard-setting activity gains momentum, power relationships may become embedded – locked into – organizational arrangements (cf. McAdam and Scott, 2005), or the institutional arrangement may make it easier for some stakeholders to consolidate their power. In this book, we focus on the creation and impact of stakeholder categories in order to analyze such structural power, which often lacks visible conflicts and resistance. Geoffrey Bowker and Susan Leigh Star (1999) pay special attention to the creation and impact of actor categories and begin their discussion by noting that it is indeed human to classify both things and people: classifications are central to the understanding of social order. A fascinating feature of categorizations is their tendency to be perceived as a given, and to be uncontested as soon as they have been established. As George Lakoff (1987) concludes, 'since we understand the world not only in terms of individual things but also in terms of *categories* of things, we tend to attribute real existence to those categories' (p. 9).

To establish stakeholder categories – the categories under scrutiny in our investigation – the standard setter makes distinctions and ascribes similarities, sorting out the commonalities within a group of actors and the significant differences in relation to other groups. In this way, the standard setter seeks to discover the heterogeneity and homogeneity in the organizational landscape. Categorizations constitute a principle of inclusion in and exclusion from organized activities; they can tell us something about who is – and who is not – allowed to participate in such decision-making arenas as standard-setting committees. As Ian Hacking (1999) reminds us, categories are the product of historical events, social forces, and ideology, all of which could well have been different. It is important, therefore, to remember that categorizations are not a given; nor are they neutral in any way. They are social constructions. A specific categorization is merely a suggestion of how to classify and organize a group of people, based on an estimation of similarities – and there are always other possible categorizations that could have been used. Accordingly, in our search for the order and dynamics of standard-setting activities, we argue that an examination of the actor classifications created and used by the standard setter as a way to organize and legitimize a standard-setting activity is of great importance.

As we elaborate upon in Chapter 8, a particular construction or categorization may favour some groups and disfavour others. George Lakoff (1987, p. 41) refers to the work of Eleanor Rosch in discussing so-called '*prototypes* – subcategories or category members with a special cognitive status – that of being the "best example"'. In each category of people there are asymmetries called prototype effects, meaning that subjects judge certain members of the categories as being more representative of the category than other members.[1] Accordingly, we argue, there is a need to examine how certain actor categories work in practice, and to study the consequences of these categorizations. In Chapter 8 we demonstrate how the way of categorizing participants into one stakeholder category or another may affect the way participants perceive themselves and others (or the asymmetries and prototype effects that are likely to evolve), as well as their abilities to perform powerful collective action.

LEGITIMACY

Legitimacy is the last component in our formula. We have already argued that this concept is central for a rule setter, and it has been referred to frequently in recent literature on governance, public-private partnerships, and non-state authority. As we demonstrate in this section, however, the relationships between legitimacy and authority on the one hand and legitimacy and power on the other are somewhat complicated.

When initiative-takers of new governance arrangements seek to establish authority for the new rules they propose, they address and criticize the legitimacy problems of traditional state-centered politics and regulation. New ways of governing and setting rules for societies typically challenge conventional methods of governance and regulation. Bäckstrand (2006) has noted, for example, that 'partnership' relates to 'the three "deficits" of global environmental politics: the governance deficit, implementation deficit, and participation deficit' (p. 291). Likewise, Biermann, Chan, Mert and Pattberg (2007) maintain that 'the emergence of partnership is often seen as a reaction to deficits in accountability and legitimacy of traditional public policy, from national governmental policies to intergovernmental agreements'. On the other hand, 'partnerships raise serious questions of their own accountability and legitimacy' (p. 297). Regulatory innovators must struggle to legitimize their own standards. As we have noted previously, the issue of organizing standardization is a question of how to organize the standard-setting activity both efficiently and legitimately.

Any type of governance relies on legitimacy (cf. Weber, 1919/1977), but we argue that new regulatory arrangements (including transnational standardization) that are built on non-state horizontal relationships face a huge structural drawback. Although traditional regulatory arrangements may have serious legitimacy problems, it is important to consider the fact that private governance, by definition, lacks the traditional enforcement capacities associated with the sovereign state (Bernstein and Cashore, 2004; Cashore et al. 2004). And private standard setters have, by definition, cut themselves off from the political system of representative democracy, which has long been assumed the ultimate source of policymaking and rule-making legitimacy and authority. We argue that regulatory innovators in non-state arenas cannot rely on such assumed legitimacy, but must achieve more active approval from a broad group of stakeholders, including state actors. No one has voted for them. They are, in a sense, self-elected, and must gain broad support for their activities and standards. In the analysis of legitimacy creation, we can therefore expect the standard setters to devote much of their organizing efforts to gaining this broad support.

There is another issue at play here, and it further fuels the legitimacy challenge. Regulatory initiators such as those examined in this book must maintain that their own rules are novel, ethically important, useful, and needed in various ways. It is crucial, therefore, for a rule setter to convince organizations in its environment that there is a value added component of the rules set by the organization. In green labeling, for instance, standard setters categorically distinguish what could be subject to labeling and what cannot, which implies a symbolic differentiation between green and grey, good and bad, sustainable and unsustainable, safe and risky. Such symbolic differentiation in labeling has often proved to be highly controversial (Boström and Klintman, 2008). Moreover, standard setters may claim their superiority by relating to previous regulatory efforts in the regulatory space, thereby sending a message to other regulatory players and wider audiences that previous regulatory arrangements and efforts have failed in some respects. ISO must claim the need for an ISO standard on SR, despite the fact that the UN already has its Global Compact and that the ILO has already set international labour standards (Chapter 3). FSC must claim the need for a new standard for sustainable forestry, although the processes of international governmental organizations (IGO) exist in parallel (Chapter 4). And the MSC must do the same, even though actors such as the Food and Agriculture Organization of the UN are developing approaches and policies in parallel (Chapter 5). Our chapters on the establishment of the FSC, MSC, and ISO 26000 committee demonstrate that such claims making is controversial. At the end of the day, the initiative takers face a complex task in trying to convince others that their own rules are (or will be) better or complementary to existing rules; and this task requires that they take a serious stance on the issue of legitimacy.

When analyzing the struggles of non-state standard setters in their attempts to establish legitimacy, it can be useful to make theoretical parallels to traditional state-centered politics and regulation. Yet we have just concluded that state and non-state governance operate under different conditions. In her analysis of public-private partnerships, Bäckstrand (2006) argues that we need to rethink notions of accountability and legitimacy: '[I]t is problematic to use criteria stemming from ideal-type national democracy to evaluate the legitimacy and accountability of global governance structures lacking a supranational authority' (2006, p. 292). Hence, concepts such as accountability, legitimacy, and authority need to be rethought (see also Boström and Garsten, 2008), although some general characteristics may be the same. At the most general level, legitimacy is a relational rather than a possessional concept (cf. Rosenau, 2003). The legitimacy of an actor's operations must be understood in relation to the perceptions of all relevant stakeholders – or audiences (cf. Cashore et al., 2004; Huckel, 2005). Relevant stakeholders can be actors with a direct interest in the policies and procedures of the standard-setting bodies, or they can be actors that are less directly influenced by the policies but have an important role in *recognizing* and *approving* the standard-setting body or activity. Both groups include states, IGOs, businesses, and civil society actors, all of which may develop distinctly different yardsticks from which to assess the legitimacy of a standard-setting activity.

Given the need to establish legitimacy, how then can the standard setter achieve this task? Several factors can be seen as essential in establishing legitimacy. In this book, we use the concepts of *input, procedural*, and *output legitimacy* to distinguish among various legitimacy bases used by the FSC, MSC, and ISO (Chapter 9). Input legitimacy often refers to aspects such as balanced representation of stakeholders and the inclusion of expertise. Procedural legitimacy concerns such aspects as transparency, accountability, and decision-making procedures. Output legitimacy has to do with problem-solving capacity, effectiveness, and market impact.

Rule setters believe that legitimacy can be established by referring to and using such sources of legitimacy (cf. Boli and Thomas, 1999; Braithwaite and Drahos, 2000; Rosenau, 2003; Bernstein and Cashore, 2004; Tamm Hallström, 2004; Garsten and Lindh de Montoya, 2008; Boström, 2006b; Bäckstrand, 2006; Werle and Iversen, 2006). In part, they are considered as intrinsically positive – seen as democratic, for instance. In part, they are considered instrumentally positive – practicing them will lead to better outcomes. In other words, it is assumed that there are positive relationships among the choice of those who set a standard (input), how the standard-setting activity is conducted (procedures), and the possible benefits of using the standard (output).

In Chapter 9, we depart from the distinctions among input, procedural, and output legitimacy, to discuss a number of *legitimacy strategies* that we observe in the material on the standard-setting processes hosted by the FSC, MSC, and ISO. We discuss the different ways in which legitimacy strategies can be combined, although they may not always fit together well and although a number of challenges are involved. They may even conflict with each other, as seen when the principle of expertise clashes with the principle of representativeness (Tamm Hallström, 2004). They are often not concrete enough to guide action, as many of them are essentially open for flexible interpretation. And practicing ideals such as balanced representation or transparency may be easier said than done.

Our aim with the analysis of legitimizing processes is to contribute further to the discussion on standard-setting legitimacy by shedding light on the critical role of legitimacy challenges that *continuously* confront standard-setting bodies. In our analysis, we demonstrate how standard setters face rigid expectations to demonstrate a capacity to practice legitimacy strategies – not merely to talk about them – and in this context we discuss *the problematic relationship between legitimacy and power*.

A continuous challenge for a standard setter trying to establish authority is the difficulty of combining legitimacy and power. Another problem arises from the fact that all sources of power – and all types of power strategies developed by stakeholders – are not necessarily seen as legitimate in the eyes of all stakeholders. Yet another challenge exists because stakeholders can use for their own purposes the fact that the definitions and framings of legitimacy ideals and principles are open to dispute, negotiation, and alternative framings and interpretations. Powerful actors may deliberately refer to ideals such as transparency in their attempt to create an impression of transparency, because real transparency involves decisions, selections, and, inevitably, judgments about what should be revealed to the public and what should remain hidden (Thedvall, 2006; Garsten and Lindh de Montoya, 2008; Klintman and Boström, 2008). The challenge for the standard setter, then, is to establish an organizational arrangement that allows stakeholders to *provide* and *use* their own power resources, and to see that all stakeholders *mutually accept* the power strategies that are developed and used by involved organizations.

In summary, the legitimizing challenges that a standard setter must handle in one way or another – challenges that we have discussed in this section – may lead to a powerful rule-making arrangement such as the FSC, the MSC, and the future ISO 26000. They have all grown to become authoritative, but in accordance with our formula and our analysis in this book, the authority tends to be strong only as long as stakeholders perceive the power of these arrangements as legitimate.

NOTE

1.   Lakoff (1987, p. 41) offers a number of examples of asymmetries (prototype effects) found within categories of things and beings: robins are judged to be more representative of the category BIRD (so-called 'prototypical members') than are chickens, penguins, and ostriches, for example, and desk chairs are judged to be more representative of the category CHAIR than are rocking chairs, barber chairs, beanbag chairs, or electric chairs.

3. International Organization for Standardization: A Standard for Social Responsibility

WORK AREAS, ORGANIZATION, AND FUNDING

The International Organization for Standardization (ISO) claims to be the world's largest developer and publisher of international standards, with more than 16 000 published. Its expressed purpose is to contribute to international economic harmonization through the development of these standards. The great majority of ISO's standards provide technical specifications for the performance and safety of manufactured goods and their interchangability and interoperability, test methods to assess conformity, design and installation requirements, physical and electronic networks, and quality of services. Since the late 1980s, ISO has also been publishing management system standards covering a growing number of aspects of corporate and organizational life. Quality assurance (ISO 9000) and environmental management (ISO 14000) standards are well-known examples.

ISO is a nongovernmental organization that, according to a current self-description:

> forms a bridge between the public and private sectors. On the one hand, many of its member institutes are part of the governmental structure of their countries, or are mandated by their government. On the other hand, other members have their roots uniquely in the private sector, having been set up by national partnerships of industry associations (www.iso.org, accessed 8 April 2008).

ISO was founded in 1946 to assume the standard-setting activities initiated by the United Nations Standards Coordinating Committee (UNSCC). Since then, ISO has grown to close to 160 members, all of which are national standards bodies (NSBs), and most of which are nonprofit. Many of these members, however, have profit-making subsidiaries with business activities such as consultation, certification, and publishing. In line with the bridge metaphor, there are clear links to governmental structures in ISO member countries, through such mechanisms as government representation on standards boards and committees at all levels – in turn implying that NSBs tend to be highly responsive to policy impulses from their national governments (Higgins and Tamm Hallström, 2007). Entanglements are also clear between ISO and intergovernmental organizations such as the UN, the World Trade Organization, the World Health Organization, the OECD, and the European Commission, all having formal cooperation with ISO.

If we look closer at the way in which ISO standards have developed, we see that the organization deploys around 200 technical committees to draft and update its standards. After a vote among its members, ISO can begin a standard-setting project in a new field. It is open for interested members to apply to hold the secretariat that administers the standard-setting activities. The actual standard writing and related administrative work is thus delegated to member organizations that volunteer to assume these responsibilities. In effect, this means that the British Standards Institution (BSI), the American National Standards Institute (ANSI), and like bodies volunteer the necessary administrative assistance and venues for meetings of international committee members – which includes the providing of experts – when a committee meets to develop draft standards. Many committees field special working groups that assume responsibility for subprojects. In both cases, the experts doing the actual writing of standard drafts are appointed through the ISO member organizations that have announced their interest to contribute. All experts participate 'voluntarily' – at the expense of their employers.[1] It has been estimated that more than 30 000 individuals serve as experts in ISO's international standardization work (Loya and Boli, 1999). A working group usually lasts for several years, meeting annually for a number of intense weeks. From beginning to end, the development and publication of a standard takes an average of five and a half years.

Compared to the vast number of voluntary experts active in the working groups, standard setters such as ISO employ relatively few administrators and technical advisors. The ISO Central Secretariat employs some 150 people from 23 countries. They supply a range of services to ISO's national members, including coordination of the standards development program; administration of voting on draft standards; the final editing and publication of standards; and information, communication, and public relations. The costs of the Central Secretariat constitute 20% of ISO's total operational expenditures. This 20% is covered through member subscriptions (60%) and income from sales of publications and other income from services (40%). The remaining 80% of the yearly operational expenditure comes from the work that ISO delegates to its members: the running of technical committees, secretariats, and working groups in which the actual standard-setting work occurs (www.iso.org, February 2008). This means that 80% of the costs are financed directly by the member bodies that hold all these technical committees and secretariats. And holding a meeting constitutes a much larger responsibility than merely hosting or arranging one. Member bodies that hold meetings must send out drafts, compile comments, and plan agendas for meetings and pre-meetings, among other things. This is a long-term commitment that requires a separate secretariat. Moreover, experts in the field conduct the standard-setting work of the technical committees, and the cost of these experts is not included in the account for the ISO operational expenditure. Yet these costs represent most of the work being performed on global standardization.

ISO EXPANDS ITS BUSINESS INTO SOCIAL RESPONSIBILITY

In 2002, ISO began discussions on the idea of expanding its activities in a new direction, by entering the field of corporate social responsibility (CSR), or social responsibility (SR) as ISO later called it. A decision was made in 2004 to embark upon this project, and the first move was to develop a guidance standard: the so-called ISO 26000, to be released in 2008 (later postponed to the present target year of 2010). The precise aim of this guidance standard is to provide a definition and clarification of the concept of SR and on the ways in which a SR approach could be integrated into the everyday operations of all organizations. In contrast to ISO's other work areas, SR focuses on responsibilities for sustainable development and the welfare of society. The general understanding is that it encompasses such issues as human rights, labour practices, and the environment – issues that several stakeholders would place within the traditional responsibilities of states, rather than the responsibility of a 'private' organization such as ISO. Predictably, several commentators expressed strong criticism of the initiative, and questioned ISO's legitimacy in this field. Other stakeholders articulated great expectations that ISO would change its structure and working procedures into more democratic ones, thus augmenting its democratic legitimacy (Tamm Hallström, 2006). In the remainder of this chapter, we examine the way the ISO 26000 process came about, and how it was organized during the period 2002–2007.

SETTING THE AGENDA FOR ISO 26000 (2002–2004)

Articulations of the Need for an ISO Standard on Social Responsibility

In May 2002, the ISO Consumer Policy Committee (COPOLCO) published a report stating that, from a consumer perspective, ISO corporate responsibility standards were both desirable and feasible. The report described corporate responsibility as a third generation of ISO management system standards, following the work with the ISO 9000 and ISO 14000 series of management system standards (COPOLCO Report, 2002). The recommendation of the committee was, however, that ISO needed to explore the issue further and that a strategic advisory group on SR should be established, with representatives of a broad range of stakeholders, in order to guide ISO's decisions concerning the development of ISO SR instruments (p. 9). One interviewee, who was involved in the ISO debates within ISO regarding this recommended work area, described how the COPOLCO report became the key stimulating force for new standards within ISO, but also how these ideas were controversial and perceived as undesirable by industry players, for example.

At about the same time, the UN pronounced support for private CSR standardization initiatives, emphasizing the significant role of the private sector in sustainable development (AG Report, 2004). In the Plan of Implementation presented at the UN World Summit on Sustainable Development in Johannesburg in 2002, states were called to encourage industry to enhance SR through voluntary initiatives. Both ISO standards and Global Reporting Initiative guidelines on sustainability reporting were explicitly cited as examples of such initiatives (AG Report, 2005). There seemed to be at least some space – some kind of complementary function to the ongoing inter-governmental work – for non-state initiatives like ISO's. One obvious perceived advantage of an organization like ISO was its international membership and well-known trademark with wide reach among corporations globally, which would render any future ISO standard the potential of being used worldwide. Moreover, ISO was experienced in the development of standards that were commodified and directly applicable to organizations (Higgins and Tamm Hallström, 2007).

It was not only the UN that encouraged the idea of ISO standards in the field of SR. Consumer organizations and service providers such as consultants and certification firms appreciated and promoted this idea. In response to these positive and negative perceptions of a new ISO standardization project, the ISO Board decided to implement the recommendation made in the COPOLCO report: to establish an advisory group with the task of further exploring whether or not ISO should proceed with standardization activities in the SR field, and if so, to determine the scope of the work and the type of deliverable (e.g. technical report, guidance standard, requirement standard). ISO managed to engage a broad range of stakeholders representing close to 30 organizations to participate in this investigative work (see Appendix 2 for a full list of organizations represented). The group was called the ISO Advisory Group on Social Responsibility, and it met five times between January 2003 and April 2004. The investigation resulted in a report published in May 2004.[2] A member of the investigative group described his initial optimism and perception of the investigation as being akin to a 'window dressing' activity to legitimize the process that everyone wanted. He soon realized that there was real tension and resistance among stakeholders, and that the process would probably not proceed as smoothly as he had first imagined, given that industry players and others were working actively against it. Yet his conclusion was that the project was worthy of support:

> ISO needs this standard. That's really why the advisory group recommended it, because despite much opposition from industry, this was a big strategic question for ISO and they had a need for this standard in order to survive and compete as an organization. So we were quite optimistic, and therefore recommended ISO to go ahead (interview with a former advisory group member, May 2006).

As the investigative report approached the end of its work, ISO began arranging for an international conference, to be held in Stockholm in June 2004, at which the report and recommendation would be debated. As the ISO conference was being organized, the Swedish Standards Institute (SIS), which was hosting the ISO conference, began preparing for a pre-conference, in order to encourage developing countries to be active in the ISO work on SR by helping them to be well-prepared for the main conference. Although developing countries represent more than 70% of ISO's total membership, they are comparatively small players in the global context; inadequate funding prevents representatives in these countries from participating actively in any of the international committees or holding any international secretariats. ISO regarded this as a major problem, particularly as it saw SR issues as being significant to developing countries. With this background, SIS took the initiative of arranging a pre-conference for developing countries only, and managed to obtain funding from the Swedish International Development Agency (SIDA), to invite approximately 30 people to participate at both the pre-conference and the main conference, with travel costs and lodging provided.

According to several commentators, an issue of debate arose at this stage concerning a specific characteristic of SR unsuitable for ISO standardization.

Given its political character, including human rights issues, it is a public policy field that is and should be occupied at the international level by a number of such intergovernmental organizations as the UN, the OECD, and the ILO. These organizations issue rules developed in representative work structures: inter-governmental agreements that ideally should be translated into national legislation, for example. According to these commentators, a new ISO standard would create the risk of crowding out existing norms and standards set by representative organizations (which some people would consider to be more important than ISO's standards), as well as those set by private organizations such as the Global Reporting Initiative. Several stakeholders were also concerned about the fast-growing industry of service providers (e.g. management consultants, certification firms) offering sustainability tools and advice as one of the major driving forces in the ISO initiative (Tamm Hallström, 2008). As one person who participated in the investigative group that ISO established in 2003–2004 remarked:

> I think that CSR has become the flavour of the month activity. But it has to come to an end some day. There is a lot of money being made on CSR, by consultants, accreditation groups etc. – it's a whole industry (interview with advisory group member, May 2004).

In summary, we can see that various opinions – some in favour of and some critical – were articulated before ISO was ready to make its final decision about beginning standard-setting activities in the field of SR. In order to understand better the dynamics of the ISO 26000 process as it began and developed over time, it is valuable to clarify the picture of the stakeholders and interests involved.

Organizations That Were Particularly Active – For and Against the Idea of an ISO 26000 Standard

Some individuals and organizations were particularly active from the beginning, and many of them maintained central positions in the ISO 26000 work during the entire drafting process. As noted, ISO can be counted among these organizations with a consumer policy committee that published the COPOLCO report in 2002. The ISO Technical Management Board ('the ISO Board') later took the initiative to form the investigative group to explore the issue further, and this step was followed by an arrangement of the international conference to discuss the results of the investigation. It was finally decided to pursue standard-setting activities.

Among the organizations that were active in the investigative work were several that continued to be active during the standard-writing phase – organizations representing a consumer perspective, for example. The position of organized consumers was generally positive toward the ISO initiative, and it usually included arguments that a third party certification was needed in order to affect behaviour in companies.

Organizations representing business interests – the International Chamber of Commerce and the International Organizations of Employers, for example – were there from the start as well, and continued actively in the standard-setting work. They typically held negative views about adding more CSR standards in general, and management system standards specifically, and preferred that organizations should be free to create their own CSR, and not steered in the specific direction of a standard. The industry group was active during the entire process – a recurrent observation throughout this book. Its representatives made their presence felt at work meetings; they provided written comments on various drafts, public presentations, and leadership positions; and they assumed as many leadership positions as possible.

Organizations representing labour interests were far less engaged, although like the industry group, they tended to be against this ISO initiative. As one labour representative interviewed said: 'We see a risk that companies want to use this voluntary standard that is lacking sanctions, in order to obtain goodwill. We would prefer that they negotiate and sign a global agreement, where there is a relationship between two parties.' The interviewee further explained that, from a labour perspective, ISO was not seen as the appropriate standard setter in this case, because SR is about politics, which requires robust procedures, whereas 'in traditional technical standardization there are expertise and scientific reports to refer to, so then it's fine with experts' (and ISO as the relevant standard setter).

There were yet other organizations that participated in the investigative group and continued their engagement, but with new representatives and new strategies. The ILO was such an organization; it was not highly positive toward this ISO activity (see also Chapter 7 on the ILO participation). As a member of the investigative group said about ILO participation:

> They [ILO members] recognize that they need ISO, for compliance, as ISO can bring exposure to the issue. But they hate the thought of needing ISO and they risk a lot in supporting ISO. To me, their support is an indication that they are discouraged about their own core ILO labour standards, but their job is to promote standardization as such ... so that is a consistent justification (interview with advisory group member, June 2004).

A few organizations, such as the WWF, decided *not* to continue their engagement after the disbanding of the investigative work. A representative of this organization explained why the WWF participated during the investigative phase in 2003–2004:

We had worked with ISO on specific issues before, and were not that happy then. We criticized ISO for its lack of stakeholder involvement. It wasn't a constructive issue. And we've kept an eye on ISO since then – particularly ecolabeling, but also CSR. We've also looked at GRI, OECD, and the Global Compact. The advisory group had been running for some time before we were invited, and we saw it as an opportunity to see if the work of ISO would be positive or negative according to our perspective – if sustainable development could be enhanced in the ISO engagement. And we wanted to know if there is a genuine gap that ISO could fill (interview with representative of the WWF, May 2004).

The interviewee also raised the issue of performance versus process-based rules – a recurrent discussion within the work of the investigative group. The interviewee was of the opinion that SR tools for corporations must be performance based, as the FSC and MSC are (see Chapters 4 and 5), and not process-based as ISO standards tend to be, in order to make a contribution to sustainable development. When the investigative report was published in 2004, there was no full consensus within the group, as the WWF requested that it be allowed to attach a minority report. In its minority view, it stated its concern about the ambiguity of some parts of the report – particularly the fact that the preconditions and the scope of the work did not address environmental issues satisfactorily.

We can conclude that there were various perspectives and organizational efforts involved in setting the agenda for the ISO 26000 process. Some organizations were active only at an initial phase; others joined early and continued their engagement throughout the process; and yet others joined only after ISO had made the decision to start developing the ISO 26000 standard. In Table 3.1, we account for the common positions of the five initial stakeholder categories established by ISO in 2004.

After the presentation of the report written by the advisory group, the ISO Board had a meeting at which ISO formally acknowledged that SR involved a number of subjects and issues that were qualitatively different from the subjects and issues that ISO had traditionally handled. Still, the ISO Board decided to move ahead and undertake SR standardization immediately, as formulated in the resolution:

The ISO Technical Management Board [the ISO Board] recognizes that the conference confirmed the AG's [advisory group's] recommendation that there is a need for a guidance document, written in plain language which is understandable and usable by non-specialists, and not for a specification document intended for conformity assessment, [and] further recognizes that the conference indicated that this work should be undertaken immediately (ISO/TMB resolution L/2004 of 25 June 2004).

Table 3.1 Overview of various perspectives on the ISO 26000 initiative. The categories used in the table are those used by ISO in 2004

Stakeholder group (according to ISO categorization in 2004)	Position at the time of the Stockholm conference in 2004
Consumers	ISO standards (management system type of standards, including certification) are good tools for regulation of TNCs.
NGO	ISO lacks democratic authority; but ISO standards as tools for regulation are good if ISO changes into proper multi-stakeholder organization, including actual participation of developing countries and small and medium-sized enterprises (SMEs).
Government	ISO lacks democratic authority; but ISO standards as tools for regulation are good if ISO changes into proper multi-stakeholder organization. ISO standards could still be problematic for developing countries though, if they develop into Technical Barriers to Trade.
Labour	ISO lacks democratic authority and is not suitable to set social standards. The ILO system is better: it implies legislation rather than voluntary standards.
Industry	CSR is not suitable for standardization; the field is still evolving, and not mature enough for standardization. It is not possible to use a one-size-fits-all-approach. It is not the role of private companies to do work of governments (set rules).

The board decided that the standardization work on SR would not be delegated to a technical committee (whether existing or yet to be formed), as would be the usual ISO procedure. Instead, the SR work was to be conducted by a special international working group – the ISO 26000 working group (called 'the ISO 26000 committee'[3] in this book) – linked directly to the ISO Board itself. Special procedural rules were to be developed by the ISO Board and the time limit for producing a guidance standard on SR was set at three years (compared to the usual five or six years it takes to produce ISO standards). One of the first steps taken by ISO was to change the structure of the ISO 26000 committee into a multi-stakeholder committee with the involvement of a much wider range of experts, originating not only from industry corporations and service-providing companies, but also from governmental, nongovernmental, consumer, and labour organizations. The idea was to respond to criticism raised during the investigative work and the ISO conference in 2004, by changing ISO from an organization that assembles 'voluntary' experts in an unspecified manner to a multi-stakeholder organization that assembles a number of experts representing a number of predefined stakeholder groups proportionately, thus turning ISO into a more democratic and legitimate organization. In an executive summary on ISO and SR, the ISO Secretariat coined the term 'expert representatives', to underline the added stakeholder dimension of participants (ISO and Social Responsibility 2006, p. 2).

The following section outlines the result of this organizing process, drawing a preliminary rough picture of the organizing activities that occurred within ISO between 2004 and 2007. The picture is improved in subsequent chapters with the addition of material on specific organizational issues of particular interest to us, and worthy of more detailed discussion and comparison with the other cases.

ORGANIZING THE DRAFTING PROCESS (2004–2007)

The Start of a Multi-Stakeholder Organization: Twinning Arrangements and Stakeholder Categories

The actual standard-setting work was to begin in 2005. By late 2004, however, an ad-hoc group within the ISO Board was established to develop procedural rules for the ISO 26000 committee. Its mandate included the establishing of requirements for stakeholder involvement and so-called twinning arrangements between individual developed and developing countries. The purpose of the twinning arrangements, to be used for chairpersonships, the secretariat, working groups, and various task forces, was to improve the balance between developed and developing countries.

Following the procedural recommendation about twinning arrangements, the ISO Board announced that the twinned countries were invited to submit joint applications regarding the positions of chairpersonship and secretariat of the new working group; only applications coming from a developed and a developing country would be considered. Sweden and Brazil won the competition among the applications received, upon which they formalized their twinning arrangement – the first formal twinning arrangement in ISO's history.

Among the other initial activities aimed at shaping ISO's new organization was the creation of six stakeholder categories to be represented in various task groups. When ISO organized the conference in 2004, it used five formalized stakeholder groups to categorize the conference participants – labour, NGO, government, consumer, and industry – but shortly afterwards added the category of Service, Support, Research, and Others (which we have labeled 'Others'). In practice, the addition of the sixth category meant primarily that the large group of service providers, such as management consultants and certification firms, obtained their own stakeholder category instead of being part of the industry group. Before this change, several industry representatives expressed their disapproval of the large number of consultants who, under the first categorization, were placed within the industry group: 'This is one of these troubling aspects in this field. People who are making money from it. It's a profession for so many people, and for them – the more complicated the better ...'.

This situation made it difficult for the industry group to attain a consensus position, because service providers such as consultants often had divergent opinions and interests that clashed with those of several large corporations. The separation of service providers (Others) from other corporations (industry) was probably appreciated not only by industry representatives but also by those of the Others group, as the change meant that the latter obtained its own legitimate category, with seats reserved for Others representatives only. In 2007, yet another category – administrative – was added. This was not an expert category, however, but solely an administrative one, the purpose of which was to distinguish NSB representatives (ISO members) from members of the Others group.

After the stakeholder categorization was settled, the secretariat submitted a guidance document defining each category, based on descriptions drafted by the stakeholder groups themselves. Its purpose was to encourage ISO members who were responsible for the nominations from each country, to ensure that the people involved in the ISO 26000 process participated under the appropriate stakeholder category (N48 rev. 1). This document had varying descriptions of the categories, not only the length and outline of the definitions, but also in treatment of the potential overlap between categories. The government stakeholder definition was one of the shortest and most precise, stating only the members belonging to this category (typically salaried civil servants). The definition of the Others group was also short, and much less precise in identifying its members; it was formulated as a residual group.[4]

The industry stakeholder definition, on the other hand, comprised enterprises that manufacture products or provide services and pursue primarily commercial interests; employer organizations; business associations; special industry organizations; and trade associations representing various industries at the national, regional, and international levels. The definition also included nonmembers of the (new) industry group, however: 'enterprises and other organizations that offer services related to standardisation, including certification, registration, accreditation, and related consulting services (SRI services) that pose an inherent conflict of interest' (N48 rev.1). We can infer, therefore, that it was critical for the industry group to ensure that no service providers were placed among the commercial organizations that should constitute the core of the industry group. There were other such examples[5] of efforts to clarify who did and who did not belong to a certain category. As we discuss further in Chapter 8, there are no given or 'natural' categories, and no firm or stable borders of such categories. Categorizations need to be created and, as we observed in the industry case, such processes can involve negotiations over the precise boundaries of a category. Once they are established, however, they quickly tend to be taken for granted and begin to be perceived almost as a given (cf. Chapter 2).

In addition to the categorization of participants into a stakeholder affiliation, ISO labeled the participants either 'experts' or 'observers'. Among the guidelines on the role of observers, the ISO 26000 Secretariat clarified that 'observers may not comment or otherwise seek to influence the proceedings, either in meetings or in correspondence', and that their name tags should be a different color than those of experts. During plenary meetings, observers were to sit only in a designated observers' section (ISO/TMB/WG SR N 72, 11 May 2006).

These instructions clarified that there were significant differences between experts and observers, the experts being the most influential participants. The distinction between experts and observers was also valid for international organizations lacking a national affiliation, and therefore classified as liaison members rather than stakeholder representatives. Yet another distinction was made between participants from developing and developed countries. Even though developing countries were never accorded their own stakeholder category, this distinction remained crucial for categorizing participants when

Table 3.2 Actor categories used to classify participants of the ISO 26000 process

Experts	Participants were invited to *participate* in the ISO 26000 process on a voluntary basis to *discuss and write* the ISO 26000 standard.* Maximum 6 experts per member country and maximum 2 experts per liaison member were allowed at the international level.
Observers	Participants invited to participate in the ISO 26000 process on a voluntary basis. *Not allowed to take an active part* (make statements) in the consensus-making process. Maximum 6 observers per member country and maximum 2 observers per liaison member at the international level.
Stakeholders (national)	Additional classification used for all experts and observers originating from specific countries and nominated through one of ISO's national member bodies. Classification was linked to belonging to 1 of the 6 fixed stakeholder categories (2 representatives of each stakeholder category and country – 1 expert and 1 observer – allowed at the international level).
Liaison members (international)	Specific classification was used for experts and observers originating from international organiza-tions being ISO liaison members (2 experts and 2 observers allowed from each liaison member).
Administrative	Officers of ISO and its members (national standards bodies) have similar status to observers. One administrative staff is allowed from each member country.
ISO 26000 secretariat	Chairman, co-chairman, secretary, and co-secretary; administration only, neutral position.

Note: * There were generally about 400 people present at international work meetings, a majority being experts.

the actual standard-setting work started, particularly when consensus decisions were being made. As we discuss in Chapter 9, it was crucial for legitimacy reasons for the views of all stakeholder groups, including those from developing/developed countries, to be considered in the decision-making processes. The distinction between participants from developing and developed countries was also important for the nominations of leadership positions, as all leaderships were twinning arrangements.

As illustrated in Table 3.2, ISO predefined six actor categories: experts, observers, stakeholders (government, labour, consumer, NGO, industry, Others), liaison members, administrative, and secretariat staff.

Division of Labour: Strategic, Standard Writing, and Advisory Task Groups

There were approximately 400 people at each international work meeting. At the beginning and the end, debates took place in *plenary meetings* convened by the ISO 26000 Secretariat. During the first two work meetings in 2005, moreover, six *stakeholder-specific discussion groups* were instituted and a number of *temporary ad hoc groups* were established to discuss the terms of reference and structure of the working group, the design specification of the standard, and the working group's procedures. As the drafting work proceeded in 2005, a number of permanent groups replaced the initial temporary ones. Three *strategic task groups* were established to support the coming standard development work: TG1 (Funding and stakeholder engagement), TG2 (Communication), and TG3 (Operational procedures). Three *standard-setting interim task groups* were also established to develop a draft of the standard: ITG4 (Stakeholder engagement), ITG5 (Core context of SR), and ITG6 (How to implement SR). These interim groups were later changed into permanent standard-writing groups (TG4, TG5, and TG6), focusing on various chapters of the standard's text. Furthermore, an *Editing Committee* was established with the task of reviewing and editing the standard document. The first drafts of the standard text were written in the three standard-writing groups, to be compiled later by the Editing Committee. The secretariat then sent the text to the entire working group for comments a number of times during the drafting process. Twinning leadership between a developed and developing countries applied to all these groups, for the positions as convenor, co-convenor, secretary, and co-secretary.

In addition to these strategic and standard-writing task groups, there were a number of other task groups with advisory functions that supported the work of ISO 26000.[6] One of these groups was the *Chairman Advisory Group*, established in 2005, giving advice to the chairs and secretaries during the course of their work.[7] In 2006, a temporary *Liaison Task Force*, comprising representatives of all six stakeholder groups, was formed to overcome problems of inconsistencies that occurred between the various working groups responsible for writing different parts of the draft standard. The Liaison Task Force proved to be efficient and was appreciated for its work, and it was decided to let the group continue to identify any inconsistencies and integration issues and to advise drafters how to ensure consistency of tone and level of detail across documents.

Later in 2007, the Liaison Task Force was disbanded and replaced by the so-called *Integrated Drafting Task Force*. According to Resolution 2 of November 2007, this new group was tasked 'to review the full text of the ISO 26000 drafts including revised texts from drafting teams; to review and revise the ISO 26000 drafts in an integrated manner, based on comments received; and to compile comments received from consultations' (ISO/TMB/WG SR N 132). In practice, the new group essentially comprised the same people as the Liaison Task Force did.[8] To conclude, wee see that the organizational structure of the ISO 26000 committee became more complex over time.

One ISO-experienced consumer representative commented that the best way to influence the content of a standard was not necessarily through active participation in standard-writing groups and through comments on drafts written by these groups, but through direct contact with members in these other groups (e.g. the Chairman Advisory Group, the Editing Committee, the Liaison Task Force):

> I guess I've helped to prepare the comments of Consumers International more than those of my national committee. I've also concentrated my efforts on communicating comments to my stakeholder group and to the consumer representatives in such groups as the LTF [Liaison Task Force]. I see this as a more important and meaningful way to influence, to concentrate on a few points instead of trying to influence [the whole text] through the 7000 comments[9] that are communicated to the secretariat. ... I think there is sometimes a blind faith in what is written and communicated [to the secretariat] – that you should make comments on every single detail. It's better to lobby against a few, selected things (interview with consumer representative, December 2007).

We return to the issue of influence throughout this book, and demonstrate that it was indeed important for those who wished to influence the ISO 26000 process to be part of such groups as the Chairman Advisory Group, the Editing Committee, and the Liaison Task Force, as membership of these groups implied certain advantages. There were, however, only a few of the 400 participants of the ISO 26000 committee that tended to be part of these groups.

In Chapter 4, we return to the 1990s, to examine the background and establishment of the FSC as well as the years of organizing that followed.

NOTES

1. ISO members (NSBs) have participated in the development of certain sponsoring arrangements, however, in response to criticism over difficulties that some stakeholders have experienced in financing their participation. Funds are provided by national governments to their NSBs to offer financial support to labour, consumer, and NGO representatives, and to national aid organizations to fund representatives from developing countries (see also Chapter 9).

2. See Tamm Hallström (2006) for a detailed account of the work of the ISO Advisory Group on Social Responsibility.

3. A committee was formed to deal with ISO 26000; we sometimes refer to it as the 'ISO 26000 committee'. When we refer merely to 'ISO' in the context of the work being done for ISO 26000, we are also referring to that committee.

4. The definition of the Others group: 1) organisations and individuals, not from other stakeholder categories, that seek to advance an understanding of SR through education, training, academic study, and research; 2) organisations and individuals, not from other stakeholder categories, that develop voluntary standards, codes of practices and SR related tools; and 3) organisations and individuals, not from other stakeholder categories, that provide services related to the implementation and support of SR activities (N48 rev. 1, p 8).

5. The NGO definition, for instance, clarified that: 'the mission of the NGO should not be the development of standards, or the provision of standards-related services; the NGO should not represent the specific interests of either government, industry, labour unions or consumer groups; and grants or membership dues from, or fee-based services to, for-profit organisations should not be a significant proportion of an NGO's overall funding or compromise the autonomy of its governance.' The labour definition was clear about including only persons designated by independent representative workers' organizations, based on the ILO Convention 135, but with the additional clarification that this definition did *not* include workers or persons from the human resource departments of companies; enterprises providing labour-related services or advice; NGOs that deal with labour or workplace issues; or representatives of organisations established or effectively controlled in any way by employers, industry, or governments.

6. 1.13.1 A group having advisory functions may be established by a technical committee or subcommittee to assist the chairman and secretariat in tasks concerning coordination, planning, and steering of the committee's work or other specific tasks of an advisory nature (ISO/IEC Directives, Part 1, Sixth edition, 2008).

7. Initially only two experts from each stakeholder category (twinning arrangement, with one woman and one man recommended) were allowed to participate in the Chairman Advisory Group. The appointment of these experts was made by each stakeholder group at the Brazil meeting. Consumers International, International Organization of Employers, International Confederation of Free Trade Unions, and Accountability were among the organizations that managed to obtain one of these scarce and attractive positions. Three other organizations were later invited to join the Chairman Advisory Group: the ILO, the UN Global Compact and Global Reporting Initiative, as well as representatives of the Editing Committee and of all strategic task groups and standard-writing groups.

8. The choice of IDTF members was clarified in the resolution: convenors and co-convenors of the three standard-setting task groups; one representative from the Editing Committee; one expert from the ILO (in accordance with its memorandum of understanding); one expert from the UN Global Compact (in accordance with its memorandum of understanding); one representative of the ISO Central Secretariat; two Secretaries, appointed by the chairs of the ISO 26000 committee; two experts from each stakeholder category (as far as possible, one was chosen from a developed country and one from a developing country), to be nominated by the stakeholder groups, including at least one who has been involved in the drafting teams of the standard-setting task groups; and two alternates nominated by the stakeholder groups.

9.   There were numerous written comments communicated to the secretariat each time a new draft was finished. The first draft of the ISO 26000 standard in 2006, for example, received about 2000 written comments to be discussed in Lisbon in May 2006; the second draft in 2006 received about 5000 written comments to be discussed in Sydney in January 2007; the third draft of 2007, amounting to some 100 pages, received about 7000 written comments to be discussed in Vienna in November 2007; and the fourth and final draft in 2008 was commented upon and discussed in Santiago in September 2008.

4.   Forest Stewardship Council

A forest crisis, existing since the late 1970s, served as a background for the market-based initiatives in forest policy during the 1990s (e.g. Elliot, 1999; Domask, 2003; Dingwerth, 2005; Pattberg, 2007). Such threats as tropical deforestation and loss of old-growth forests in temperate and boreal zones, as well as threats to biodiversity, ecological functions, and the land rights of indigenous people, fuelled social movements in their targeting of forest-related industries during the 1980s. Between 1980 and 1995, the planet lost 7% to 8% of the world's total tropical forests, an area roughly the size of Mexico (Domask, 2003). Intensive and escalating campaigning eventually led to a concerted effort among social and environmental nongovernmental organizations (NGOs), certain actors from forest-related industries, and a few other actors to establish the Forest Stewardship Council (FSC). The FSC was formally established in 1993 as an international nongovernmental association of individuals and organizations with the aim of promoting environmentally appropriate, socially beneficial, and economically viable management of the world's forests. The FSC has established a framework with principles and criteria from which accredited certification bodies can certify forests. Through chain-of-custody certification, the products that come from certified forests can be given the FSC label.

Fifteen years after its establishment, the FSC can report a positive trend in certified forests. By August 2008, FSC certification existed in 81 countries and covered roughly 10% of the world's managed forests (FSC, 2008). Many scholars are fascinated by the FSC initiative – by the notion of a non-state actor trying to regulate forestry – and researchers have sought to address the varied impact and implementation of the FSC (see for example Cashore, Auld, and Newsom, 2004; Meidinger, Elliot, and Oesten, 2003; Pattberg, 2007; Gulbrandsen, 2009). In this context, however, our primary focus is not on the FSC's diffusion worldwide, but on organizational aspects at the global level, including such topics as power, legitimacy, and stakeholder interaction. This chapter describes the establishment and further development of the FSC, as well as some of the challenges and criticisms that have confronted the organization as it entered the transnational regulatory space and tried to maintain its position there.

THE ESTABLISHMENT OF THE FSC[1]

Before Forest Certification and the Establishment of the FSC

In the late 1970s, governments, international governmental organizations (IGOs), and environmental NGOs began to call for action at the international level to conserve forests, and in the 1980s public concern about deforestation increased considerably. In 1983, a first attempt to regulate the issue of deforestation was taken by timber-producing and timber-consuming countries in their International Tropical Timber Agreement, under the auspices of the UN Conference on Trade and Development, which entered into force in 1985 (Pattberg, 2007). The agreement called for the establishment of an International Tropical Timber Organization (ITTO), which began operation in 1986. The agreement and the organization should, on the one hand, promote expansion of international trade in tropical timber and, on the other hand, encourage implementation of forest management systems that consider measures to conserve tropical forests. The ITTO and other UN units did contribute to a growing awareness of environmental problems, while simultaneously demonstrating an incapacity to solve or deal effectively with the global forest crises (Synnott, 2005).

From the mid-1980s onwards, environmental NGOs sharpened their focus on forest issues in their global campaigning activities. Early on, Friends of the Earth (FoE) took initiatives by linking UK timber companies with tropical deforestation. Indigenous civil society groups in developing countries with tropical forests staged protests, and social movement organizations in northern countries targeted both governments and retailers in the Do-It-Yourself markets. '[T]he anti-DIY demonstrations proved to be highly successful and garnered considerable media and public attention. Customers began to write letters to the retailers and to confront store managers and employees with tough questions about timber sourcing' (Bendell and Murphy, 2000, p. 69).

Boycott campaigning led some large private companies to stop using tropical forest products and many municipal governments in the UK, USA, Germany, and the Netherlands to ban the use of tropical forest products in their procurement policies (Domask, 2003; Pattberg, 2007). Yet, the new mobilizations, boycotts, and institution building did not lead to a reduction in deforestation rates. The WWF observed that the boycotting strategy led to a devaluation of the standing timber in tropical forests around the world, which in turn actually caused accelerating deforestation, as forests were cleared for farming, grazing, and building.

Another problem was the one-sided focus on tropical forests. In 1987, Friends of the Earth in the UK (FoE-UK) published the first edition of its

Good Wood Guide and launched its *Seal of Approval* for dealers and retailers. Although it was one-sided in its total rejection of tropical timber, thereby implying that all other sources, such as temperate timbers, were environmentally benign, 'it set the scene for the next steps, and showed the potential power of the concept of identifying well-managed forests' as explained by Timothy Synnott, first Executive Director of the FSC (Synnott, 2005, p. 8).

Yet in spite of their best of intentions, environmental NGOs found that their campaign messages were being misinterpreted. 'By focusing on tropical timber, the message the general public understood, was "tropical timber is wrong and non-tropical timber is right"' (Fern, 2001, p. 15). Companies were being branded as contributing to forest destruction based solely on their use of tropical timber, and as their legitimacy was threatened, business actors began to search for solutions. Manufacturers created labels for their products, claiming sustainability of their forest sources (Synnott, 2005; Pattberg, 2007). But as labels began to appear in abundance, confusion spread, and some manufactures and retailers expressed a willingness to learn more about the source of their raw materials.

In the late 1980s, FoE and other actors tried to encourage the ITTO to consider certification and labeling as mechanisms for improving tropical forest management. Although this topic was discussed for some time, no concrete results were produced. Some developing countries responded negatively, fearing that NGOs could introduce labeling as a disguised means of promoting timber boycotts. Others believed that certification was simply not feasible. A number of environmental NGOs concluded that the IGO process had been a failure that would not yield significant improvements in tropical forest management over an acceptable time horizon (Elliot, 1999; Synnott, 2005; Dingwerth, 2005; Pattberg, 2007). Yet, certification and labeling had by now, through the discussions within this IGO, 'entered the consciousness of those interested in shaping global forestry management' (Cashore et al., 2004, p. 11).

Timothy Synnott, who also was a key founder of the FSC, summarized his reflections in his notes on the early years. According to him, the tensions within the ITTO showed:

> ... that workable and acceptable solutions would not arise unless representatives of all sectors participate equally in their formulation and design. They also showed how ITTO's abilities were constrained by restricting its mandate to tropical timber, and by its polarizing division into producing and consuming countries. These lessons were learned in the FSC, which was designed from the start to be open and participatory, for application in all forests, worldwide (Synnott, 2005, p. 10).

Something more sophisticated than the FoE's *Good Wood Guide* was needed, as the experience with this guide showed 'that a single campaigning NGO could not reliably identify sustainable sources, based on its own sources and policies, in an arena as complex as forest management. This demonstrated the need for criteria or standards, and *multi-stakeholder participation*' (Synnott, 2005, p. 10, our emphasis).

Someone had to take a path-breaking initiative, however, and Hubert Kwisthout, a manufacturer of bagpipes, was just the person to do so. As he explained to us in an interview, he needed tropical timber for the bagpipes: '[A] tropical timber boycott would not benefit me greatly. So I thought, "what can we do to ensure that you get timber from better-managed sources?"' He started the Ecological Trading Company, and tried to import timber from well-managed sources through his small company. 'We found it difficult to market our timber', he continued during our interview, 'because there was nothing that distinguished our claims from those made by other timber companies; they all claim to get their timber from well-managed sources'.

In 1990, Kwisthout proposed the establishment of an independent body for the verification of sources and for monitoring and standard setting. He initiated discussions with key persons from the WWF-UK and the retailer B&Q, both of which expressed a supportive attitude and provided initial funding. This group soon obtained sufficiently wide support, and a pro-certification network was formed. It included these actors, as well as a few representatives of the timber industry, science, retailers, and other civil society organizations representing woodworkers (Woodworkers Alliance for Rainforest Protection) and environmentalists (e.g. Rainforest Alliance). This core group established a certification working group in 1991, and 'most of the activities that led to the founding of FSC were associated with this group or its members. However, it remained quite informal, as a gradually expanding circulation list or forum, rather than a fixed membership' (Synnott, 2005, p. 13).

So far, we have seen that a number of factors facilitated the establishment of the FSC:

- perceptions of an escalating forest crisis;
- perceptions that little was happening on the transnational policy scene (regulatory space) increasing media campaigning activities, including consumer boycott mobilizations, among environmental and social NGOs;
- a growing understanding among NGOs and companies such as large image-conscious retailers that an effective and credible solution to the problem had to be developed; and

- a few initial efforts to establish consumer guides that provided ideas for certification.

Toward the Establishment of the FSC: Defining Basic Structural Elements

The Certification Working Group arranged two meetings, the first of which, held in San Francisco in April 1991, attracted 17 people, 14 of whom were from North America (Synnott, 2005). Although Kwisthout described it as a brainstorming meeting, it appeared to be a formative gathering. According to Synnott, some of the basic elements within the certification strategy had became firmly established within the core group: that the new organization under consideration would not itself certify forests, but would be responsible for developing some type of standard; that a standards organization, tentatively called the Forest Stewardship Council (FSC), would be established; that the FSC would cover certification of forests in all parts of the world; that a system of labeling should be used; and that the FSC should conduct accreditation (albeit under the term 'umbrella-monitoring'). 'The discussions and the minutes included all the key concepts that were adopted later by the FSC itself' (Synnott, 2005, p. 14).

The second meeting was held in Washington in March 1992, and attracted 43 participants from ten countries. Group members began calling themselves the 'FSC Founding Group'. The Interim Board of the FSC Founding Group (Interim Board) was established with the mandate of overseeing further consultations and preparing for the founding assembly of the FSC. Synnott recalls the Washington meeting:

> This was the first of many FSC meetings where strong differences of opinion emerged, including some that were personalized and entrenched. Disagreements that emerged during and after the meeting included the participation of people with economic or commercial interests, and the status and decision-making powers of the 'Interim Board'. However, an embryonic FSC emerged from this meeting with draft statutes, standards, mission statement, and a group of people that could take decisions, raise funds, and initiate actions in its name. From then on, FSC had a de facto operational existence, although it was still 30 months away from legal existence (p. 15).

Before the formal establishment of the FSC, the Interim Board conducted national consultations in ten countries from all parts of the world. These national consultations gave firm assurance to the Interim Board that it was on the right track and that it could expect substantial support from many interests worldwide. This rising support helped the Interim Board 'to carry them through the hazards of the Founding Assembly' (p. 15), which we describe in the next section. The FSC idea was presented at the Rio conference in 1992, and the failure of the Rio summit to establish a binding forest convention provided an additional incentive to move on with the FSC initiative (Cashore et al., 2004; Pattberg, 2007).[2]

One notable disagreement that appeared in the early discussion related to the scale of operation that should be relevant for FSC certification. In these early years, Synnott maintains, there was a common perception that FSC would or should focus mainly, or even exclusively, on small-scale or community-managed forests. The NGO World Rainforest Movement found it 'bizarre in the extreme' to invite people exercising large-scale highly mechanized logging, while WWF-UK saw no reason to disapprove the automatic inclusion of medium- and large-sized producers (Synnott, 2005, p. 15).

Establishing the FSC – a Turbulent Founding Assembly

The Interim Board organized the Founding Assembly in Toronto in October 1993. It had to consider carefully the representativeness of the stakeholders, as Synnott recalls:

> The Interim Board was well aware that the credibility of the new organization would depend on the scope, conduct and success of the founding assembly. They recognized that a completely open participation would run the risk of being dominated by particular interest groups, or by those people and organizations best able to pay the expenses. Great care was taken in selecting the invitees, to ensure a reasonable balance of interests between tropical, temperate and boreal regions, and between social, environmental and economic interests (Synnott, 2005).

The list of invitees included 134 people from 24 countries, most of whom came from northern countries. The organizers paid for a limited number of participants, giving priority to people from NGOs in the tropics. The participants included representatives from industries, social and environmental NGOs, and several governments. Among the participants were representatives from the WWF, Greenpeace, and the FoE, as well as labour unions, indigenous groups, retailers, and the consulting sector (Dingwerth, 2005). A draft of the *Principles and Criteria for Natural Forest Management* (Principles and Criteria) was approved, and by 1994 the final versions of that document and of the FSC statutes were approved by the FSC members.

Kwisthout remembers there were people invited from some companies in the pulp and paper industry 'with a very bad reputation ... so it was an enormous consternation amongst some of the more radical NGOs, environmental NGOs, that these people were invited at all'. Synnott (2005) reports that troubles began immediately at the founding assembly. Even before the meeting, an NGO, based in Germany, circulated a paper in which serious doubts were expressed: 'At best the FSC initiative is naïve, at worst it provides a framework for the timber industry to achieve a much desired "green veneer" and defuse pressure to attack the real issues of illegal trade, indigenous people's rights and over-consumption' (Rettet den Regenwald, in Synnott, 2005, p. 22). As the meeting began, some of the participants from a few social and environmental NGOs immediately protested the composition of the assembly and the decision-making procedures. They objected the participation in discussions and decision making by people with a commercial interest in the exploitation or marketing of timber. According to Synnott, however, skilful chairing and the establishment of subfora to avoid confrontations, made it possible for a dialog to begin. As more NGOs acknowledged that committed dealers and manufactures would play a valuable role and should have a voice in the FSC, the objecting faction was increasingly reduced. A general agreement was settled despite remaining controversies, but '[t]he agitation of the Founding Assembly foreshadowed the next few years of the FSC debate' (Synnott, 2005, p. 23).

One of the key decisions to be made in the founding assembly was whether or not to establish the FSC as a membership organization or a foundation. Worries were expressed among Interim Board members that a relatively open membership would be unwieldy and expensive, while creating severe limitations on the flexibility and decision-making capacity of the organization and encouraging the dominance of one interest group or another. The majority of the participants in the founding assembly believed, however, that an association (membership organization) would be a better structure for achieving FSC's goal (and in which they could exert influence in the future). 'This crucial decision involved introducing the chamber system [described below], to avoid the risk of any one group dominating FSC decisions' (Synnott, 2005, p. 24). As we show in Chapter 5, the same topic was discussed regarding the MSC, but with a different outcome; we further discuss the critical topic of maintaining a power balance in Chapter 10.

THE STANDARDS, ORGANIZATION, AND GOVERNANCE STRUCTURE

Although the FSC was formally established in October 1993, it operated for several months with no funds, staff, or office; and it was still two years away from attaining a legal status. In October 1995, the FSC was legally registered as a Mexican NGO, or Associación Civil (FSC A.C.). During the first years, 'the FSC framework was laid down: manuals, guidelines, protocols and contracts for certification bodies, National Initiatives and staff, together with the procedures for meetings: formal general assemblies, and less formal annual conferences and working groups' (Synnott, 2005, p. 28). In the next two sections, we briefly describe the standards, policies, and strategies that were established, followed by the organizational structure.

The FSC Standards, Policies, and Strategies

People from the FSC's core group wrote seven standard drafts, the sixth of which was broadly discussed during the national consultations. A firm conclusion of the consultations was that forest stewardship must be defined equally by environmental, economic, and social considerations; that the Principles and Criteria must apply equally to boreal, temperate, and tropical forests, defined by global principles but operating locally under ecosystem-specific standards; that these standards should apply equally to plantations and natural forests, and equally to small and large scale operations. And, as Synnott (2005) stated, 'the FSC programme has remained consistent with those conclusions ever since' (p. 21). Indeed, the largest number of controversies did not seem to be on the exact formulation of the FSC standards, but on types of organizational issues we have mentioned previously.

The basic FSC standards are known as the FSC Principles and Criteria. The ten principles are the fundamental rules formulated at a general, abstract level (see Appendix 3), which are to be worked out in more concrete processes of standard setting and certification at the national or regional level. The criteria should clarify the application of the principles. Each comprises an aspect of a principle, quantitatively or qualitatively formulated. The criteria, as well, require considerable interpretation.

Another main component of the regulatory framework of the FSC is accreditation manuals covering both forest management and chain-of-custody certification, which are used to accredit certifiers. Certification is performed by an accredited certification body (for-profit or not-for-profit) which, in turn, must follow either a national/regional adjusted FSC standard or FSC's Principles and Criteria directly, in case such national- or regional-adjusted FSC standard is not in place.

As can be seen by browsing the FSC website, the FSC has, over time, developed and refined a huge number of associated standards, guidelines, policy documents, and strategies. Several interviewees from the FSC Secretariat maintain that standards and policies are being constantly revised in the light of new experience. It is possible to mention only a few key examples here. In his report, Synnott (2005) notes, among other things, the development of policies for percentage-based claims[3] and the use of chemical pesticides (forbidden vs. restricted). It soon also became evident that

Principle 9, on the maintenance of natural forests, was unsatisfactorily formulated and required revision, as the criteria provided insufficient guidance on the identification and management of the site, in order to ensure compliance with the principle. The phrase 'high conservation value' was eventually invented in this concretization work. The FSC's tenth principle on plantation, established in 1995, two years later than the other principles, has given rise to controversy, particularly regarding social aspects. And again, in 2004, the FSC launched a two-year Plantations Review process to accommodate increasing criticism raised by NGOs.

One important strategy has been the 'social strategy' (FSC, 2003), launched because the FSC faced extra difficulties in fulfilling its social goals – problems regarding the fragmentation and underrepresentation of members from the social chamber, for instance (see also Chapter 8). Furthermore, the majority of FSC-certified forests appeared in the developed part of the world under the large forest companies, rather than in small family or community-based forestry (Pattberg, 2007). This outcome is ironic, as the FSC attempted from the beginning to encourage certification in developing countries and for small-scale operations (cf. Meidinger, Elliot, and Oesten, 2003). Preparing for certification is not without costs, however, and requires some level of administrative, management, and technical skill, as well as access to international market structures. One outcome of the social strategy is the FSC's Small and Low Intensity Management Forest (SLIMF) standards, as applied for example to community-managed forests operations. Although several of our interviewees appreciated this and other measures, most of them maintained that the problems remain, and, as stated in the current FSC global strategy, 'FSC has not made as much impact on small forest owners, community forests, or low intensity managed forests as was initially hoped' (FSC, 2007, p. 8). Another ongoing project is a recent collaboration with the Fairtrade Labelling Organization International. The two organizations have launched a pilot project with the hope and aim of establishing a dual-certification system that could bring benefits to small-scale forestry.[4]

A topic for the future is to relate FSC certification to the climate issue, as forests play an important role in combating climate change (carbon sequestration, biofuels). This perspective provides new opportunities for the FSC (FSC, 2007). A standing forest can indeed bring a number of 'ecosystem services' and relate to ecotourism – issues that were not considered when the organization began. Thus the FSC has recently seen several new opportunities to increase its profile.

The FSC's Multi-Stakeholder Organizational Form

The FSC was formally established as a membership organization, having both individuals and organizations as members. The FSC is governed by a General Assembly of members divided into three chambers (the environmental, the economic, and the social) – discursively affected by the concept of sustainable development and its three dimensions of social, environmental, and economic sustainability (cf. Pattberg, 2007). Each chamber has one-third of the voting power. In addition, the voting power is divided equally between developed (northern) and developing (southern) country members in each of the three chambers.[5] The main aims of the chosen organizational design are to ensure that no group can dominate policymaking and that the north cannot dominate at the expense of the south. The latter goal was deemed necessary because of the strong north-south controversies around tropical deforestation during the late 1980s, which arose again during the Rio summit in 1992. Furthermore, organizations were allotted 90% of the voting power and individuals 10% in each chamber. The General Assembly, which meets every third year (1996, 1999, 2002, 2005, 2008), is the highest decision-making organ. An affirmative vote of two-thirds of the voting power is required to adopt a motion.

The original organizational structure adopted in 1993 involved only two chambers: one with social and environmental interests that was accorded 75% of the votes; and one with economic interests, with 25% of votes. This was a compromise, instituted because some stakeholders at the founding assembly found it difficult to accept any formal decision-making power by economic interests. By 1996, however, the strongest criticism appeared to accumulate from the trade and industry players, which considered themselves underrepresented (Dingwerth, 2005). The FSC was criticized for being 'anti-industry' (Elliot, 1999), and it responded in 1996 with the current tripartite structure. Many industry players, globally and nationally, still think that economic interests should have more than one-third of the voting power, because, at the end of the day, companies have the ultimate responsibility to implement the standards. Such criticism has led to the development of the competing certification schemes discussed later in this chapter.

Individual or organizational members of the FSC are categorized in accordance with the three chambers, and two existing FSC members are required to support applications for membership. FSC has been steadily growing from its inception.[6] By May 2009 it had 827 members, 366 from developed ('northern') countries and 461 from developing ('southern') countries; 328 of the members belonged to the economic chamber, 346 to the environment chamber, and 153 to the social chamber.[7]

The FSC has not allowed governmental actors to be members, primarily because of inertia in governmental and intergovernmental policymaking and a concern that governmental participation would unbalance the dialog among economic, environmental, and social stakeholders (Dingwerth, 2005). The FSC's exclusion of state actors is somewhat problematic, however, given the multi-stakeholder rhetoric of the FSC, and has led some actors to reject non-state certification and to see it as an unnecessary or unwelcome addition to governmental control over forest management (Elliot, 1999). Moreover, state actors are often forest landowners as well. As a response to such criticism, the General Assembly of 2002 passed a motion to include an exception to the rule and to allow government-owned or government-controlled companies to be members of the economic chamber of the FSC under special conditions. The latest General Assembly gave support to the introduction of a new type of membership for such organizations as government agencies and academic institutions – supporting members that could provide financial support to the FSC but could not participate through voting (FSC, 2008).

The General Assembly elects the nine-member FSC Board of Directors, comprising three members from each of the three chambers. Northern or southern members may account for no more than five members. The board of directors, which meets three to four times a year, is responsible for such issues as overseeing the organizational activities of the FSC, providing strategic guidance to the secretariat, approving national certification standards, and allocating budget. Rather than pushing for the interests of the organization with which they affiliate, board members are expected to provide their expertise and represent the views and concerns of their respective chamber and category (for example economy/south).

The FSC International Secretariat in Bonn, Germany, conducts the daily work of the FSC. It is staffed by fewer than 30 employees, headed by the Executive Director who is responsible to the board. The secretariat is divided into operational units: the Policy and Standards Unit, the Communication and Marketing Unit, the Finance and Fundraising Unit, and the Office Management and Human Resource Unit. In 2005, the previous Accreditation Business Unit was separated into an independent body, as a way of adapting to globally recognized ISO standards in the field of accreditation and certification (ISO 65). The unit is now an accreditation service company called Accreditation Services International (ASI), wholly owned by the FSC, but operating independently. The FSC has another subsidiary called the FSC Global Development, which is responsible for the FSC trademarks and brand.

The secretariat is tasked with the effective implementation of FSC policies and programs, promotion and fund-raising, and collection and distribution of information about the FSC activities; the presentation of annual reports; the coordination of regional office activities; assistance to the National Initiatives in various ways; preparation for the general assemblies; collaboration with actors supportive to the FSC; the consistency of FSC policies and practices worldwide; and the handling of certification bodies. The secretariat plays an influential role as an interpreter of the FSC Principles and Criteria and FSC policies (Dingwerth, 2005; Pattberg, 2007). We further discuss the role and increasing power of the secretariat, in greater detail in Chapters 6 and 7.

Another key organizational element of the FSC is the *National Initiatives*, which are approved by the FSC Board. National Initiatives exist in 56 countries. It was assumed from the start that national standards would be best developed by national stakeholders working together in a national working group, and that national and regional certification standards should be developed through multi-stakeholder consultative processes in national FSC working groups that mimic the FSC's tripartite organizational structure (equal representation of the three chambers). These working groups must be approved by the FSC's international board. The parent organization, the FSC, would play a coordinating (and pushing) role, but would not develop the national standards.[8] Interviewees from the secretariat maintain that they often engage with contact persons from National Initiatives, and they claim that National Initiatives are involved in many issues: marketing, standard setting, dispute resolution, and they also act as stakeholders by giving comments.

The basic three-chamber structure is now firmly rooted. Other constitutional aspects in the governance structure of this growing organization have been topics for continuous discussion and reforms, however. Soon after the millennium shift, a group called the Change Management Team was formed and commissioned to investigate coming challenges and strategic issues for the FSC (FSC, 2002). The group conducted a range of interviews with stakeholders and staff members to identify internal and external challenges. The General Assembly of 2005 decided to establish a comprehensive review of FSC's operational and decision-making structures. These review processes and the FSC strategy documents (e.g. FSC, 2002, 2005, 2007, 2008) have suggested changes in the relationship between the board and the secretariat (for a discussion of this issue, see Chapter 7), in the relationships among FSC units at various levels, in the separation of the accreditation and standard-setting functions, in measures to secure an independent financial basis, and in the professionalization of communication activities (cf. Pattberg, 2007). Based upon these and other documents and upon comments from interviewees, it is fair to say that one of the most central organizational issues has been the challenge of maintaining the efficiency of the FSC throughout its growth, while maintaining its structure with democratic input from social, environmental, and economic interests worldwide. The FSC has reached a level of complexity that creates serious governance challenges for the organization. Kwisthout, who at the time of the interview was also a staff member of the secretariat, reflects on the decision to establish the FSC as a member organization rather than a foundation (cf. the case of the MSC, Chapter 5): 'Now, that's fine from a democratic point of view, but it creates an enormous amount of administration, because now I think we've got about 900 members – still not a lot, but it is a lot of work to administer.' He talks about organizational and funding issues as the two most challenging current issues facing the FSC. Another interviewee, with experience in both the FSC and the MSC, talks about a key difference between these two organizations: 'FSC has this global concept of National Initiatives and national standards', which makes the FSC 'very difficult to manage' (see Chapter 5 on the MSC).

Funding has proved to be an incessantly challenging issue, and many commentators (including several interviewees; cf. FSC, 2002; 2008) argue that the FSC is drastically under-financed. As the financial challenges faced by the FSC and the MSC are similar, we have decided to elaborate on this topic only in relation to the MSC, which we have done in Chapter 5.

Except for the Accreditation Program (by FSC's subsidiary Accreditation Service International), from the beginning the FSC has relied heavily on donors from governmental and nongovernmental organizations and private foundations, with membership accounting for only 5% of its total income (see also Dingwerth, 2005).[9]

THE FSC IN THE TRANSNATIONAL REGULATORY SPACE – COUNTERMOVES AND RELATION TO IGOS' REGULATORY FRAMEWORKS

We have mentioned that the initiation and founding of the FSC gave rise to intensive critiques and controversies, some of which were channeled within the FSC system. According to Kwisthout, who was active from the start, radical environmental groups have been and remain serious critics of FSC. They do not believe in developing a dialogue or engaging in negotiations with large forest companies. Several interviewees mention Simon Counsell, and his NGO Rainforest Foundation in this regard. Counsell was engaged in the FoE and timber boycotting during the 1980s. He participated in the early FSC development, but would later appear primarily as a critic, raising serious concern over dubious FSC certificates. Later, he co-authored the well-known critical report, *Trading in Credibility. The myth and reality of the Forest Stewardship Council* (Counsell and Loraas, 2002), in which the topic of dubious FSC-certified forestry was discussed with reference to a number of case studies. Counsell is no longer a member of the FSC and eventually formed the FSC watch, which is an independent observer of the FSC developed by FSC supporters, members, and nonmembers concerned about what they perceive as 'the constant and serious erosion of the FSC's reliability and thus credibility'.[10] The group critically examines several FSC certifications in a number of countries, and reports their results on its website. Its members argue that the FSC is increasingly captured by vested commercial interests (the economic chamber) and criticize the FSC's inability to address the problem, as well as its tendency to report only success stories (see also Chapter 9).

The FSC initiative has also been controversial for a large number of business actors in the forest sector. Some forest companies have not accepted the invitation to participate in the FSC's tripartite structure, and have initiated competing processes and programs. One early counter-initiative taken by forest industries was to seek forest certification through environmental management systems (ISO 14001). In 1995, the Canadian and Australian standards bodies also proposed to ISO that a guide be prepared for the application of ISO 14001 in the forest sector. Greenpeace and other environmental NGOs opposed such initiatives, however, on the grounds that an environmental management system is an insufficient basis for claims of sustainability, because it lacks performance levels (Elliot, 1999). They also criticized the lack of stakeholder participation in ISO that could allow credible discussions on sustainable forest management. The Canadian/Australian proposal was eventually withdrawn. According to one of our interviewees from an FSC-certified forest company, a new perspective regarding the relationship between ISO 14001 and the FSC, eventually emerged, and it came to be seen that the two standards were compatible rather than competing. In order to establish legitimacy as a global standard setter, it has also become important for the FSC to make certain references to ISO 65.

More challenging for the FSC has been the development of competing programs by forest-industry and forest-landowner associations in Canada, the USA, Europe, and most other countries in which the FSC is active (Cashore et al., 2004). Such separate initiatives were later merged into the Programme for the Endorsement of Forest Certification (PEFC) schemes. These competing programs mirrored the ISO 14000 family, by emphasizing organizational procedures and discretionary, flexible performance guidelines, in contrast to the FSC's insistence on substantive, nondiscretionary, and fixed performance requirements (cf. Cashore et al., 2004). Moreover, these competing models were dominated by business interests, in contrast to the equal distribution of voting power among environmental, social, and business interests in the FSC. Their standards were narrower in scope, stressing only forestry management rules and continual improvement, whereas the FSC includes rules on labour and indigenous rights and wide-ranging environmental impact. Although the FSC and the PEFC, for instance, remain competitors and opponents, many scholars have observed that the systems have gradually moved closer together, and are not completely independent of each other (e.g. Cashore et al., 2004; Domask, 2003; Boström and Klintman, 2008).

From the beginning, the FSC has also felt the need to establish links with the policies of other IGOs, while emphasizing an independent position in the transnational regulatory space. We saw earlier that the FSC was established in part as a reaction to failures within IGO policy processes to establish effective regulatory frameworks for dealing with the global forest crisis. To side-step IGOs completely, however, would likely trigger devastating conflicts. Many public actors are actively involved in defining and developing strategies for what is termed 'sustainable forest management'. Such UN units as the Food and Agriculture Organization of the UN and the ITTO are engaged with this task. They maintain some distance from the FSC, and are not always in agreement with the FSC and its potential effectiveness. Yet, they embrace its 'broader mandates for nongovernmental participation and oversight in community forestry' (McNichol, 2003, p. 24) and have:

> moved from early positions of suspicion about certification (as a potential non-tariff barrier to trade, and as diverting attention from government-led forestry improvements), to tracking progress in certification (the annual ITTO updates being particularly useful), to acceptance of FSC, and of certification amongst many instruments for SFM [Sustainable Forestry Management] (Bass, 2003, p. 39).

At the same time, such organizations compete over symbolic dominance in the transnational regulatory space (cf. Gulbrandsen, 2004). The Change Management Team repeatedly stressed in their report the critical need to position FSC globally and in relation to its competitors, and argued the FSC has to be 'the ISO of forest certification' (FSC, 2002). This report emphasized the 'serious competitive threats that FSC is facing' (p. 3). It is critical that the FSC be recognized as *the* international standard because, '[s]hould lower standards be accepted as the international framework by the WTO, stricter FSC standards would be deemed *de facto* trade barriers' (p. 4). The result would be the watering down of FSC standards either through mutual recognition of the accepted standard or through the marginalization of the FSC system.

The Change Management Team recommended the development of proactive strategies for dealing with competition, including work with allies in the transnational arena, through such means as linking with progressive retailers. One way to guard its positions and credibility in the transnational regulatory space is to also be involved in a meta-organization for labeling organizations. The FSC – as well as the MSC – is a member of the International Social and Environmental Accrediting and Labelling Alliance (ISEAL Alliance) – a membership that requires it to follow its Code of Good Practice for Setting Social and Environmental Standards (see Chapter 6). Linking to such other organizations is critically important for maintaining power and legitimacy, and ultimately for maintaining authority, for such an organizations as the FSC (see for instance Chapter 9).

We have demonstrated that the FSC must constantly guard its position in the transnational regulatory space as it faces criticism from radical social and environmental NGOs and competition from other standard setters, and as is being assessed by IGOs. When we asked Kwisthout what he thought about the achievement so far, he replied 'we are still here'. He argued that the FSC could certainly be better, but it could be worse – it could cease to exist. This is indeed an intriguing observation because, as we argue in this book, it requires substantial organizing and legitimizing efforts to establish and maintain such a non-state authority as the FSC.

NOTES

1. Several scholars have written fascinating and informative texts on the establishment of the FSC, which we refer to in this section. See, for instance, Elliot, 1999; Cashore et al., 2004; Dingwerth, 2005; Pattberg, 2007; and Gulbrandsen, 2009. The main reference in this section, however, is that of Timothy Synnott (2005), first Executive Director of the FSC, who also took an active role in the establishment of the association. His text, which is available on the FSC website, provides a rich description and reflection of events before and during the early years of the FSC. We recommend it to anyone looking for more historical detail on the FSC. We have also conducted some informative interviews with people who were active from the beginning, including Hubert Kwisthout, who kindly agreed to allow us to use his name.

2. Many commentators saw the UN Conference on Environment and Development in Rio as failing in forest regulation. There were concerted calls for the implementation of a forest convention, but the international negotiations revealed that northern and southern societies had greatly differing perspectives on the issue (Elliot, 1999; Pattberg, 2007). Whereas northern governments saw deforestation as a global environmental problem that had to be addressed, southern governments were reluctant to sign agreements that would weaken their sovereignty over these resources. The only results of the Rio conference were a set of nonbinding 'Forest Principles' and a chapter in Agenda 21.

3. i.e. how much of a FSC-labeled product that would come from certified forests (100% or less, how much less, how to handle recycled material, how to assure traceability, and so on).

4. http://www.fsc.org/news.html?&txttnews[ttnews]=129&txttnews[backPid]=107&cHash= 24d 26b2268, accessed 15 September 2008.

5. The FSC defines 'northern members as those based in high-income countries and 'southern members as based in low, middle or upper-middle income countries (Pattberg, 2007, p. 115, p. 149).

6.   See trend, p. 21 of the FSC annual report of 2007: http://www.fsc.org/fileadmin/web-data/public/document_center/publications/annual_reports/Annual_Report_2007_ENG.pdf, accessed 15 May 2009.
7.   http://www.fsc.org/fileadmin/web-data/public/document_center/publications/newsletter/newsletter_2009/FSC-PUB-20-07-04-2009-05-07.pdf?PHPSESSID=b662bcd51697726becb87b42bee35f09, accessed 15 May 2009.
8.   National Initiatives are no longer the only groups entitled to develop national standards. Balanced stakeholder working groups may be set up to develop national (and regional) standards without the necessity for these to be accredited as national initiatives.
9.   Figures taken from p. 28, available at http://www.fsc.org/fileadmin/web-data/public/document_center/publications/annual_reports/Annual_Report_2007_ENG.pdf, accessed 20 May 2009, referring to the FSC and its subsidiaries.
10. See www.fsc-watch.org, accessed 28 June 2009.

5. Marine Stewardship Council

During the last two decades, the depletion of fish stocks through industrial overfishing and destruction of marine habitats have been among the most infected and debated environmental issues globally. Controversies have escalated: marine scientists versus fishers; big fishing industries versus environmental NGOs; large-scale versus small-scale fisheries in the high seas and coastal waters; and conflicts among fishing nations, including developed versus developing countries. Various regulatory efforts to counteract this escalating global crisis have been undertaken; and for the purpose of this book, we find it particularly interesting to focus on the non-state standard setter, the Marine Stewardship Council (MSC). The directors of the WWF and Unilever made a remarkable – and controversial – announcement in February 1996, when they signed a joint statement of intent to establish the MSC. One year later, in February 1997, the MSC was formally established in London with a specific mission: to work for sustainable marine fisheries through a system of certification and labeling. The MSC's *Principles and Criteria for Sustainable Fishing* (Principles and Criteria) were developed to encourage sustainable fisheries – regardless of their size, scale, complexity, geography, or technology – to be assessed for any commercial fishery anywhere in the world. MSC certification began in 1999. In June 2009, 48 fisheries had been certified, and more than 2000 products were carrying the MSC label.[1]

In this chapter, we describe the early and later development of, the MSC organization and its standards and policies, including the challenges faced by the organization. Indeed, the WWF and Unilever initiatives were both novel and provocative in the eyes of several stakeholders.

THE WAY TO A MARINE STEWARDSHIP COUNCIL

As was the case with the FSC, the MSC was established in response to a crisis: global fisheries. A huge and increasing amount of the world's most valuable commercial fish stocks were over-exploited, fully exploited, depleted, or recovering from over-exploitation. And there was no sign that this negative trend was about to be altered. A painful experience that occurred some years before the establishment of the MSC was the collapse of the Grand Banks cod fishery of Newfoundland, Canada, and the loss of over 40 000 related jobs in the industry (Howes, 2005).

The alarming international situation was and is frequently blamed on the rapid growth of the industrial fishing fleet and harvesting capacities, unrestrained market forces, and paralyzed intergovernmental regulation (Oosterver, 2005). Scientific evidence, when available, has been neglected for political reasons, quotas are set higher than recommended, and controls are often ineffective creating considerable space for illicit fishing (e.g. Kuntzsch, 2003). Regulating fisheries is especially problematic because fish is an open access resource, leading to a 'tragedy of the commons' (Hardin, 1968).

The first convention trying to deal with overfishing was the UN Convention on the Law of the Sea of 1982 (e.g. Porter, Brown, and Chasek, 2000; Hoel, 2004). Several key fishing countries have been unwilling to implement that convention, however, and the rules are often criticized for their laxness. Additional rules and policies, such as the 1995 FAO Code of Conduct for Responsible Fisheries and the UN Fish Stocks Agreement, have since been implemented. Although such regulatory arrangements have encouraged a precautionary ecosystem approach to fisheries management, they are not legally binding, and have had only limited success in preventing further decline in fishing stocks worldwide.

Given such rule-setting inertia among IGOs, the major transnational environmental NGOs gradually introduced fisheries as a key issue on their agenda (Hoel, 2004). WWF International launched its Living Planet Campaign in 1995, with 'Endangered Seas' as one of its main issues. The organization targeted IGOs and national bodies with limited success. There were some previous labeling efforts in the fisheries sector such as dolphin-safe tuna or turtle-safe shrimps, but they referred to only one attribute, and did not focus on overfishing (Chaffee, Leadbitter, and Aalders, 2003). As WWF experienced positive achievements with the FSC initiative, it identified an opportunity to initiate a similar approach in this sector. Unilever, an important buyer in the seafood industry, began to take the same perspective, as declining fish stocks presented the company with an obvious risk: 'Unilever, one of the world's leading buyers of frozen fish, recognised that, unless major fisheries took stronger steps to become sustainable, the company would no longer have access to its valued raw material' (Weir, 2000, p. 119).

Unilever had recently developed a sustainability policy and had contacts with scientists that were researching the state of future global fish stocks. In 1995, researcher Jackie McGlade informed Unilever and WWF of their mutual interest in this issue (Fowler and Heap, 2000), and a consultant from

Burson-Marsteller working with Unilever 'advised Unilever that WWF was a more suitable partner than Greenpeace on the grounds that WWF is a more "conservative" NGO with previous experience of working with business through the FSC' (p. 138). As one Unilever interviewee, Volker Kuntzsch, informed us, Greenpeace Germany began a public campaign at that stage, and Unilever was bombarded with postcards from German consumers. Kuntzsch continued, 'So we were very aware that we had to do something, and at the same time WWF tried to find the best way to approach fisheries in order to improve sustainability'.

The two organizations initiated a dialogue, but not without initial resistance from some of their members: 'There was a lot of tension in the beginning, yes, and it required a great deal of communication and discussion to get it done', Kuntzsch told us (see also Fowler and Heap, 2000; Weir, 2000). He said that the main obstacles were about trust: 'knowing each other's history, Unilever knowing that WWF was very much about campaigning, putting ads into newspaper about how bad the fisheries are'. He continued:

> We also had to learn a lot about WWF at that stage, trying to find out if they were really serious, whether this is not just an idea to get closer into the Unilever business to see what they really do and maybe turn the whole thing around into a campaign, now that they had all the data.

WWF members were concerned about the way a partnership could affect their relationship with key IGOs, other environmental NGOs, and the fish workers' unions. Another worry was that WWF would indirectly legitimize all other operations of Unilever or that WWF could be in conflict with the company. The strategy of forming a partnership, however, fits with WWF's identity as a cooperative, constructive, and solution-oriented environmental NGO. Key members of each organization played a crucial role in overcoming internal political obstacles. WWF and Unilever then hired the international consulting firm, Coopers & Lybrand, to develop implementation plans for the MSC. In February 1996, the directors of WWF and Unilever signed a joint statement of intent to establish MSC.

The similarity between the names *MSC* and *FSC* is obviously no coincidence. Indeed, staff members from the WWF's forest team, who were active in the work with the FSC, were also engaged in developing the Marine Stewardship Council. Although the FSC was seen as a positive model, its governance structure and processes were seen as cumbersome and time-consuming (Fowler and Heap, 2000; Synnott, 2005; Gulbrandsen, 2008). Coopers & Lybrand consultants attended the first General Assembly of the FSC, and, according to one of our interviewee, 'were pretty horrified':[2]

And they said essentially, as I understood it: "whatever you do when you set up the MSC, don't make it democratic, like the FSC". So the MSC was set up with much more hand picking of the board ... and that the approach to standard development would be more scientific and technical rather than consultative. ... You wouldn't have a hundred random members, members of the FSC, debating and drafting standards and then voting on them. So the FSC was much more democratic in its structure than the MSC was. And intentionally so.

Based on such concerns, the consultant advised that the MSC be established as a foundation rather than a membership organization like the FSC. Volker Kuntzsch from Unilever, who was active in the process, also explained:

We didn't want to be seen as an organization that is owned by anybody or one that is made up of certain green interests, or a number of companies or environmental organizations [with their own agenda] ... It should be an independently governed body without influence from a specific majority.

From the outset, the MSC established a governance structure that was strikingly less democratic than that of the FSC. As it eventually became independent of WWF and Unilever, however, its feature as a multi-stakeholder organization was strengthened. Before describing this organizational development, we first describe the development of the standards framework.

DEVELOPING THE PRINCIPLES AND CRITERIA

The MSC's Principles and Criteria were developed in a process that stretched over 18 months (May, Leadbitter, Sutton, and Weber, 2003). The core group comprising selected marine experts and people from the WWF and Unilever developed an initial draft of Principles and Criteria, which was presented at a workshop in the UK in September 1996. This document was drawn from a number of sources, including the FAO *Code of Conduct for Responsible Fisheries* and the UN *Agreement on Highly Migratory Species and Straddling Stocks*. This draft was reviewed at eight meetings with a wide range of stakeholders in the USA, Germany, Scandinavia, South Africa, New Zealand, Australia, and Canada. The core group at the workshop, which arranged the eight stakeholder meetings, included environmental and marine experts and scientists, members of the fishing industry, seafood buyers and processors, and governmental officials and regulators. The core group also had contact with such organizations as the World Conservation Union (IUCN), the World Bank, and OECD. Further considerations were conducted in developing countries in Africa, Latin America, and Asia. A final draft of the Principles and Criteria was prepared at a second workshop in Washington, DC, USA, in December 1997, and forwarded to the MSC's Board of Directors. Before the final adoption of the Principles and Criteria in 1998, several test cases were conducted. In spite of the extensive set of stakeholder meetings that was arranged, this initial period of standard setting appeared to be primarily in the hands of experts from environmental NGOs (particularly WWF), marine and environmental experts and scientists, and representatives of retailers and processors in the seafood industry. As we describe later in the chapter, criticism soon surfaced, particularly from fishing communities, fish workers, and some governmental actors (e.g. from some developing nations and from Scandinavia).

The MSC set three general principles, which, in turn, form the basis for 23 detailed criteria that are used to evaluate fisheries seeking MSC certification:[3]

1. A fishery must be conducted in a manner that does not lead to overfishing or depletion of the exploited populations and, for those populations that are depleted, the fishery must be conducted in a manner that demonstrably leads to their recovery.
2. Fishing operations should allow for the maintenance of the structure, productivity, function and diversity of the ecosystem (including habitat and associated dependent and ecologically related species) on which the fishery depends.
3. The fishery is subject to an effective management system that respects local, national and international laws and standards and incorporates institutional and operational frameworks that require use of the resource to be responsible and sustainable.

MSC Principles and Criteria were aimed at global application, considering the fact that fisheries vary extensively along a number of parameters. The standard formulations tend to be indicative rather than absolute. They state what should be achieved rather than precisely how to achieve a particular outcome.[4]

In striking contrast to the FSC case, the MSC standards did not cover SR or sustainability, although they were advocated by a number of commentators. As Kuntzsch from Unilever said:

> What we were definitely trying to influence during the standard-setting process from Unilever's point of view was not to put too much emphasis on the social sector, but ensure that we are talking about fisheries management practices in order to ensure the sustainability of fish stocks. In the beginning, there was a great deal of emphasis placed on [articulations such as]: "Yes, but we need to take care of the developing nations and we need to make sure that people are not negatively influenced and we should consider aquaculture, and all these things." And we said:

"Well, for us, this is really about making sure there will be wild fish out there in the ocean in the future that can be caught, and that everything else should be regarded as a second priority and should maybe be included in the future in some stage." But our first priority should be on how do we ensure the sustainability of wild fish stocks. That was basically the direction given by Unilever.

Accordingly, the MSC institutionalized a standard that focused chiefly on environmental matters.

As with the FSC, MSC labeling requires chain-of-custody tracking to ensure that products carrying its logo actually originate from a certified fishery. All companies in the supply chain – from boat to plate – must have MSC's Chain of Custody certification. A first version of this standard was established in December 1999, and a second one in August 2005.[5] This standard states, for example, that businesses must demonstrate their effective storage and record-keeping systems, making it possible to separate certified fish and noncertified fish.

As the Principles and Criteria are formulated at a generic level, indicators must be more specific – developed individually for each fishery. The actual certification process plays a critical role in determining the definition and interpretation of the Principles and Criteria.[6] The first certifications were 'very much a learning phase for the MSC' (Cummins, 2004, p. 90), and one key lesson was the level of guidance material that must be given to both certification bodies and other stakeholders. The Fishery Certification Methodology was developed early on and has been updated continuously in parallel to experiences of certifications. Worries about significant variations in the quality of assessments encouraged the MSC to launch the Quality and Consistency project in 2006, which led to the introduction of the Fishery Assessment Methodology in 2008. The aim of the 2008 document was to provide certification guidelines and to assist accredited certification bodies and other stakeholders to make the actual certification process more effective, streamlined, and transparent. The MSC has gradually implemented a number of other strategy and policy documents as well – the recently introduced *Guidelines for the Assessment of Small-Scale and Data-Deficient Fisheries*, for instance, which is part of the MSC's Developing World Programme.

THE ESTABLISHMENT OF THE MSC AND ITS MULTI-STAKEHOLDER FORM

The MSC was established under an Interim Board comprising members of WWF and Unilever. The Board was disbanded in February 1998, and the MSC was eventually rendered independent, with funding from a number of charitable trusts. Unilever and WWF had a strong agenda-setting role in the formative years of the MSC (cf. Fowler and Heap, 2000) and continued to play key roles. Weir, from Unilever, maintains '[a]lthough the MSC now operates independently from the partners, both Unilever and the WWF clearly have a large stake in the successful introduction of the certification scheme among fisheries around the world' (Weir, 2000).

Since the time of the MSC's independence, it has been critical to the legitimacy of the MSC and its image as an independent unit that WWF and Unilever (particularly Unilever) maintain their distance (Fowler and Heap, 2000; Constance and Bonanno, 2000). The MSC faced criticism, primarily from NGOs, that it was much less democratic than the FSC (see further discussion in the final section of this chapter) and that WWF and Unilever controlled it. It had to develop into more of a multi-stakeholder organization, which happened gradually. The governing body that was initially established included a board, a standards council, an advisory board, an approvals committee, and an informal senior advisors' group. As the MSC progressively implemented the governance structure, however, it became evident that, in addition to insufficient stakeholder inclusion, it was inefficient and expensive to operate (MSC, 2003). Commentators spoke of 'decision paralysis' (Ward, Phillips, and Chaffee, 2003). In response to comments and critique from a number of stakeholders, the MSC commissioned an independent panel in 2000 with representatives from industry and NGOs (albeit with eight persons already firmly integrated into the MSC network). The role of the panel was to review the governance of the MSC in order to achieve greater transparency and openness, while maintaining its efficiency. This panel conducted a ten-month review while they 'consulted with hundreds of individuals and groups' (MSC, 2003). The process led to a new governance structure, which was relatively complex but more positively recognized.[7] It now includes the main Board of Trustees, Technical Advisory Board, and Stakeholder Council, each of which is described in the following sections. In addition, there are committees with specific mandated tasks, informal working groups, and regional and national working groups. These working groups are not established as separate units, as they are in the FSC structure, with its 'National Initiatives'; rather, an

MSC executive (which we call 'secretariat' in this book) is accountable to the board and supports all these bodies.

The Board of Trustees

The Board of Trustees, which meets formally four times a year, has maximum 15 members appointed in their personal capacities. Its members are nominated for a three-year term. The board should be balanced with representatives from different sectors and geographical regions. It makes final decisions regarding the approval of a fishery that has applied for MSC certification and makes decisions about overall organizational strategies. It also considers issues relating to funding and appoints chief members of the Board of Trustees, Technical Advisory Board, committees, and the secretariat. The Board of Trustees delegates much of its work to the committee structure (in which board members can participate), which includes the Finance Committee and the Executive Committee.

Given the review of the governance structure, the MSC has worked to get broad and balanced sector and geographical representation in the Board of Trustees. In order to ensure representation and input in decision making from both the Technical Advisory Board and the Stakeholder Council (described below), the chairmen from each group have positions on the Board of Trustees. In August 2008, the 12 members of the Board of Trustees, including the WWF, had a background in marine science, fishery management, the seafood industry, and the environmental community.[8]

The MSC's Technical Advisory Board

The MSC Technical Advisory Board comprises members from scientific and standard-setting backgrounds. They are appointed by the Board of Trustees and elected in their personal capacity for their expertise in matters relating to the Principles and Criteria. The Technical Advisory Board, which meets approximately twice annually, advises the Board of Trustees and the Stakeholder Council on matters relating to MSC standards. It can also make decisions on issues delegated by the Board of Trustees.

As we discuss in Chapter 8, one could argue that the word 'advisory' serves to undervalue the role and power of this unit. It has, for example, a key role in developing policies and guidelines for assessment and certification. The frameworks of the MSC and the FSC are different. The MSC has only one universal standard (Principles and Criteria), whereas the FSC, as a complement to its global standard, has a structure with nationally or regionally adjusted standards. Because fisheries in different seas and regions vary along many dimensions, having only one universal standard implies that the MSC guidelines for assessment and certification – the Fishery Certification Methodology and Fishery Assessment Methodology, for instance – attain extra importance. And it is the responsibility of the Technical Advisory Board to develop and refine these central MSC documents in a continuous manner. The profile of the members of the Technical Advisory Board is strikingly similar to the profiles of the members of the Board of Trustees. As of August 2008, the webpage lists 16 experts. It is notable that at least half of them are marine scientists or marine researchers from natural science backgrounds, most of the others are from fisheries management or the seafood industry, and a few have specific standard-setting expertise (one such member was a key person in the early establishment of the FSC).[9]

The Stakeholder Council

The Stakeholder Council comprises 30 to 50 members. It meets annually to allow participants to express concerns and deliberate on current challenges, and the Council has the mandate of sending recommendations and opinions to the Board of Trustees and the Technical Advisory Board. The Board of Trustees must consider the views of the Stakeholder Council. Basically, the same type of issues that are discussed in the other units are debated in the Stakeholder Council (see Chapter 8), but it is the task of this unit to ensure that the interest and knowledge of all relevant stakeholder categories are voiced and considered.

The Stakeholder Council was initially divided into eight categories, each of which had equal weight. Four belonged to the 'Public Interest Category': Scientific, Academic and Resource Management Interests, General Conservation NGOs and Interests, Marine Conservation NGOs and Specialist Interests, and General Interests and Organisations. The other four belonged to the Commercial and Socio-Economic Category, Catch Sector Interests, Supply Chain and Processing Interests, Retail, Catering and Distribution Interests, and Developing Nation and Fishing Community Interests. Although these subcategories may have been helpful for achieving broad coverage of interest representation, members of the Stakeholder Council did not consider them particularly useful (see MSC, 2007). Our interviewees actually speak of a two-chamber structure, by referring to 'the Public Interest Category' (some say 'the NGOs') and 'Commercial and Socio-Economic Category', and did not give much weight to the subcategories. The MSC also established a Stakeholder Council Steering Group comprising eight people – one member from each subgroup. This steering group was established in order to facilitate regular interaction with the other organizational units. It has appointed two chairs: one from the group of constituencies that fall into the public interest sector and the other from the commercial sector. Both co-chairs have positions on the Board of Trustees. The MSC now refers to these two categories, as well as a third 'Developing World Category'. In practice, however, the two-chamber structure appears to be the norm. The Stakeholder Council Steering Group has only two chairs in the Board of Trustees, for example, and they are occupied by people from the other two categories.

It has been difficult to recruit members from the Public Interest sector and to obtain representation from small-scale fisheries, developing countries, and consumer associations. In July 2009, the MSC reported on its website[10] that the Stakeholder Council had 11 members in the Public Interest category, all but one from developed countries. It had 16 members from developed countries in the Commercial and Socio-Economic Category and 4 from the Developing World Category. An interviewee who has participated in the Stakeholder Council says that although it represents NGOs, industry, and academia, it generally comprises 'people from Anglo-Saxon countries, sharing the same culture and background'.

Whereas the Technical Advisory Board is an organ for the representation of science and standards expertise, the Stakeholder Council was established to represent commercial, environmental, and other public interests. Accordingly, there is a clear organizational distinction made between 'technical' and 'political' issues, and between 'expertise' and 'stakeholder/interest representation', an issue we discuss further in Chapter 8.

In contrast to the FSC case, participants in the Stakeholder Council are not members, in the true sense of the word, and have no formal voting power. According to Gale and Haward, the MSC structure, compared to that of the FSC, is better-adjusted to a fast-moving business environment: 'Its managerial structure is designed to insulate the Board of Trustees from the political influence of civil society actors' (quoted in Ponte, 2008, p. 163). Others argue that there is a need for the council to strike a balance between democracy and efficiency, between public interest and timely progress. 'It is very easy (and a well tried strategy for some) to tie up organisations in the bureaucracy of consultation and input' (May, Leadbitter, Sutton, and Weber, 2003, p. 25). As one interviewee argues, although the Stakeholder Council 'has relatively little formal power', the structure 'does acknowledge that a variety of stakeholders must be involved in the development of policy'.

The council appoints half its members, and the MSC Board appoints the other half after consultation with the MSC Secretariat. Each sub-constituency in the Stakeholder Council is responsible for its own nominations and appointments. Accordingly, there is a clear barrier to cross if a stakeholder wants to be a 'member'. There is an upper limit in the number of participants allowed in each stakeholder category, so in order to be a member, one must fill an existing gap that corresponds with a relevant category, or wait until a vacancy occurs.

The MSC Secretariat

The MSC also has a secretariat ('executive' in MSC terminology), with an administration conducting its daily work. The main office of the secretariat is in London, with regional offices in Seattle and Sydney and local offices in Edinburgh, Berlin, The Hague, Cape Town, and Tokyo. The secretariat is responsible for day-to-day activities, including fundraising, education, contributions to the interpretation and development of MSC standards and policies, development and licensing of the MSC logo, and promotion and publicity of the MSC's work. The MSC Board appoints the Chief Executive, who heads the secretariat. The secretariat has grown significantly over time, and the MSC is predicting a continuation of that trend. By March 2007, it had 27.5 full-time employees.[11]

Across the offices, the secretariat has a departmental structure: the policy department, a commercial outreach team, a fishery outreach team, a communication function, the fundraising team, and administrative support. According to an interviewee from the secretariat, it ensures that the standard principles and criteria are credible, transparent, and consistently applied. The staff is engaged with the quality and delivery of the program, and communicates extensively with fisheries, retailers, certification bodies, customers, and other actors. According to interviewees from the MSC Secretariat in London, their job during the initial years was primarily to present and seek recognition for their work: 'There was a strong focus on making people aware of what we do, very heavily focused on persuading a small number of people to experiment with us.' That phase has changed, however: 'Now we are a more accepted part of the landscape, and there are different challenges now. We've got lots more people coming to us knowing who we are, having an idea of who we are.' But all these people coming to the MSC demand various types of information and assistance. The staff of the secretariat therefore engages in the training, education, and guidance of various stakeholders. According to the interviewees from the secretariat, the current struggle is addressed primarily at meeting theses demands. Members talk about a mismatch between the size of the staff and a drastically increasing workload. According to the MSC's Integrated Strategic Plan, the 'commercial outreach' team and the 'fisheries outreach' team should work relatively aggressively to increase both supply (which is the responsibility of the fisheries outreach team) and demand (which is the responsibility of the commercial outreach team and which should target the retail sector in particular).

FUNDING

Since the early period, the majority of MSC funding has come from the USA, and, to a lesser extent, from the UK. Critics soon emerged, accusing the MSC that it was overly reliant on donors representing specific interests, particularly environmental interests (Hoel, 2004). When the MSC was formed, it was expected that logo-licensing revenue to the charity would quickly fund the costs of the organization (May et al., 2003), but these expectations turned out to be unrealistic. Now, at the end of the first decade of the new millennium, financial support still comes from only a few sources:

> Accusations of being in one pocket or another were inevitable. The two founders, Unilever and WWF, were still perceived to be bankrolling an operation that was largely there to serve their interests at the expense of others. That was never the case, but perception is always more important than reality. The MSC, like so many embryonic charities, faced constant danger of financial collapse and loss of funder confidence (May et al., 2003).

With such concerns as background, the MSC's funding strategy has been to diversify its sources. It has been seen as critical not to be too financially dependent on either US sources or US foundations. Moreover, donors 'seldom stick to one issue indefinitely. Many like to provide start-up funds and then move on to new pressing issues' (p. 30). Hence, there is a constant need to increase percentages of income from license fees. 'The number and volume of MSC certified fisheries are critical factors. It is crucial, therefore, for the MSC to engage high-volume, commercially valuable fisheries in its programme without compromising its environmental standards as a means to that end' (p. 31).

The MSC has largely failed in its goal of significantly increasing income through license fees, however. By 2006/2007, only 8% of the revenue comes from certification and licensing fees.[12] The MSC is virtually reliant upon charitable grants (79%) and receives some donations from governments (6%) and companies (4%). That year the MSC had 41 donators, and a total income of £3 million. In the Integrated Strategic Plan of 2006–2009, the MSC acknowledges that logo-licensing revenue is unlikely to make a significant contribution to funding in the short term. The MSC will continue to rely primarily on US donors and UK donors, although the hope remains that 'this will change over the medium and long term as the MSC supplies critical mass of certified product in the developing world'.[13] 'Growth' is the key word here. The entire Strategic Plan is permeated by insistence on the need to increase market demand and supply. In Chapter 9, we discuss some of the implications of such an orientation in terms of output legitimacy.

THE MSC IN THE TRANSNATIONAL REGULATORY SPACE

The introduction of the eco-labelling concept in marine fisheries has provoked reactions ranging from enthusiastic acceptance to harsh rejections across all stakeholders in fisheries worldwide (Kuntzsch, 2003, p. 176).

As the MSC entered the regulatory space, it faced considerable criticism. Environmental NGOs, the governments of developing countries, and small-scale fishermen in a number of countries raised concerns about the cost of certification and requirements for sophisticated management systems preventing small-scale fisheries and fisheries in developing countries from obtaining certification (May et al., 2003). Some stakeholders criticized the MSC for having an undemocratic structure, which they compared unfavourably with the FSC's structure. The major involvement of a single transnational corporation, Unilever, was a source of great suspicion and critique, particularly among governmental actors and fish workers' unions. Again, the contrast with the FSC was striking, even provocative, to some commentators, as the FSC was based on a much larger and broader group of stakeholders. The fact that the MSC arranged many stakeholder consultations worldwide was not seen as good enough. Constance and Bonanno (2000) researched the intensive debate that appeared in *Samudra*, a journal issued by the International Collective in Support of Fishworkers (ICSF), soon after the establishment of the MSC. Whereas some editorials and articles were in support of the MSC, there were numerous debaters, such as the following, raising serious criticism:

... these last years of the century are giving birth to a new alliance: a type of ruthless, unsentimental, large-scale action which entirely bypasses governments. After years of mutual suspicion and tension, the environmentalists and the industrialists, the sandals and the suits, are working things out together (quoted in Constance and Bonanno, 2000, p. 131)

The MSC was pictured as just another example of northern eco-imperialism (p. 132; cf. Fowler and Heap, 2000). As in the case of the FSC, the MSC had to face strong criticism, but it is noteworthy that the criticism did not initially lead to efforts to present alternative transnational standards. Although the MSC was challenged on many fronts during this period, Constance and Bonanno (2000) report that a careful planning and campaign secured sufficient support and initial success. Kuntzsch (2003), who noticed this extensive criticism, also emphasizes that the 'MSC has gained a remarkable recognition within the fishing industry, amongst politicians and NGOs in a relatively short time' (p. 179). In our interview with him, he said that the company was intensively involved in networking and mobilizing efforts within the sector, in relation to both competitors and suppliers. He also mentioned that WWF played a similar role in relation to other NGOs (see also Weir, 2000).

As for IGO regulation, it is significant that certification in the fisheries sector, compared to the forestry sector, occurs in a much denser transnational institutional environment (Gulbrandsen, 2005). There is a comprehensive global framework of the conservation and management of living marine resources, as opposed to the situation in forestry (Hoel, 2004). The European Commission (EC) is sometimes mentioned by MSC stakeholder interviewees as a competitor or opponent, as there is ongoing discussion in the EC about applying regulations to labeling, or even about a public labeling system in fisheries. In relation to the UN, the MSC has developed a noticeably friendlier approach compared to the FSC. In developing its Principles and Criteria, the MSC took the UN's Food and Agriculture Organization Code of Conduct for Responsible Fisheries as its starting point. Yet, the MSC's relationship with FAO was ambiguous and somewhat infected initially, particularly the relationship with some of FAO's member countries. Indeed, much of the initial criticism directed at the MSC was raised within an FAO setting (Hoel, 2004). A number of industrialized countries wanted FAO to develop guidelines for the application of ecolabeling schemes in fisheries, in order to ensure that such schemes were developed and applied in an orderly way that did not impose excessive restrictions on the fish trade.

Although several developing countries opposed any FAO involvement in the issue, FAO gradually shifted to a more positive attitude toward labeling. After two years preparatory work, it launched its *Guidelines for the Eco-labelling of Fish and Fishery Products from Marine Capture Fisheries* in 2005. According to Gulbrandsen (2005), the issuing of these guidelines for fish and fishery products ecolabeling could be seen as 'an effort by governments and FAO to regain control of an issue area predominated by nonstate organizations' (p. 13). Yet, in the perception of the MSC, the guidelines were easily made compatible through the MSC approach, and MSC people did participate in the FAO process. In 2006, the MSC announced 100% consistency with FAO guidelines. The MSC saw (and sees) the FAO as a main reference and source of legitimacy, and MSC staff do not see the guidelines as a move to restrict MSC authority.

In order to be 100% FAO consistent, however, the MSC had to make organizational reforms. First and foremost, the accreditation of certification bodies had to be separated from standard-setting functions. The MSC contracted out the accreditation to the FSC's Accreditation Service International, which gave the benefit that the MSC could claim is entirely consistent with both ISO and the FAO guidelines. Lack of control over certification bodies is compensated by trust in an accreditation body that springs from the 'credible' FSC. Second, the objections process had to be independent of the certification program and paid for by the objecting party. The MSC had previously a board member in the objection panel and could cover the costs through charitable funding sources.

Through these moves, the MSC lost some direct control of the actual certification, and there was some concern that objecting parties must pay the cost for objecting (which several 'weak' stakeholders might not be able to afford). But it was apparently important for the MSC to stress the compatibility of its system with FAO guidelines, and proudly concludes that no other organization comes close to FAO compliance.

Another key organization for the MSC in the transnational regulatory space is the International Social and Environmental Accreditation and Labelling Alliance (ISEAL Alliance), described in Chapter 6.

The MSC has been successful in carving out a unique, if not to say monopolistic, position as a non-state standardizer and certifier of sustainable fisheries at the global level. Yet the MSC faces a need to be constantly aware of possible competitors on the transnational regulatory scene in the marine sector, and, as noted by several interviewees, various state and non-state labeling initiatives have been taken. Interviewees maintain that it is a key concern for the MSC to check what its competitors (several mentioned 'Friend of the Sea') are doing, and the impact they will have on the MSC program over the short and longer term. As one interviewee says:

> It continues to be a challenge for the MSC to be able to maintain, particularly in the face of industry, that people should go for what we consider to be the gold standards, when there are other options that may be much cheaper out there, and particularly if the consumers don't recognize there are any differences.

From the beginning, the retail sector has been a key ally of the MSC in the transnational regulatory space. 'The MSC is a market-driven initiative. Critical to its success is engaging retailers' (MSC 2003, p. 38). The Integrated Strategy Plan for 2006–2009 shows a remarkably strong commercial outreach strategic focus on retailers, particularly retailers in the UK, Germany, and the USA. The MSC has chosen to work closely with retailers because their MSC commitments and sourcing policies can encourage suppliers to apply for MSC assessment and certification. In March 2003, Sainsbury's became the first retailer to commit to having all wild fish sold in its supermarkets sourced from sustainable fisheries by 2010 (Cummins, 2004). A milestone in the MSC's history occurred in early 2006, when Wal-Mart announced its intention to use MSC-labeled seafood in sourcing all of its wild-caught fresh and frozen fish for the North American market – a market in which the MSC had previously had limited impact. In the view of one interviewee from the MSC Secretariat: 'It is such a famous name, and it caught the attention of media in the fishing sector – iconic in a way ... that has changed the environment in which we operate, I think.'

Although the MSC is increasingly seen as an 'accepted part of the landscape', as an interviewee from the secretariat expressed it, the MSC must still devote a great deal of communicative effort to maintaining its position. The MSC is continuously facing various types of criticism. From the industry side, a key criticism has been that the MSC is not fast enough in delivering certified raw material. Other stakeholders, including a few interviewees with positions in the Stakeholder Council, address the lack of social criteria in the MSC standards framework and its failure to reach the developing world. Furthermore, the MSC often faces criticism because of stakeholders' negative attitudes toward certain MSC-certified fisheries (May et al., 2003; Hoel, 2004). The New Zealand Royal Forest and Bird Protection Society strongly criticized the granting of the MSC label to the Hoki fishery, for example, because of the killing of seals and albatross by the fishery (Oosterver, 2005). Greenpeace, which previously had a representative on the MSC Board, developed a more critical attitude after such observations (Greenpeace also criticizes the MSC's use of the term 'sustainable', which it does not consider honest) and maintains that no fully credible certification system for sustainable wild-caught seafood currently exist. We return to the role and position of Greenpeace later in this book.

The MSC's defenders tend to refer to such aspects as the inclusive and transparent assessment procedures, the use of 'expert judgment' and 'objective assessment', the possibilities for any stakeholder to raise objections, the use of corrective measures (e.g. May et al., 2003, p. 24). Such statements draw attention to the role of legitimacy and standard-setting ideals around science, expertise, good procedures, balanced and effective participation, and several other issues – a topic we return to in Chapter 9. In Chapter 9, we also discuss the trial-and-error character of the legitimacy aspirations of the standard-setting process. Indeed, the entire MSC story shows an organizational development with such features, and which, rather than linear, is dialectical between the incessant calls for 'more effectiveness' versus 'more democracy'.

NOTES

1.   Figures from the MSC website: www.msc.org, accessed 28 June 2009.
2.   The same interviewee said that when 'FSC evolved, the next GA was much more efficient; it matured a bit and had a better system, or a bit of assistance, and was better able to accommodate its democratic side, whilst being more efficient'.

3. http://www.msc.org/documents/mscstandards/MSC_environmental_standard_for_sustain able_fishing.pdf, accessed 11 August 2008.
4. See http://www.msc.org/documents/msc standards/MSC_environmental_standard_for_sus tainable_fishing.pdf, accessed 11 August 2008. See also May et al., 2003.
5. http://www.msc.org/about-us/standards/msc-chain-of-custody-standard, information accessed 11 August 2008.
6. According to the MSC procedure, certification requires a series of steps, beginning with pre-assessment by an MSC-accredited certifier and ending with full assessment by an evaluation team, nominated by the certification body. All steps in the certification process must be transparent and open to all stakeholders, except in the pre-assessment stage, which is confidential. Any stakeholder can raise objections, using a formalized complaint procedure. A certificate is given for a five-year period, after which a new and full assessment must be conducted, in addition to annual audits. The certification body writes a final report with a recommendation and the MSC Board makes the final decision on certification approval.
7. In recognition of MSC's drive for openness, transparency, and the highest standards of internal management, it was presented with the UK *Charity Times* Best Practice Award in September 2002.
8. http://www.msc.org/about-us/governance/structure/board-of-trustees/whos-on-the-msc-board, information accessed 14 August 2008.
9. http://www.msc.org/about-us/governance/structure/technical-advisory-board/whos-on-the-msc-tab, accessed 14 August 2008.
10. http://www.msc.org/about-us/governance/structure/msc-stakeholder-council/whos-on-the-msc-stakeholder-council, accessed 16 July 2009.
11. http://www.msc.org/documents/MSC-Statutory-Accounts-2006-07.pdf, accessed 12 August 2008.
12. http://www.msc.org/documents/annual-report-archive/MSC_Annual_report_2006-07_EN.pdf, accessed 8 August 2008.
13. http://www.msc.org/documents/governance/strategic-plan/MSC-Strategic-plan.pdf/view, accessed 13 August 2008.

6. Actors and Capabilities in the Regulatory Space

In this chapter, we examine our three standard-setting processes in their wider context of a regulatory space, and discuss a number of actors that are typically involved in transnational standard-setting activities. The purpose of this analysis is to draw a map of actors and interests in standard-setting activities, and to provide an overview of the capability of organizations to participate – to influence others. Such capabilities are hugely differentiated globally – something that an organizer of a multi-stakeholder process must consider. We understand differences in the capability of participating in terms of pre-existing power asymmetries, which, in turn, can be analyzed as asymmetries in access to various types of power resources: material, symbolic, cognitive, and social. We do not believe, however, that the capability of participating can be explained only by access to resources, and throughout the remaining chapters we return to this issue and discuss yet other perspectives.

The reader will notice that we use actor categories in this chapter that are commonly found in scholarly literature on transnational governance: international governmental organizations (IGOs), transnational corporations (TNC), and nongovernmental organizations (NGOs), for example. Such organizations clearly play essential roles in a regulatory space, but the categories are not sufficiently informative to allow us to obtain an adequate understanding of our empirical topic. As a complement, we have therefore developed a typology of actors that is introduced in this chapter. We have made a distinction according to the basic relationship between these actors and the standards produced:

1. Value-driven organizations (e.g. environmental NGOs and trade unions) and knowledge-based organizations (e.g. research institutes and think tanks).
2. Direct and indirect users of the standards produced (e.g. corporations implementing standards and consumers buying products originating from corporations implementing standards).

3. The standard setter hosting the standard-setting process (including the secretariat) and allied service providers (e.g. consultants, publishers, and certification companies).
4. Competing rule setters in the same regulatory space (e.g. IGOs and private standard setters).

VALUE-DRIVEN AND KNOWLEDGE-BASED ORGANIZATIONS

Within transnational multi-stakeholder standardization, there is, by definition, a large group of organizations representing various interests, values, or bodies of knowledge and expertise that are to be reflected in the standards established (or to be reflected in standard proposals defeated). In our cases, we observed a number of organizations specializing in or focused on one or several issues relevant to the subject matter of standardization. In the ISO 26000 case, for example, there were NGOs, social movement organizations (SMOs), community-based associations, think tanks, professional associations, and research institutes representing such values- and knowledge-based areas as human rights, the environment, consumers' rights, and labour rights. They all sought membership to become involved in and contribute to the development of the ISO 26000 standard. Similar organizations participated in the work of the Forest Stewardship Council (FSC) and the Marine Stewardship Council (MSC). We label these types of organizations value-driven and knowledge-based, to stress the fact that they represent specific values or bodies of knowledge that they consider crucial to promote.

Some of these organizations are fully committed to the ideologies, visions, and aspirations behind the standard-setting work. Most of them, however, understand ISO, FSC, or MSC standards as one tool among several in the work toward socially and environmentally responsible economic practices. Some of them perceive the standard-setting work as a second-best strategy, implemented because other transnational private or public initiatives have failed.

In all three processes, the range of stakeholders is wide. The issue of social and environmental responsibility-taking is a global concern, but it is especially relevant in those parts of the world where living conditions, working conditions, and environmental conditions are less well-developed and in need of improvement. These stakeholders may lack many types of power resources. Maybe it is better to speak of 'affected publics' (Mason, 2005) in such circumstances, in fact, because the term 'stakeholder' implies an actor that is already organized and who has at least managed to address a viewpoint in relation to a political topic. There are several affected publics with the potential for many viewpoints, but no capability of addressing or even grasping the issues at stake. Certain affected publics may be illiterate or live with poverty and starvation. Although the standards developed by the FSC, MSC and ISO may be relevant to their concerns, one would not expect many people from such environments to be considering such an abstract strategy as standardization and certification as a political aspiration.

The members of both the FSC and MSC experience frustration in trying to involve communities living in such circumstances. Even if affected publics are organized – if they have developed some form of civil society – the step toward routine participation on a transnational standard-setting scene is certainly a big one. An interviewee representing an environmental NGO from a southern, developing country in the FSC reflects upon this:

> There are very few big NGOs that can afford to participate – like Greenpeace, WWF. They are big and can participate. But a lot of the small ... for example in the south ... there is almost no environmental organization that can participate and have well-paid people that keep following the policies (interview with previous FSC member, environment/south).

The same interviewee, who did participate in a working group in one standard review process, was even more concerned about the much greater capability for participation among stakeholders representing economic interests:

> In the consultations, you send mail to the list and say: "Look, we are dealing with this, this, and this. What do you think?" Like 70% or 80% of the answers came from the economic chamber. You see, they have people; they work for companies; they have time to follow these documents and to spend time on this (interview with previous FSC member, environment/south).

Characteristic of many of the NGOs participating in FSC work, the interviewee continued, was the necessity of sending voluntary, unpaid participants to meetings; whereas stakeholders representing the economic chamber were well-paid employees.

Other knowledge-based or value-based organizations, however, are more resourceful and capable of participating in the three standard-setting processes: large environmental and human-rights NGOs such as the WWF or Amnesty International for example. Both these organizations possess specific expert knowledge and have large budgets (e.g. the income of the WWF in 2002 amounted to 332 million USD; Mason 2005), extensive networks (e.g. the WWF has offices in 90 countries), and unique research opportunities. Because of actors' differing histories and their locations in the social landscape, they have different access, experiences, and abilities to provide knowledge, experience, and information (cf. van Rooy, 2004). Having material power resources provides them with the time for investing in cognitive power resources, which, in turn, allows them to contribute expertise. Several interviewees returned to this issue on several occasions:

> The more resources you have, the easier it is for you to make yourself heard. And it is easier for you to investigate different things and so on, making sure what you consider important is also dealt with, and that any important detail is not forgotten. That's the way it is. The more resources you have, the greater impact you can make (interview with previous board member, economic/north).

There can also be asymmetries in relation to symbolic power resources. Although social organizations as a group have the same formal status as environmental organizations within the FSC, according to some interviewees, they do not have the same symbolic status. The following interviewee indicates that social NGOs have less symbolic power than do environmental NGOs:

> In mass media, you only read about labour unions when there are problems. You read about how labour unions organize strikes. We're often seen as something negative ... workers are causing troubles and so on ... That is the common picture of a labour union (interview with representative of a meta-organization for labour unions).

Accordingly, some NGOs may have a symbolic advantage in relation to transnational standard-setting processes. It should be noted, however, that symbolic power is partially dependent on the profile and orientation of the standard-setting organization in question, including the categorizations that have been made (Chapter 8). The relative symbolic weight between social and environmental NGOs seems to be the opposite in the ISO case, in which the social dimension takes precedence over the environmental dimension. In the ISO case, however, stakeholders were not categorized according to a distinction between social and environmental dimensions. It is not obvious, therefore, that we can compare the symbolic strength of these two dimensions in this case. We return to the issue of categorization and further analyze this type of variation and consequences in Chapter 8.

Finally, there are asymmetries in power and the capability of participating that are connected to *social power resources*, which include the capability of forming networks and organizing, and even the ability to create an efficient and effective organizational structure. Certain NGOs may be extraordinarily well-trained and organizationally structured to establish links, networks, or alliances among groups on a global scale (cf. Kekk and Sikkink, 1998; Smith, 2005; Scholte, 2005). The power asymmetries relate to variation in the strength of local civil societies. Many parts of the world have weak or nonexisting civil societies. Having a weak civil society locally means lack of organizational resources to participate in the transnational civil society. An interviewee working for a meta-organization for labour unions argues that labour unions from Northern Europe tend to be stronger than they are in most other countries. It is difficult in some countries to recruit and keep members and create strong local labour unions, which considerably affects the ability to participate and to have a forceful voice on the transnational standard-setting scene.

While reflecting on the social power resources, it is worth noting the differences involved in being an organizational representative (or even having an organizational affiliation) versus participating as an individual. The type of transnational regulatory organization we analyze in this book tends to be an interorganizational network (Waddell and Khagram, 2007), implying that it is difficult to be strong without organizational affiliation. This is particularly relevant to the FSC, which has both organizations and individuals as members. Interviewees in this case maintain that those without affiliation to an organization tend to be weaker. An individual who wants to be strong, on the other hand, needs to be backed by an organization and have access to its collective resources (Ahrne, 1994). This situation is even truer on the transnational scene. In fact, the FSC has two problems linked to the social category: the fact that it is generally difficult to mobilize members from southern countries representing social issues, and the fact that the social chamber is overrepresented by nonaffiliated members. According to an interviewee from the FSC Secretariat, this combination contributes to the weak power position of members from the south and the social chamber.

Although a value-driven organization has access to a number of power resources, it can still be an insufficient condition for effective participation, as we can see, for example, in the case of the Greenpeace refusal to participate in the MSC. The WWF was deeply engaged in both the FSC and MSC, and, at an initial phase, in ISO 26000 work. Yet Greenpeace, in spite of its key concern for marine issues, restricted its resources to FSC work, and developed a much more critical attitude toward the MSC. There had been engagement at the beginning, but a number of problems were observed, including, according to Greenpeace, questionable fisheries that had received the MSC label and were able to market their fish products as 'sustainable'. Thus Greenpeace refused to expend extensive resources in trying to improve standard setting:

> We are not doing anything like that, mainly because we think it won't work. ... It would take us a lot of work to get somewhere. Our opinion is: "OK, they [MSC] aren't the biggest threat to the worlds' oceans", and we are putting our resources elsewhere at the moment and are campaigning for sustainable and equitable

seafood by focussing on the retailer sector directly (interview with Greenpeace member).

In spite of Greenpeace's relatively strong capability of participating in standard-setting activities, this Greenpeace interviewee believed that a supreme effort would be required in order to make a significant impact. In Chapter 10, we return to the material and ideological obstacles facing NGOs and other similar organizations, in participating regularly in transnational multi-stakeholder standard-setting processes.

DIRECT AND INDIRECT USERS

The standard setters produce standards that are adopted by *indirect users*: individuals or public and private organizations buying products that are certified according to the standards. The standards can also be adopted by *direct users*: public or private organizations certifying themselves or their products according to these standards. Moreover, the same organization can potentially be both an indirect and a direct user.

CSR- and image-conscious TNCs represent a large number of direct and indirect users. And many of them participate in the standard setting, and, needless to say, have strong financial capabilities of doing so. Charles Lindblom (1977) has written about 'the privileged position of business', by which he was referring not merely to the ability of large corporations to accumulate and control various types of resources. Rather, he meant that business is always indispensable in politics, because any decision that affects corporations will necessarily have societal consequences. In relation to the MSC, FSC, and ISO, at least some segments of big business are necessary if these standards are to be authoritative and have any impact on the market. Certain actors, then, have both a free ticket into the regulatory space and an extraordinary capability to participate.

There is at least one type of power resource, however, that TNCs generally lack or that they have a somewhat problematic relationship with: symbolic power. To be sure, corporations such as IKEA have strong symbolic power, in that their brand is widely known, recognized, and trusted. Yet, most corporations face a huge legitimacy challenge regarding their work with social and environmental responsibility, and are aware of the fact that they are constantly at risk of being targeted by journalists and social movements. 'Transnational corporations and business organizations have a great deal of power but little legitimacy. Social movements, on the other hand, have only little power but high level of legitimacy' (Beck, 2005, p. 75).

To use our terminology, value-driven and knowledge-based organizations such as social movement organizations and NGOs may have an advantage in symbolic power (high legitimacy, strong moral authority); they can use this power to challenge users like TNCs, not least within standard-setting activities. Ulrich Beck (2005) argues that the 'legitimation trap' in which global business power is caught provides considerable potential for politicization. Reputation damage and legitimacy crises make world markets highly unstable (see also Power, 2007; Boström and Garsten, 2008):

> The more they [TNCs] "emancipate" themselves from voters and state institutions, the more dependent they become upon consumers and their trust, on markets and competitors. Credibility thus becomes a crucial form of capital, as world markets presuppose the existence of trust – on the part of both the public and consumers. ... The fragility of shareholder and consumer trust point to the fragility of global corporations' legitimacy. This is their Achilles heel, and this is what social movements have in their sights when they embark on their spectacular campaigns (Beck 2005, p. 75).

Several TNCs are therefore willing to compromise with NGOs, expert organizations, or social movements within standard-setting processes. Social movements get a free ticket, but they may have less capability of participating. As we observed from our ISO case, however, corporate representatives, who traditionally constitute the main expertise within ISO standard-setting processes, obtain a high (expert) status in comparison to NGO representatives. One representative of a social NGO within the ISO 26000 process did not think there were experts with higher or lower status, but that it boiled down to who would implement these standards. According to this interviewee, the users would be corporations rather than NGOs, trade unions, or consumer organizations, and corporations can be in a particularly influential position for standard setting:

> It's industry that will implement this, so it's important that they have influence in the process. There are technical issues, and if something is important for industry, then it's ok that they have more influence about that, unless it's a political issue of course (interview with a social NGO representative, June 2008).

The fact that ISO is a relatively old organization with traditions in other, technical fields of standardization can partially explain this observation. In various green labeling standardization processes, however, knowledge in such areas as technology, production methods, processing, distribution, and marketing is often indispensable, and it is often corporations that possess this expertise (Boström and Klintman, 2008). The MSC and FSC standards are aimed at product labeling (as opposed to the ISO 26000 standard that will label organizations). In the case of product labeling, we compared organizations at the beginning of the production chain (producers) and the middle of the production chain (retailers, processing industries, and Do-It-Yourself business actors, for instance), and found a difference between motive on the one hand and capability of participating on the other. In the case of the FSC, we observed that large corporations such as IKEA, B&Q, and Home Depot played key roles and expressed strong interest in standard-setting activities. In the case of the MSC, we noted the driving role of Unilever, and the supporting role of Wal-Mart, as well as a noticeably strong focus on the part of the MSC to engage closely with the retail sector.

Boström and Klintman (2008) emphasize that business actors in the middle of the production chain often play key roles within product labeling processes, identifying positive economic values in green niches or in green public relations. They also see green labeling as a means of reducing the risk of negative publicity. In the cases of the FSC and MSC, direct users have been less eager to endorse or participate in the standard-setting activities. Initially, there was no general push for certification from forest companies or fisheries. Rather, as we discussed in Chapters 4 and 5, much of the criticism and counter-initiatives came from the production side – from direct users. One reason for their negative attitude was that they would have to bear most of the cost of implementing and complying with the standard criteria – a reason for their negative attitude. Producers rather than retailers would have to make the on-the-ground changes and be audited by a third party.

One may also look at this from the viewpoint of capability to participate. On the one hand, large and transnational companies clearly have sufficient material – cognitive and social resources (e.g. collaborating within meta-organizations) – to be able to participate in standard-setting activities. Small enterprises (often family-owned or community-based as in forestry and fishery), on the other hand, may lack both incentives to comply with abstract non-state standards (Boström and Klintman, 2008) and the capability to participate in the standard-setting processes. Direct users in the sectors of forest and marine certification can, in principle, be small economic actors, such as family-owned forestry businesses, and may come from poor, developing countries. If certification to a standard represents something highly abstract and infeasible, participating in transnational standard-setting work is even more unrealistic. And should they have the incentives to participate, they simply have no resources.

Finally, it is important to acknowledge another type of indirect use of standards: governmental organizations orienting their own regulatory frameworks to the created standards. State actors could, of course, use standards in their procurement activities, but they could potentially refer to standard criteria as well when they develop principles and criteria in their own rules or establish new public policies (cf. Rametsteiner, 2002). Their participation within standard-setting processes can be hindered by factors other than those related to different power resources. In the case of the FSC, for example, state actors are formally excluded. They are not allowed to participate unless they own forests, which make them eligible for membership in the economic chamber. There can also be regulations on the domestic level that set limits for such organizations to participate in non-state-driven rule-setting processes. As shown in our analysis of the ISO case – with its background within technical standardization dominated by industry interests – state organizations were invited to participate, and a few of them even obtained special status through the negotiation of their own memorandum of understanding (see Chapter 7).

THE STANDARD SETTER HOSTING THE PROCESS (INCLUDING THE SECRETARIAT) AND PROVIDERS OF ALLIED SERVICES

The FSC, MSC, and ISO are 'multi-stakeholder' organizations, which implies that their relevant stakeholders are supposed to negotiate and thereby determine the outcome of their standards. According to this perspective, the organization hosting a multi-stakeholder process is a neutral arena with no stakes of its own. On the other hand, we must look at the organization as such, the organization as a 'bureaucracy', including an organizational dimension and organizational elements that go beyond an arena for stakeholder communication and negotiation. This is what Barnett and Finnemore do in their book, *Rules for the world* (2004). They discuss International Organizations (IOs), which we call intergovernmental organizations (IGOs), and the relationship between IOs and their member states. They criticize the mainstream literature on international relations, and argue that the literature has failed to see IOs as autonomous actors that exercise power in world politics. This literature mainly presents the development, expansion, interest, success, failure, function, and dysfunction of IOs as an effect of state interests and state power. Barnett and Finnemore argue that IOs are part of the explanation for such tendencies. By referring to Max Weber's discussion on bureaucracies and rational-legal expansion, they contend that IOs should be seen as bureaucracies, which is a distinctive social form of authority. Looking at IOs from this perspective helps the researcher to understand the strengths and expansion of certain IOs, as well as the failures and weaknesses of such organizations from the perspective of its members.

Although our topic is not IGOs such as the UN or the IMF, these authors draw attention to the internal work of rule-setting organizations. The multi-stakeholder standard-setting organizations we analyze can be understood by examining the motives, strategies, and power of participating stakeholders, such as value-driven and knowledge-based organizations or direct and indirect users. Although these actors are certainly essential to the process, Barnett and Finnemore suggest that IOs can create their own authority by developing specialized expert knowledge in various areas and becoming skilled at defining problems and solutions and classifying and categorizing the world, often through moral and scientific argumentation.

One actor that is particularly relevant in this regard is the secretariat. As Barnett and Finnemore notice in their study of IOs, secretariats are staffed with specialized expertise, and it is through investment in expertise that the bureaucracies establish authority and, consequently, autonomy and power. The secretariat comprises the staff members that work with all the day-to-day issues surrounding the standard-setting activities. ISO's *central* secretariat is based in Geneva, where the president and the ISO Technical Management Board are also located. As noted in Chapter 3, however, the day-to-day administration and leadership for the drafting of standards within a specific area of standardization is delegated to one of ISO's national members. In the ISO 26000 case, the secretariat constitutes a twinning arrangement between Brazil and Sweden, with offices in Stockholm and Rio de Janeiro. Work meetings of this secretariat are held in both countries during international work meetings of the entire ISO 26000 committee. There is no fixed location, but a system of rotating responsibility between participating members for hosting these meetings. In the case of FSC, the secretariat is situated in Bonn, and the MSC Secretariat is located in London along with a number of regional offices.

We observe from both the FSC and MSC cases that the role and power of the secretariats has increased over time, as the standards and the governance structures became institutionalized. We can summarize a number of manifest or latent roles and responsibilities that the secretariats of the FSC, MSC, and ISO have undertaken:

- pushing and assisting in national or regional standards development or assessment processes;
- ensuring consistency of standards and policies and the interpretation of standards and policies worldwide;
- doing work for decision-making bodies within the standard-setting arrangement (e.g. boards and general assemblies);
- developing and communicating new procedural rules and organizational structures;

- organizing and convening international work meetings, and handling rounds of comments in connection to meetings;
- taking responsibility for fundraising issues and oversee the finances of the organizations;
- handling information, training, and education in relation to national and regional offices, to members, and to other stakeholders (e.g. certification bodies and direct users); assisting in the interpretation of standard principles, criteria, and policies; and
- performing moderating roles in stakeholder discussions.

It is clear that the standard-setting organizations de-emphasize these organizational units when they provide information about themselves and market their standards. In self-descriptions of the FSC, for example, it is the well-balanced tripartite governance structure, including all multi-stakeholder arrangements, that appears in the forefront. The MSC tends to stress similar aspects and prefers to highlight the Technical Advisory Board and Stakeholder Council rather than the secretariat. The ISO employs an organizational novelty that helps to ensure its legitimacy in this field: the secretariat and its coordinating role tends to be highlighted, as the secretariat constitutes a twinning arrangement between one developed (Sweden) and one developing country (Brazil). When it comes to public presentations of standard writing, however, the multi-stakeholder structure, expertise of stakeholders, and the consensus principle are heavily emphasized. Hence, it is not part of the identification work of these standard setters to highlight their secretariats. The secretariats are assumed merely to follow procedural rules, assist, and perform an executive role in relation to the other organizational units driven by 'stakeholders' – all with neutrality. One could say that the secretariats do not have strong symbolic power resources.

Some of our interviewees had concerns about the under-financing of the secretariats and the need for them to expand in relation to expanding workflows and increased expectations. Nevertheless, the staff of the secretariat has resources and is in a unique position to develop cognitive and social power resources that, in turn and through time, enable it to develop an action capability and an authoritative position. Such a picture emerges simply by reflecting upon the list of latent and manifest roles and responsibilities. The secretariats gradually assume more decisions, tasks, and responsibilities. A number of interviewees, such as the following FSC member, commented on this situation:

> At this moment when you speak about the FSC, you always think about the head office in Bonn. That's the FSC for many people. But the FSC is all of us working in the system. I'm not paid by the FSC. I don't receive any salary – I don't receive anything. I'm a volunteer (interview with FSC stakeholder, social chamber/south).

This interviewee said that many decisions were made at headquarters, and argued that responsibilities should be more decentralized and given to FSC groups at the country level, thus offering more room for stakeholders. The quote indicates that it is necessary to focus on the host, including the staff (secretariat), when analyzing processes that are supposed to be driven by stakeholders.

The 'administration' of the standard-setting process, however, does not exactly correspond with the 'secretariat', because other stakeholders could assume core administrative roles. In the ISO case, for example, we observed how a few strategic task forces, such as the Chairman Advisory Group, the Liaison Task Force, and the Integrated Drafting Task Force, included (a few) stakeholders that became influential in this way. The role that such task forces play and their impact on the standard-setting activity is considerable, as they offer advice and support, thereby influencing the work of the secretariat. They help to resolve the main problems to be handled – establishing priorities among problems, for example; setting the agenda for international work meetings; and shaping the decision-making structures, including procedural rules and definitions of those with access to crucial decisions. These activities, however, were limited to a small group of people possessing the necessary administrative expertise. In Chapter 7, after our review of participation strategies, we examine such inner circles or elite groups more closely, and further analyze the role of the secretariats.

Barnett and Finnemore (2004) discuss another relevant aspect of the 'host' of the standard-setting process: IOs do not merely exercise power, but can also 'authorize their own expansion' (p. 34). We may see the entrance of ISO into the field of SR through these lenses by simultaneously considering ISO and the way commercial interests are entangled in the so-called ISO system. These commercial interests include such service providers as consultants, certification auditors, and publishers of literature related to the use of standards. The ISO Board comprises delegates from a number of ISO member bodies (national standards bodies), most of which are nonprofit organizations with profit-making subsidiaries engaged in consultation, certification, and publishing (Tamm Hallström, 2006; Higgins and Tamm Hallström, 2007). Consequently, seen as an aggregate of interests or allies (cf. Rose and Miller, 1992), including numerous companies providing services around the implementation and diffusion of ISO standards, ISO has had a stake in turning the ISO 26000 process into a successful standardization project. To achieve this goal, ISO must convince organized interests in its environment that it is successful and legitimate in its endeavours, which in this case meant that it acts as a 'neutral arena' for the standard-setting process, for example, and ensures that representatives of all stakeholder categories come to its meetings and are seen to participate on equal terms. This is the image that ISO promotes in public presentations of the ISO 26000 committee. In reality, ISO needs this standard to complement its earlier success with the ISO 9000 and ISO 14000 standards, thus bolstering its standing in the global regulatory space for management system standards. Although ISO does not seek to thrust accountability onto others, it does have an interest in and the services to support the launching of a new management system standard (Tamm Hallström, 2006; 2008). The more stakeholders ISO manages to involve in the process and convince of the advantages of the ISO 26000 standard, the more missionaries it has to promote and encourage the use of the standard, and the better the odds that the standard will attract sales and compliance across all types of organizations around the world. Thus even though ISO presents itself as a neutral arena, we should also see it as an actor – part of a wider commercial network, with its own interests at stake. As noted by a member of the ISO investigative group quoted earlier: 'this was a big strategic question for ISO, and it had a need for this standard to survive and compete as an organization' (Chapter 3).[1]

COMPETING RULE SETTERS – OR DO THEY COMPETE?

It is necessary to consider potential competitors in the regulatory space, and here we focus on transnational competing rule setters. To be sure, a single nation state could also be seen as a competing rule setter in relation to the FSC, MSC, and ISO, at least as seen from the national viewpoint. A transnational rule such as the FSC standard can surely compete with national regulatory frameworks (e.g. see Cashore, Auld, and Newsom, 2004 for the US case). For our purposes, it is more relevant to keep the focus at the transnational level. Soon after the FSC was established, it had to experience serious counter initiatives with competing industry-dominated programs, such as the Programme for the Endorsement of Forest Certification (PEFC) schemes (see Chapter 4). Although the MSC has not experienced competition to the same extent, it is crucial for this standard setter and its stakeholders to consider the potential power of competing certification schemes. If competing schemes develop and grow, the integration and collaboration among stakeholders may be disturbed (cf. Chapter 8) and the output legitimacy challenged (cf. Chapter 9).

Our three standard setters claim that there is a need for new rules, and they are definitely not alone with their aspirations on the transnational scene (cf. Mörth, 2004; Djelic and Sahlin-Andersson, 2006; Pattberg, 2007). The following quote illustrates that standard-setting bodies usually enter a transnational regulatory space that is already covered, to some extent, by rules and rule-setting bodies. The implication is that tensions tend to emerge when a new rule setter tries to create a new position and a space for its rules:

> The ILO case was so obvious: their negative attitude. They were worried that the ISO process would become a normative process. But GRI has also expressed skepticism. They're afraid that this will intrude on their territory, and GRI is a fairly new organization. They're still in the process. Their view is that they have "the one" standard on reporting today, but it is still a very young organization. They work according to special procedures, a multi-stakeholder process. They issue guidelines, have working groups, and promote transparency through posting documents on their website. They have experience, as they see it, and they want to share their experiences with ISO, but they also want to ensure that ISO doesn't get its hands on the reporting part (interview with government representative active in the ISO process, May 2005).

Note that this remark was made in 2005, and referred to the defensive reactions toward the ISO 26000 initiative on the part of the Global Reporting Initiative (GRI) and the ILO. In Chapter 7, we return to the ILO example in a discussion about participation strategies that change over time. Another competitor that we discuss in a similar way is the UN Global Compact.

The democratic legitimacy enjoyed by ILO and, to a lesser degree, the UN Global Compact, differentiates them from other potential competitors – the Global Reporting Initiative, for example. The Global Reporting Initiative is a private organization and a relatively young one – at least compared to the ILO. Strong democratic legitimacy (offered to ISO through formal cooperation) can be regarded as an important symbolic power resource in the ISO context, as ISO was criticized by several significant stakeholders for its lack of democratic legitimacy. Such rule setters also have unique cognitive power resources, in that they are already familiar with existing rules and principles, having jurisdictional and other types of expertise, understandings, and 'correct' vocabulary in the relevant problem area.

The OECD, the Social Accountability International, and AccountAbility can also be analyzed as competitors in the ISO 26000 case, in so far as they all have their own established norms, standards, guidelines, and principles. These organizations, which typically have less democratic legitimacy within the ISO process, need to defend their own position in the regulatory space. Given that they could not stop the ISO initiative in the early phase, they seek instead to use the standard-setting process as the occasion arises, in order to promote their own standards. They try, for example, to make their own standards appear on the list of relevant normative references that, it was proposed, was attached to the future ISO 26000 standard. ISO, in turn, has a major advantage in its operational capacity, its high-profile trademark, its experience of standardizing management systems, and its standards being widely used among businesses globally.

In the cases of the FSC and MSC, the other rule setters (the Global Reporting Initiative and the OECD, for instance) did not enter these two standard-setting processes on forest and fishery certification. Like ISO, the FSC and MSC had to ensure visibility in the transnational regulatory space in relation to competitors, allies, and other rule setters. And they had to manage their relationships carefully with other global rule setters. In Chapter 4 on the FSC and Chapter 5 on the MSC, we observed the apparent need for these organizations to establish links with the policies of other IGOs, while simultaneously emphasizing an independent position. Some of the most significant IGOs are the ILO (for the FSC), the Food and Agriculture Organization of the UN (for the MSC), ISO (for both the FSC and MSC), and the WTO (for both; see Boström and Klintman, 2008 on how the WTO discourse has had an impact on the standardization of green labels). Although there was, and is, a dialogue on various topics, these other global rule setters appear to perceive little need to enter into the internal standard-setting work of the MSC and FSC. They have affected the conditions for standard-setting work within the MSC and FSC, and arguably are indirectly affected by their activities. But they do not intervene directly.

Because of their somewhat narrower scope compared to ISO, organizations such as the FSC and MSC have seen a need to unite, forming a common front in relation to other international organizations such as ISO and the WTO. The International Social and Environmental Accreditation and Labelling Alliance (ISEAL Alliance) was founded in 1999 by, it claims, eight leading international standard-setting certification and accreditation organizations that focus on social and environmental issues. Both the FSC and MSC were among its founding members.[2] The aim of ISEAL Alliance is to assist, debate, and facilitate exchange and harmonization among its members. ISEAL Alliance has recently developed its Code of Good Practice for Setting Social and Environmental Standards, which is mandatory for ISEAL Alliance's full members and which emphasizes such characteristics as openness, transparency, and broad stakeholder dialogue in standard-setting work. By following this code, ISEAL Alliance's members can ensure that they all commit to high standards of credibility, and thereby prevent negative publicity and increase the authority of the entire movement of these standard setters (see also Boström and Klintman, 2008). Another important role for ISEAL Alliance is to monitor the actions of other global standard setters such as WTO, OECD, and ISO. ISEAL Alliance was established to help solve the problems faced by individual members. The members share a concern, for instance, about the effects on labeling of WTO's free trade rules and ISO's standard-setting rules and doctrines. Consequently, ISEAL Alliance examines the relationships among various labeling and certification systems and among such systems and other standards and regulations worldwide. Thus ISEAL Alliance has been established on the transnational scene to carve out some regulatory space for credible certification and labeling instruments, in a partly conflicting relationship with such other global players as the WTO and ISO (Boström and Klintman, 2008). ISEAL Alliance does not try to compete or engage in open conflict with these organizations; rather it finds ways to relate to their regulatory frameworks while engaging in minimum compromise with the members' goal of rewarding high social and environmental standards.

NOTES

1. Another noteworthy aspect that is part of the 'big strategic question' for ISO, is that the field of social responsibility (SR) has connections to one of ISO's other work areas: environmental management and the so-called ISO 14000 standards. Should ISO have chosen not to expand into SR, which includes environmental aspects, a competitor might have developed a SR standard and become a leader in the field, creating the risk of rendering ISO 14000 obsolete. Thus ISO probably saw the need to take action in this area, even though it might have meant that there was a risk of a new SR standard ruling out one of its current best sellers (ISO 14000). Yet another example of an issue or area of standardization that is closely linked to the field of SR is the issue of occupational health and safety. A few years before the work on the ISO 26000 standard began, ISO was involved in discussions about a possible new ISO standard on occupational health and safety. Those discussions never lead to a standard-setting process for ISO, however, and many people later perceived this to be a strategic mistake (see Chapter 9 for a discussion of this example; Ruwet, 2009).
2. See http://www.isealalliance.org/index.htm (accessed 23 January 2007). Full members are FLO, FSC, IFOAM, MAC, MSC, SAI, and Rainforest Alliance (see list of abbreviations).

7. Dynamics of Preferences and Strategies of Participation

In this chapter, we examine people and organizations as they participate in multi-stakeholder standardization processes, and discuss a number of *strategies of participation* that we have observed in our material. Thus we leave the discussion of *which* actors participate in a regulatory space and in standard-setting activities, and turn to the question of *how* they participate and *what* strategies of participation they use. This focus helps us to obtain an understanding of the complexities that characterize the daily practice of standard setters in their organizing and legitimizing efforts. More specifically, we continue our examination of the interests and motives of participants by observing and asking them about their doings in these processes. We identify various motives linked to the relationship between participants and the standard, and the role and benefits of the standard that participants believe they can enjoy. We also discuss the way motives and strategies of participation form and change during and within the process itself. We demonstrate that the diverse and changing interests of participants, together with their relatively diverse resources and opportunities to influence the process, increase the complexity of these processes and constitute a great challenge for the standard setters in their quest for authority.

In the presentation of our analysis, our observations are generated primarily from the ISO 26000 case, because our ISO research was conducted as a process study in real time and therefore serves as a suitable starting point. We do, however, make comparisons among the motives and strategies of participation of the three cases when we believe that the differences tell us something intriguing.

STRATEGIES OF PARTICIPATION

Some organizations involved in the ISO 26000 process were active from the start, with many members present at their initial meetings (cf. Chapter 3). Presentations were given and position papers presented to ISO (Tamm Hallström, 2006), both for and against the ISO 26000 initiative. Service providers such as management consultants articulated their support from the beginning in 2004, as did consumer associations and a group of developing countries. Service providers in particular, had strong presence at the initial ISO meetings before and around the time the actual standard was being written. Competing standard-setting organizations such as the UN Global Compact and the OECD, as well as a number of NGOs and governmental organizations were also relatively positive toward this standard-setting initiative – with some reservations and requirements for changes of the ISO procedures, however. The competing standard setter, ILO, together with trade unions, was reluctant to send representatives to articulate their negative position through a voice strategy. A number of individual corporations that were possible users of the future standard, and industry and employer associations representing such users were also negative toward the ISO 26000 standard. They exhibited a much more active strategy, however, both in numbers present at the initial meetings and in their articulation of written comments communicated to ISO.

This was how it looked at the beginning of the standard-setting process. As we demonstrate in this chapter, however, the positions and strategies of these organizations did not remain constant during the time-consuming work of drafting the ISO 26000 standard. Turning now to participation during the first years of work, most of the strategies discussed here are strategies of participation, either for or against. Yet we believe that it is valuable to discuss the strategy of nonparticipation as a way of resisting a standardization initiative. We have identified eight strategies of participation and nonparticipation, some of which are aimed at influencing *the contents and future status of the standard*; others are aimed at influencing *the status of the organization or stakeholder* that participates. Thus participants were there:

- to influence the contents of the standard,
- to ignore the initiative and deliberately fail to participate,
- to delay or stop the process,
- to protect their own standards,
- to speed up the process and ensure that it resulted in a usable standard,
- to learn about CSR,
- to develop their social networks or keep an eye on others, or
- to increase their status.

It should be emphasized, however, that participants may have used more than one strategy during the entire process, sometimes combining several or changing direction, depending on the moves of other participants.

Those Who Were There to Influence the Contents of the Standard

Many of the stakeholders tried to influence the contents of the standard in various ways, using various methods. One strategy was to have many representatives present at work meetings, performing various *voice strategies* such as disseminating written comments on standard drafts and participating in debates in standard-writing task groups. A complementary strategy was to act indirectly through participation in various strategic task forces, trying to influence the organizing process (e.g. definitions of leadership positions, shaping of procedures) or the members of special task forces. Yet another way of exercising influence on the standard and its status in relation to other standards and instruments in the same field was the *threat to exit*. This strategy was particularly effective for high-profile actors, as their mere presence granted legitimacy to the standard-setting activity (see Chapter 9).

At the center of disagreement was a number of substantial issues that were up for debate and 'manipulation', to use Christine Oliver's terminology (1991, p. 157–158). There was disagreement over the *appropriate target group* of the standard. Should it be applicable only to corporations, as in assumed in the notion of corporate social responsibility (CSR), or to all types of organizations, as in social responsibility (SR)? And should it be directed primarily at large corporations, or should the language subsume small and middle-sized corporations? These issues were unclear during the initial work phase; there were several corporations, business associations, competitors, value-driven organizations, and service providers that were for or against these options. Over time a convergence emerged toward the SR approach, including multinationals, small- and middle-sized companies, and other types of organizations.

Another issue concerned the *limits of the scope*. Should the standard cover all three pillars of sustainable development – economic, social, and environmental – or should it cover social issues only? Companies or service providers that had invested time and resources in implementing ISO 9000 and ISO 14000 standards generally pushed for the new ISO standard as a complement to existing standards on the environmental dimension (e.g. ISO 14000) and the economic dimension (e.g. ISO 9000); they focused solely on social issues, as implied by SR. One representative of an individual corporation worked hard for the adoption of SR, because it would likely be interpreted as representing only the social dimension. Other corporations and industry associations lobbied for CSR and one standard including all three dimensions. In general, organizations that were already using a CSR terminology, having their own CSR standard or providing services around a CSR approach, for example, tended to prefer that direction. And over time convergence developed toward the three-pillar approach – economic, environmental, and social – and toward SR. Still, after a few years of standard-writing work, criticism arose regarding the paragraphs in the standard on environmental issues that were perceived as weaker than other parts of the standard, and concerns arose about the lack of authoritative environmental NGOs such as the WWF among the participants. One interpretation of this evolution is that the limits of the scope – whether or not to include environment – was perhaps not clear-cut in practice.

A related intensive debate concerned the definitions of *core principles* of SR, which included respect for human rights, recognition of stakeholder rights, accountability, and transparency, for example, and of *core issues* of SR. At the beginning of 2007, consensus evolved around seven core subjects that were eventually labeled environment, human rights, consumer issues, labour practices, organizational governance, fair operating practices, and community involvement and development. Consumer organizations were clearly satisfied with the fact that consumer issues were among the final core subjects, whereas several interviewees representing industry interests were not happy to include operational governance or fair operating practices – or at least believed that fair operating practices could be included under operational governance. Eventually a decision was made to include these seven core subjects in the standard, whereas intensive debates continued about the definition of such related concepts as stakeholder engagement, ethical behaviour, supply chain, sphere of influence, and sustainable development.

Participants also argued about the appropriate *level of requirements* in the standard. Should it be a short and generic text for all types of organizations, or a more elaborate and precise text with an inclusive definition of stakeholders, including business-specific requirements such as the supply chain? The debate also addressed the degree to which a *management systems approach* should be introduced as a model in the standard text. Should it merely be a list of the existing instruments (e.g. standards, and conventions) or should it be similar to management systems standards, in that it included precise and detailed recommendations for implementation? In 2007 an interviewee described how the task group responsible for the implementation chapter struggled to make the existing draft more practical, while 'de-managementifying' it to suit those who resisted a management systems approach. She told us that someone in that task group said that their task was to make something that 'looks like a dog, smells like a dog, and barks like a dog, but isn't a dog'. Many service-providing companies, but also other types of stakeholders, were among those engaged in filling the ISO 26000 standard with practical guidance to organizations, preferably through a management systems approach similar to the one used in the ISO 9000 and ISO 14000 standards. Industry associations representing direct users tended to be of the opposite opinion, struggling hard to delete any wording that could be connected to a management systems approach.

A related concern was about the *type of verification and reporting mechanisms* appropriate for the standard. Certification could be a solution (as it is for the ISO 9001 and ISO 14001 standards) – a solution that could be linked to a management systems approach. Many stakeholders spoke in favour of such a solution, but the issue of certification was delicate, and industry associations, in particular, argued against it from the beginning (Tamm Hallström, 2006). Indeed, it was stated in the official purpose of the ISO 26000 committee not to develop a certification standard, although this debate was far from closed.

And if the standard should include a *reference list of existing CSR tools* to be recommended, what should be considered 'existing tools' or 'authoritative intergovernmental instruments' or 'international norms of behaviour', which were other terms used in this debate during the time of drafting the standard? Should such a list contain only intergovernmental agreements, such as the core labour standards of the ILO and the UN declaration of human rights? Or should it be a more inclusive list that would include the Global Reporting Initiative guidelines, the Social Accountability International SA8000 standard, and the UN Global Compact principles?

In their analysis of substantial issues that were debated within the ISO 26000 process, Ruwet, and Tamm Hallström (2007; 2008) followed a single debate: the choice between CSR and SR – and analyzed the arguments around this choice. They found a number of sub-debates involved in the overarching debate framed as 'CSR versus SR'. What types of organizations are concerned by the standard? What sizes of organizations are concerned? What tone should be used? What should be the level of requirement and specificity? What issues should be the focus? Should a new name be created (Ruwet and Tamm Hallström, 2007; 2008)? This analysis thus reveals that issues of disagreement may be activated in various contexts, albeit under disguise – invisible to the large majority of participants. Later in this chapter, we return to this point, as we examine the aspects and decisions that are typically visible and open only to a few participants forming inner circle or elite group within standard-writing processes.

Those Who Consciously Ignored the Initiative and Did Not Participate at All

An action that could be considered the opposite of the manipulation strategy is to ignore or criticize, and not to participate in the standard-setting activity at all (cf. Oliver, 1991; Alexius, 2007). There is obviously a methodological issue involved in the examination of such a strategy, as it can be difficult to reach conclusions about people who are not there. Yet a few observations can be discussed. Some of the most CSR-progressive corporations were among those missing throughout the ISO 26000 process. One labour representative expressed concern by saying:

> A relevant question is: Who is here from industry, and why? Not one of the companies from our country that is participating here has signed a global agreement, and you can wonder about that. Why are [the large companies] not here in the ISO 26000 process? We think that they're very good, and some of them have signed global agreements, and they follow up on issues like child labour and work environment. When we ask them, they reply: "Why should we be there? It's of no relevance to us" (interview with labour representative, April 2007).

Some of these large companies may have had their own standards. IKEA, for example, launched IWAY (short for 'IKEA way') in 2000, for the purchase of home furnishings – a standard that includes general legal requirements, environment block, work conditions, and wood procurement. IKEA did not appear to be threatened by or in need of a new ISO standard. The company's absence in the ISO 26000 process could be explained by a reluctance to expend resources developing an unnecessary, irrelevant standard that was not seen as a competitive threat. As it turned out, however, the ISO Board decided to proceed with standard-setting activities in the CSR field despite the absence of a few important potential stakeholders, and the perceived resistance from several corporations, industry associations, and the ILO.

Stakeholders may also criticize or develop antagonist strategies as outsiders. We note in Chapters 4 and 5, for instance, that strong criticism was levied toward the FSC and MSC during the initial phases. As the FSC eventually became established and gained momentum, it became difficult to ignore this organization, and critics began to develop competing programs, such as the Programme for the Endorsement of Forest Certification (PEFC) schemes. Hence, a strategy of participation, in a broader sense of the term, is to enter the transnational regulatory space as a new competitor (cf. Alexius, 2007). Others develop watchdog organizations such as the FSC Watch.

Those Who Were There to Protect Their Own Standards

Referring to the investigative work on SR that ISO initiated in 2003 and to an Occupational Health and Safety (OHS) initiative[1] discussed a few years earlier within ISO, an ILO representative made the following statement:

> I was there [in the ISO investigative group on SR during 2003–2004] to keep an eye on it, so that ISO didn't go against ILO interests, and develop something lower than the ILO standards, because ILO makes real standards in the social area. We had experience from ISO, from the occupational health and safety issue. ILO then

decided not to participate, because of lack of representation in ISO work. And ISO had no mandate to work in occupational health and safety, and no proper representativeness, no balance between industry and labour. They were closer to a decision then, but they never went ahead with that project. But they were well-prepared and we didn't want to participate in that. So we didn't have a completely harmonious relationship with ISO ... Here ISO was more careful, though. They set up an advisory group. ISO has learned from the past. So we were there (interview with ILO representative, June 2004).

As described in this quote, the ILO thus used a strategy of nonparticipation a few years earlier when ISO discussed a possible standard on occupational health and safety (see also Ruwet, 2009 on this example). We can assume that the strategy of resistance performed by the ILO – being a central standard setter in the field of work practices, including occupational health and safety – was indeed effective, as it meant that ISO was not granted legitimacy from this authoritative stakeholder (cf. Alexius, 2007). As ISO started to plan for its standard-setting activity in the field of SR, the ILO was again less than supportive. As described by the ILO representative, it did not use the same nonparticipation strategy as in the OHS case, however, as it eventually decided to participate in the ISO investigative group to 'keep an eye on it' and to protect its own standards. All the competing rule setters that were mentioned in Chapter 6 (the UN Global Compact, the Global Reporting Initiative, the OECD, the Social Accountability International and AccountAbility) can, in fact, be understood as participating to protect their standards and positions in the regulatory space.

Those Who Were There to Delay or Stop the Process

Among those who were resisting the ISO 26000 initiative in the early days, there were several – some corporations and industry associations in particular – that remained skeptical, and continued their resistance throughout the entire standard-writing process. After the first international work meeting of the ISO 26000 committee in 2005, a representative of a TNC wrote to the ISO Secretary General expressing his views on the seriousness of problems with the ISO 26000 process. His concerns, which were also perceived by other participants, regarded the integrity of the future process, the credibility of the future standard, and the reputation of ISO (Guertler, 2005). The letter addressed problems of stakeholder balance and other procedural issues of the standard-writing work as well as the future substance of the standard.

As we observed and as reinforced by interviewees, a few negative voices originating from corporations and industry associations created loud objections. Some interviewees believed, in fact, that participants representing corporations were typically raising the same critical questions (e.g. over business-specific formulations) repeatedly in order to create debate, as a delaying tactic. They acted as sticklers for details playing for time, these interviewees believed.

Participants representing labour issues in the ISO 26000 process also appeared as strong critics. Several trade union representatives said that they did not want to speed up the process, as that would risk insufficient consideration of stakeholder interests would force consensus decisions, and ultimately harm the credibility of the process. Several trade union interviewees also raised the negative view that trade unions often have toward voluntary standards (as opposed to compulsory legislation) as a regulatory instrument or approach. As one trade union representative said of this issue and ILO's negative attitude toward ISO:

> There is strong resistance toward management systems and certification. ILO sees ISO as an organization with a history of developing management system standards that are linked to other kinds of verification mechanisms with business-oriented certification firms. ILO perceives ISO almost as a competitor. It is now proposed that ILO standards with agreements that states, employers, and trade unions together have developed, that are translated into national legislation, are to be replaced by ISO standards and the business interests following that system. ILO considers itself as more representative and more authoritative, and ISO is something completely different. It's a private initiative (interview with expert labour representative, April 2005).

For participants with such negative attitudes toward the ISO system and with a critical view of the lack of democratic legitimacy of the standard-setting work, it became crucial, then, to assure that the procedures were acceptable and taken seriously. It seemed better to allow the process to evolve over whatever time was necessary than to speed the process of getting a standard onto the market. It also became crucial to see to it that the ILO standards were not replaced by ISO standards, but that they constituted an important reference in the coming ISO standard (cf. Chapter 6).

In analyzing the material, we often found that the participation strategies observed in the ISO case were prevalent in the other cases as well. We believe, however, that there is a significant difference between the FSC and MSC, on the one hand, and ISO, on the other. It was and is considerably more difficult for organizations to delay or stop the process from *within* the FSC or MSC; they must criticize these organizations from the outside or try to defeat them through competing rule-setting activities. It is not impossible, however, to delay, stop, or encumber the standard-setting processes in these organizations. One interviewee from the FSC Secretariat referred to a strategy used by a previous member in circulating critical reports about the FSC prior to the FSC General Assemblies. The interviewee suspected that the member was strategically timing the reports to receive as much attention as possible among FSC members during the General Assemblies. He said that this tactic was not constructive, however, as it merely led to upset discussions and a misdirected focus. Yet, *ceteris paribus*, we would argue, it is more difficult to delay or stop the process by participating in FSC and MSC arrangements than by participating in ISO arrangements, because of the control mechanisms in and a narrower scope of the FSC and MSC.

Both the FSC and the MSC have institutionalized *control mechanisms* of members and participants to avoid such participation strategies stalling the process. Especially within the MSC, participants must, according to these control mechanisms, show commitment to its goals. The MSC is not a membership organization, and therefore has highly restrictive rules about the inclusion of stakeholders (leaving aside the actual certification processes in which any stakeholder is allowed to voice concern). One could argue that it is not relevant to compare an ongoing ISO process with the more institutionalized processes of the MSC and FSC. Yet during the early phases of these organizations, a core group of stakeholders had a great deal of control over the standard-setting process, and could invite those they thought were in favour of the standard-setting initiatives. Although an extensive review process, including consultations with stakeholders from a number of countries, preceded the establishment of the FSC and MSC, there was a core group of some 25 people that controlled the process and set the agenda (see Chapters 4 and 5). To be sure, there were internal tensions during initial phases, particularly within the FSC. Yet, fundamental criticism toward these organizations was raised mainly from outside.

The MSC and FSC have a *narrower scope* than does the ISO. Whereas the MSC addresses only marine life and the FSC addresses only forests and forestry, ISO's new standard targets all types of organizations globally. Within the FSC and MSC, moreover, there is an implicit assumption that not all organizations within these sectors are relevant for certification according to the FSC or the MSC standards. They aim at 'best practices' in sustainability in their respective industries, although there are various interpretations of how to measure best practice.

Those Who Were There to Speed the Process and Ensure That it Resulted in a Usable Standard

There were service providers such as management consultants and certification firms that wanted the process to advance more quickly. In 2007, after two years of writing, the ISO Secretariat proposed that they end the drafting work and move forward to final revisions and publication, and several service providers supported this move:

[We] want to get this standard published as soon as possible. It's becoming embarrassing now, when people outside already work with this standard using the second draft as a basis, and we in this working group just continue and continue to revise the text. I think it's matured to a satisfactory level now. It's good enough (interview with a representative of Others, November 2007).

As critics pointed out, however, there could be serious consequences of moving forward too quickly; the multi-stakeholder structure that was developed for the drafting work would be abandoned and replaced by ISO's ordinary national voting structure. National delegations would have to force consensus in order to establish a national vote, thereby further weakening the voices of the weaker stakeholder groups. This, in turn, could risk the quality of the standard as well as the consensus needed for a successful acceptance, diffusion, and implementation.

In the cases of the FSC and MSC, it was the retailers – a large group in the middle of the production chain – that seemed unconcerned about the exact formulation of standard contents, as long as they were feasible for users, but that urgently demanded standards (cf. Boström and Klintman, 2008).

Those Who Were There to Learn about CSR

Some of the service providers and representatives of national standards institutes (thus the members of ISO) explained that they participated in the ISO 26000 process to learn about CSR and the new standard. For such participants, the ISO 26000 work was an international arena assembling highly regarded experts in the field, and as such, it functioned as a school. It was also an arena for the discussion and development of new markets for services linked to the implementation of standards (cf. Tamm Hallström, 2004, regarding the ISO 9000 work).

A similar motive for participation was to learn about CSR at the international level in order to work consistently at the national level:

[I'm here to] see how it works. I cannot actually participate, because I'm an observer. I'll bring news of what's happening back home. We have a national sustainability standard in [my country] for corporations. So it's important that there is coherence, consistency, between what's done here in ISO and our standard (interview with an Others representative, November 2007).

Several participants from developing countries also explained that one motive for their participation was to learn about CSR ideas that were not yet established in their countries.

Those Who Were There to Develop Their Social Networks and Keep an Eye on Others

Linked to the learning strategy, was the motive of participating in standard-setting work in order to develop social power resources: to meet with colleagues, potential customers, and partners, to develop personal and professional networks. There was intense networking activity during coffee breaks at international work meetings, with talks and the exchange of business cards (cf. Tamm Hallström, 2004, regarding the ISO 9000 work). During ISO 26000 interviews, interviewees described how much communication was held through continuous e-mail correspondence, and there were special address lists for email communication that were used within a specific stakeholder group, in which debates were held and texts exchanged between the international meetings. These e-contacts were maintained and developed through social networking activities during actual meetings.

Consistent with these findings, Boström and Klintman (2008) found, in their study of green labeling processes, including forest and seafood certification, that active participation in the processes helped various groups to develop closer contacts, which, in turn, resulted in mutual learning, understanding, trust, and expectations. Yet the rapprochement usually seemed to be an unintended, albeit positive consequence of participation rather than an intended strategy of participation. Although fishers, for instance, did not expect to find common ground with environmental movement organizations, participating within multi-stakeholder work has been seen as an opportunity to check what other actors in the network, or regulatory space more broadly, are thinking and doing (Boström, 2006a). Participation can be seen as a way of decreasing the risk that other actors invent rules that everyone will have to adapt to in the future – perhaps a subset of being there to protect one's own standards.

Those Who Were There to Increase Their Status

For some participants, such as management consultants, participation provided them with a professional or moral status advantage in their regular workplace, allowing them to reference their contribution to the ISO 26000 process, and thereby strengthening their symbolic power resources. Ahrne and Brunsson (2008) note that meta-organizations are often established in order to create, confirm, and reinforce a certain identity among their members. In an analysis of the standard-setting work of the former International Accounting Standards Committee, Tamm Hallström (2004) has observed that auditors sometimes applied to become project managers for a few years in order to gain experience and increase their status as part of these international standard-setting processes. She found that their participation had clear positive effects on their work with clients.

People could also be there for a related reason: to improve the status or social recognition of the stakeholders they represented rather than their own status. When asked 'Why is your organization here to support the FSC work?' one interviewee said:

> It's mainly a way to acknowledge labour rights. In many countries, the degree of organization is very low and there's strong pressure on those who try to establish trade unions. People can get sacked, and in some parts of the world, it's even worse – people can be threatened. Through FSC, we try to protect the rights of workers and see that they are protected and followed. When we hear about noncompliance, we can inform FSC about it – if an area is certified and the rules are not followed – in areas in which trade unions are persecuted, for instance, then we can call attention to these circumstances and try to do something about them (interview with a representative of a meta-organization for labour unions).

We have tried to demonstrate the complexity and the diverse interests and strategies of the daily practices of the standard setters that we have examined. Consequently we can expect that the work of organizing all these interests into a legitimate process can be demanding, not least if we consider the fact that participants often have diverse resources to use for influence (cf. Chapter 6). Yet to complicate the situation, all stakeholders do not keep the same positions and strategies throughout the process, which often lasts for several years.

CHANGING PREFERENCES AND PARTICIPATION STRATEGIES

In this section, we demonstrate the flexible nature of preferences and participation strategies by discussing two competing standard setters that participated in the ISO 26000 process: the ILO and the UN Global Compact.

Early in the ISO 26000 process, some participants raised concern about the future position of the ISO 26000 standard in a norm hierarchy and the risk that it might crowd out existing norms and standards set by such representative organizations as the OECD, the ILO, and the UN, and those set by private organizations such as the Global Reporting Initiative. The relationship between ISO and the ILO was unique in this context, as the ILO was the first competitor to request a special status through its own memorandum of understanding (MoU) with ISO. To provide some background, many trade unions were of the opinion that there were better regulatory solutions than voluntary ISO standards regarding the issues of SR, and of course, the ILO was the key reference to these stakeholders:

> To us, ILO is the only organization with the legitimacy to set rules for these social issues that we consider to be political. Thus there is an explosive force embedded in this ISO project, as we see it. Moreover, there are already sufficient tools at the global level, such as agreements between the ICFTU – the International Confederation of Free Trade Unions – and multinational companies. We're already working on that (statement made by a labour representative at an open seminar in Stockholm about the ISO project, May 2005).

When a participant at an early ISO conference asked a representative of the ILO why ILO could not be considered as an appropriate standard setter for SR, the representative explained:

> It's difficult to define exactly where the ILO mandate stops, but we have defined a number of core areas: health and safety, work environment, labour ... If the ILO mandate is broadened to include external environment issues, that must be a political decision from governments. Maybe ILO would also have to change to a multi-stakeholder organization. But there are problems, such as the lack of resources and expertise and other organizations doing some of these things already (statement made by ILO representative at the Stockholm conference on SR, June 2004).

After the 2004 conference in Stockholm, the ISO Board decided to start drafting the ISO 26000. One of the formal requirements, presented to ISO by the advisory group before the conference, was the necessity of recognizing ILO's unique mandate through some type of communication. The ILO claims to have a unique mandate, in that it defines international norms on a broad range of social issues, on a tripartite basis. Although ISO passed a resolution about its action to respond to the requirement, the period following the conference was filled with tensions around this topic, with stakeholders worrying about ISO's response. Thus around six months after the resolution was taken, and just in time for the first international work meeting of the newly established ISO 26000 committee, an agreement on a proposed MoU between ISO and the ILO was finally reached. In its Article 1, the ILO is given a special role:

> [The ILO] cooperation is subject to ISO decisions respecting all the provisions of Article 2, including that, in the ISO SR standards development process, any committee or enquiry draft or final draft International Standard (CD, DIS, FDIS) will not be circulated for vote and/or comment before seeking prior full and formal backing by the ILO as to all elements relating to issues involving ILO's mandate ... The areas of cooperation between the Parties will include the development of any ISO International Standard in the field of SR; any activities and publications for the promotion, support, evaluation and approval of any published ISO

International Standard on SR, and any periodic review of such ISO International Standard for confirmation, revision, or withdrawal (MoU, 4 March 2005).

A representative of the ILO interviewed in 2006 made the following comment on the value of the MoU:

> We are here to protect our labour standards. The MoU between ILO and ISO is very important for us. It means that we have the right to be on all committees and in the promotion of the standard. We are not here so much to say what ISO should do – it's an ISO process. However, if they talk about labour standards, they should talk about it correctly (interview with ILO representative, May 2006).

A few years before the ISO 26000 process was initiated, as noted previously in this chapter, the ILO used a strategy of ignorance toward the standard-setting activity in occupational health and safety that was proposed within ISO at that time. As the current ISO 26000 process was initiated, however, the ILO changed its strategy and decided to participate, albeit somewhat passively, keeping an eye on the evolution of this ISO process. During the early phases of the ISO 26000 process, the ILO did not engage in debates about specific details on the substance or orientation of the proposed standard. As soon as the MoU was signed, however, the ILO adopted a highly active role, which included actions aimed at influencing the content of the future standard.

The UN Global Compact is another example of a competitor struggling for its position while changing both preferences and strategies of participation. The UN Global Compact was present in the early stages (see Chapter 3) through participation in the ISO's 2004 conference. At the ISO conference in Stockholm, in June 2004, a Global Compact representative gave a highly positive presentation, assuring the audience that the UN Global Compact Office would work with ISO to internalize the principles of the ILO, the Rio Declaration, human rights, and anti-corruption: 'ISO and Global Compact stand together!' he said.

Even if this statement expressed support of the ISO initiative, there was some hesitation around Global Compact involvement in this process. In 2005, when we contacted the UN Global Compact for a possible interview, their response was negative; they were uncomfortable about discussing this sensitive issue, and were actually reconsidering their involvement in the whole process. One year later, the UN Global Compact had changed its strategy in favour of the ISO initiative, had become more active in the process, and was preoccupied with negotiations with ISO about a possible MoU. As a former UN employee said, in speaking of the UN Global Compact's acceptance of the ISO 26000 work:

They have their principles, but they are all about rights, and nobody cares about rights. So now they want to work with ISO on this. They are curious and have sent more representation lately. They check it out and say that they are interested. They look around. If anything goes wrong they'll leave. They are here to push the principles into the ISO standard. To join this bandwagon (interview with former UN employee, May 2006).

During our visit to the Global Compact Office in New York in 2007, one of its staff members who was engaged in the ISO 26000 process made the following remark about the driving force behind Global Compact's engagement in this process:

We are 14 people working in this office. Our operational capacity is zero. But that is something that ISO and the GRI have, for example. We encourage all these frameworks and then we let the market decide what initiatives will win. We have legitimacy to offer, and that makes it a win-win situation ... We work hard to see to it that our 10 principles are included (interview with Global Compact officer in New York, April 2007).

We can see how the UN Global Compact has changed from being a relatively passive participant to becoming highly involved in critical task forces of the ISO 26000 committee, struggling for its own principles by influencing the content and orientation of the ISO 26000 standard. The ILO was particularly involved in all the debates around labour issues, in accordance with their MoU, in which the ILO core labour standards were presented as crucial, authoritative references. The principles of the UN Global Compact did not enjoy the same high status as the ILO standards did, and it had to struggle to have its principles considered for citation as authoritative references in the ISO 26000 standard (for a further elaboration on the concept of high-profile actors and their status, see Chapter 9).

In this section we have used only two examples to illustrate the point of changing preferences and strategies; these example are specific, as they concern two organizations that managed to obtain a special status, which can at least partly explain why they changed strategies. The conclusion about changing strategies, however, can be applied to other organizations that changed and combined their strategies of participation in various ways, requiring the standard setter to react. During the initial phase of standard-writing work, for example, several NGOs that were engaged in shaping the content of the standard pushed for a CSR approach – a standard designed mainly for large corporations. As the process developed, ISO decided to aim for a broader line, and target all types of organizations globally as possible users of the standard. NGOs had previously been against such an approach, based on the belief that there was a risk that the 'CSR agenda' had been lost. Then they changed course and worked hard in this new direction. One advantage of the new approach, according to some interviewees, is that it is easier to argue for strict requirements in the standard if all organizations, including NGOs, are targeted (Ruwet and Tamm Hallström, 2007; 2008). A number of organizations representing industry interests that initially were totally against the making of this standard changed over time to become highly involved in the shaping of its content and character into a 'nonmanagement systems standard'. In Chapter 8, we return to the interests of entire stakeholder groups, such as the industry group referred to here, to discuss how they sometimes managed to present themselves as united and homogeneous, while representing a number of diverse groups below the stakeholder surface.

ACTIVITIES VISIBLE TO ONLY A FEW – THE INNER CIRCLE AND THE SECRETARIAT

Before we reach a number of general conclusions about strategies of participation, we argue that a group of people and units deserve special attention: the inner circle and the secretariat. The first example attended primarily to influence the contents of the standards.

An Inner Circle

A distinctive characteristic of the standard-setting practices investigated here, and of policymaking in general, is the existence of a small group of people who are particularly influential in holding most of the leadership positions and exerting power over the contents of a standard. We call such a group an *inner circle*. Their influence can be direct, through debates and written comments, or indirect, through the organization of standard-setting work and its procedures. The inner circle should not be confused with the unit that we have called the *host* of the process (discussed in the next section in relation to the secretariat), although they do overlap. Rather, the inner circle should be seen as a group or small network of people representing the host and a few other key stakeholders. One characteristic shared by those who managed to exert power over the contents and the organization was their presence and activity at international work meetings:

> It's important to be here. Personal relations are everything. Between the meetings you can e-mail etc, but to meet and to have eye-to-eye contact really tells you about what is at stake, what possibilities there are. That isn't happening at plenary meetings, but during breakfast, lunch etc. But it's also important to give your point

of view in public – at plenary for example (interview with consumer representative, May 2006).

The interviewee continued to explain that there were 20 to 25 people among the approximately 400 at ISO 26000 work meetings who were doing almost everything:

> These are very important people – influential. It's like all political processes, I think. It's good that you can meet and talk over a cup of coffee and hear what different stakeholder groups think, and discuss with just a few people. But having said that, the others in these stakeholder categories are also important, and they can also influence. It's hard work, but you can really influence if you want to (interview with consumer representative, May 2006).

Those who managed to become part of the inner circle typically had a clear view of and worked actively to shape the contents of the standard in their preferred direction. There were competitors to ISO such as the ILO and the Global Compact, with their MoU and the Global Reporting Initiative, and there were industry associations, service providers, and value-driven organizations. We also observed that these types of organizations held one or several positions in various smaller task forces and strategic advisory groups – the Chairman Advisory Group; the Liaison Task force; and, later, the Integrated Drafting Task Force – important groups that assisted the leadership and the Secretariat of the ISO 26000 committee (cf. Chapter 3). Many of the same people appeared in all these task forces and advisory groups, forming an inner circle or elite among participating experts. We can infer that control over the organization, its procedures, and the setting of the agenda mattered a great deal to participants that wanted to influence the outcome of the process – the substance and the status of the anticipated standard (cf. Lukes, 1974/2005).

One NGO representative even suggested that the voices of some five to ten highly influential people stood out across all areas in the ISO 26000 process. Characteristic of those people, the interviewee continued, was their ability as orators, fluency in English, comfort with the jargon, and negotiating experience, giving them the ability to exclude newcomers. Similarly, in Chapter 4, on the establishment of the FSC – especially when we discussed the early phases of the process – we described how a relatively small core group, calling themselves the FSC Founding Group, and including an interim board, established some of the basic elements well before the Founding Assembly in 1993. Initially, this group comprised a little more than a dozen persons, whereas the Assembly gathered more than 100 people.

The founding process of the MSC was firmly controlled by a small group of people with affiliations from the WWF, Unilever, and an international consulting firm. Both the FSC and MSC networks have expanded dramatically over the years, but the organizational literature has often confirmed that what happens during the initial stages of institutionalization is essential to the development of processes (Stinchcombe, 1965). There are a number of mechanisms causing inertia and path dependency, making it difficult to introduce major changes in an organization once it has been firmly established (Ahrne and Papakostas, 2002). This timing issue was also seen in a number of our interviews. In the FSC case, one interviewee from a large Do-It-Yourself (DIY) chain discussed a standard revision process by saying that 'FSC has listened to our input', but that it was extremely difficult to make an impact because of the high complexity of the standard-revision process. He continued: 'We learned that we should have been more active from the start, to be able to govern this. Now, when we look at the result, it isn't particularly good. So now looking back – someone should have roared earlier and said "this is not good".'

In the MSC case, the founders – the WWF and Unilever – deliberately dissociated themselves from MSC somewhat, because of the need to establish a more independent structure for the MSC. A general conclusion is still that the few people forming an inner circle in our three cases ensured that they kept their positions in one or several of the working committees or supporting task forces that focused on organizational issues. One of Tamm Hallström's earlier investigations of an international standard setter in the field of accounting came to similar conclusions. A British expert maintained that a small group of policy players in each country that competed, in a kind of horse-trading, for the few positions in the (former) International Accounting Standards Committee. In Tamm Hallström's (2004) investigation of the ISO committee that drafted the ISO 9000 standards, experts seemed to develop a specific expertise and interest in participating in ISO work and tended to appear as experts in various ISO groups. Djelic and Sahlin-Andersson (2006) highlight how such participants in transnational rule setting can act strategically using 'the first mover advantage':

> Those participating in defining the rules of the game are more likely to understand the rules better and to be able to maneuver within and around them. Knowledge means control and power and understanding of the rules of the game gives a head start to those actors that were involved early on in rule-setting (Djelic and Sahlin-Andersson, 2006, p. 396).

Vifell (2006) developed the concept of *enclaves* as a special type of organizational form that tends to evolve in international rule-making processes. Characteristic of members of enclaves is their sharing of a vocabulary and a common knowledge about the evolution of the process – a sharing that can be used to exclude others:

The enclaves had clear boundaries to actors on the outside and the common language and history that were necessary to incorporate in contacts in the international processes became a hindrance for entrance to the enclaves. The cognitive frames supplied by the international processes made ideas presented in other ways and in other vocabulary irrelevant to the groups. The results showed that the organisation needed to be well co-ordinated in order to "speak with one voice" in different committees and at different levels in the policy process (Vifell, 2006, p. 363).

Such administrative expertise, along with language skills, constitutes a power resource in rule-setting processes. Even though a small group of experts often develops into an inner circle or enclave, with a common understanding of the process and vocabulary used, the material presented in this book demonstrates that there were diverse and often conflicting motives and interests driving actor participation. We can conclude, therefore, that the members of an inner circle do not necessarily hold the same positions on the content and orientation of the standard being set.

A few experts in the inner circle changed organizational affiliation during the course of events. One person in the ISO 26000 process, for example, began as a government representative of one country, but later became a representative of an IGO, and therefore a liaison member. In that case, the change of organizational affiliation led to a change in stakeholder categorization. Another person was first an NGO representative and later went to work for a consulting firm; yet the role change did not seem to affect this expert's status or categorization as a stakeholder. The unclear conditions of representation were, in fact, general to all participants, including participants who were not part of the inner circle. We observed consultants who were hired to represent NGO interests in the standard-setting activity or people working for an NGO who represented the interests of developing countries. The intricate issue of representation is clearly an area requiring more thorough investigation. Classification according to type of stakeholder knowledge base and issues of representation has implications for the participants' opportunities to influence the process and its outcome (see Chapter 8).

The Secretariat

The other unit that deserves special attention is the secretariat that administers the standard-setting activity. As a general assertion, the need for a strong secretariat grows in parallel to the growing market impact of standards. In our three cases, the degree of market impact differs. The new ISO standard was being developed during the period investigated, whereas the FSC and MSC standards have been in operation for a number of years and are continuously being revised; reinterpreted; or complemented by policies, strategy documents, and methodology guidelines. The management of a standard that is in operation requires additional administration, which is clear in the FSC and MSC cases – the cases that we are primarily using for this analysis.

The MSC staff almost doubled over a short period, after the organization had been in operation for a few years. The FSC's Change Management Team, which conducted a general review of the FSC's work soon after the millennia shift (see Chapter 4), gave strong recommendations for hiring key additional staff when they noticed that the FSC was 'extremely understaffed' and that existing staff had been working at 'heroic levels' in their attempt to handle the workflow. Since then, the number of staff members has increased and new positions have been added, including a professional fundraiser, public affairs and communication officer, and regional coordinator. We have seen similar developments with the creation of new positions for fundraising and communication in other international standard-setting bodies – within the (former) International Accounting Standards Committee, for example, which, during the 1990s, was expanding and strengthening its position as a rule setter in the regulatory space (Tamm Hallström, 2004).

A growing secretariat results in growing autonomy, authority, and consequently, power (Barnett and Finnemore, 2004). Although the secretariats, headed by executive directors, should be responsible to their boards, our interview material suggests that secretariats are gaining increased autonomy vis-à-vis the boards of the FSC and MSC. At least on paper, a board is closer to the stakeholders because there is an assumed link (representation) between a board member and a particular stakeholder category, whereas staff members are hired only on professional merits. Although other researchers have reported tensions between the staff of the FSC Secretariat and current or previous board members of the FSC (see e.g. McNichol, 2003), our interview material suggests that there is agreement over the relationship and the allocation of tasks and responsibilities between these units. Our interviewees agree that the board was previously too involved in various detail issues, because of its closeness to specific stakeholder interests. It could be difficult for a board member representing, say, social/south, to refrain from pushing for details that the majority of social/south members addressed, despite an urgent need for the board to reach consensus. Board members operated under time constraints, however, and all the time spent digging myriad details rendered the work of the board cumbersome and ineffective. There was a broad agreement, as expressed in the Change Management Team report, for the need to redefine the roles and responsibilities of the board to focus on strategy, leadership, and governance issues for the entire FSC network, while delegating greater authority to the executive director and the secretariat to handle routine operational matters (see also FSC, 2008). In practical terms, this change created greater autonomy for the policy unit of the secretariat to develop and refine policies and standards. The new role of the board was to monitor the standards-development process and ensure that it followed the rules for the best standard-setting practice (as defined by ISEAL Alliance, for instance), including the important task of assuring a sufficient degree of stakeholder consultation.

One consequence of these changes was the board not being allowed to modify a standard once it was submitted for approval; it could merely say 'yes' or 'no'. Hence, it should not be possible for a board member to introduce personal or company backgrounds, for example, to change the standard at the last minute. Proponents of these changes refer to both efficiency and transparency gains. This may be true, but it is important to bear in mind that regardless of whether one considers it to be a good or bad development, it fosters autonomy, authority, and power in the secretariat.

An interviewee from the FSC Secretariat claimed that the policy and standard unit within the FSC should assure that policies and standards 'are up-to-date, are developed in accordance with the expectations of our stakeholders, of our members, according to general principles of transparency, participation'. This unit should work to maintain the rigidity and integrity of the system on the one hand, and to allow solutions for upcoming questions on the other hand. As this interviewee said, the process of making the FSC standards work and having an impact on the market was an ongoing one. In addition, new sectors may develop an interest in certification, and there is a need for some preparedness to assume such opportunities. Hence, this interviewee and others describe the policy unit as constantly working with review, clarifications, and specifications for certain cases. Since the establishment of the FSC Principles and Criteria, policies and standards have emerged in many directions at various geographical and functional levels, which in turn imply that the secretariat must continuously make revisions. Once standards are developed, 'we have the task of constantly revising them', as one interviewee expressed it. Some issues are less controversial, meaning that the secretariat can conduct reviews on its own. Other reviews, such as the extensive review process of the FSC's Principle 10 (the plantation review process) required great stakeholder involvement.

It is also clear, for instance in the plantation review process, that the secretariat plays a moderating role. As one interviewee maintains, 'It can get really difficult when stakeholders would like to have a say in the development of standards. Maybe they do not have the full picture'. The interviewee indicates that the secretariat is in a position to have the big picture, whereas an individual stakeholder sees only one part of the picture. Hence, there is a need, the interviewee continues, to assemble a group of experts and to try to keep them as representative as possible, by including different types of manufactures, certification bodies, and NGOs that are aware of and concerned about specific issues. The interviewee argues: '... but then each of these technical experts has its own background, has its own kind of objectives or personal interest, I might say. Then it is our role, actually, to make all aware of the whole picture in a way' (interview with staff member at the FSC Secretariat).

In addition to the capability of providing the big picture, the secretariat has the capability to link various stakeholders to each other (the broker role), and it can combine formal and informal channels. Although the secretariats are not part of decision-making fora, they do have direct relationships with them. A staff member at the MSC Secretariat illustrates its unique position in connecting both formal and informal networks in the MSC arrangement. She talks about two parallel tracks. On the one hand, there is the formal forum where things 'pop up for discussion':

> But on the other side, there is a lot of interaction between different members of our team [staff at the secretariat] with different groups and stakeholders. And through these contacts and the relationships, the executive [the secretariat] is attuned to whatever issues are emerging. And through these relationships, we start making connections and patterns, because this is something we need to respond to, as well as having our own ideas. And then things might pop out in the more formal settings as well. And these two things are both working quite well actually, because now we are in a position to have many contacts with the stakeholders.

The staff of the secretariat has a unique position, in that its members can combine formal and informal channels to voice their views. In our three cases, we see that the host of the standard-setting body present itself as the unit that has the overview and can function as a neutral arena, in front of mutually mistrusting stakeholders that lack experiences in communicating and negotiating with each other (cf. Boström and Klintman, 2008, on mutual mistrust). They are in a good position to develop skills and address their viewpoints, which are framed as being based on 'technical or administrative expertise' rather than 'stakeholder interest'. They establish authority by claiming themselves as representatives of neutrality, impartiality, and objectivity (cf. Barnett and Finnemore, 2004). They have gained particular strengths in both cognitive and social power resources. By putting these secretariats 'in authority' (that is, having formal positions to do certain things), they have been able to strengthen themselves as 'an authority' (which derives from demonstrated expertise, training, experience, and credentials, for instance; Barnett and Finnemore, 2004, p. 25).

In summary, when analyzing standard-setting work in transnational multi-stakeholder arrangements, we need to include the organization that hosts the process, both at the abstract and more concrete levels. Our cases show that there is a growing need for a relatively autonomous organization with resources, professional training, and time to conduct day-to-day work and to monitor the standard-setting activity, while engaging in networking and moderating among the stakeholders. The staff develops a unique overview of the growing repertoire of standards, policies, and documents. As the regulatory framework grows in size and complexity, a parallel demand for expertise on the framework is developing. New rules and policies are emerging, explaining how separate rules and policies should fit together. Knowledge about specific details as well as the entirety of the process is required. And it is among those who host the standard-setting process that this type of expertise is found. Unique expertise provides power. The secretariat is in a unique position to 'see the whole', and, consequently, has the power to speak about further need for revision – often instituted because of inconsistencies and clashes among strategies, criteria, and principles. This development creates some ambiguity (which shares similarities with efficiency-versus-democracy dilemmas in an analysis of politics and administration or within principle and agency theory). The staff within the secretariats should act on behalf of someone else, even as it gradually develops autonomy, unique expertise, and insight into a number of activities. Some stakeholders observe this development skeptically. In Chapter 10, we further discuss some implications of such power shifts and imbalances for multi-stakeholder standard setting.

CONCLUSION

As discussed in Chapter 1, we believe that it is crucial to understand a standard-setting activity as part of a wider regulatory space. The preferences and strategies of participation among the stakeholders are affected considerably by the roles these organizations play and by their capabilities and relationships *outside* the standard-setting arena. In this chapter, however, we have demonstrated that preferences and strategies can evolve and change over time *within* a standard-setting process. The conditions of participation may change, therefore, depending on who is taking part in the process and the action that such actors are capable of pursuing. There is a core group of stakeholders that must be considered in any analysis of standard-setting processes – a group that is intensively involved. We have highlighted the inner circle and the secretariat as constituting such a group. This core group can, over time, even strengthen its own position and authority within the arrangement, which in turn may create power imbalances that threaten the authority of the multi-stakeholder arrangement (see Chapter 10). The complexity that we have demonstrated so far makes the work of organizing and legitimizing multi-stakeholder standard-setting activities a difficult task, and one that needs to be attended to continuously, in order to establish non-state authority. In the next chapter, we add yet another perspective to this complexity by demonstrating that there are internal structures that shape the capabilities and doings of participants: the stakeholder categories that are established by the standard setters hosting a multi-stakeholder process.

NOTE

1. A few years before the ISO 26000 committee began its activities, the ILO used the strategy of avoiding participation in another ISO standard-setting activity that was debated at that time. ISO had worked on a proposal about drafting a standard in the field of Occupational Health and Safety (OHS), but eventually ISO decided not to proceed with that proposal.

8. Power and Actor Categories

One feature of multi-stakeholder work is the need to create actor categories –
stakeholder categories – to classify all participants in the multi-stakeholder
standard-setting activity, in order to allocate tasks, responsibilities, and
decision-making power. Thus standard setters need to aggregate their views
through the creation of various actor categories, and in that way achieve both
effective and legitimate standard-setting work. As argued in the introduction
to this book, however, the creation of stakeholder categories is not merely an
organizing and legitimizing activity for the standard setter. It also contains a
power dimension that has received little attention in research on standard-
setting activities. To establish stakeholder categories, the standard setter
makes distinctions and ascribes similarities. Categorizations constitute a
principle of inclusion and exclusion to organized activities; they can tell us
something about who is and who is not allowed to participate in such
decision-making arenas as standard-setting committees. Another intriguing
issue related to power resources is the way positions or preferences can be
created within a category consisting of several members. Yet another power
issue is the impact of classifications on the groups of people being classified;
categorization usually favours some people over others – those who would be
better off categorized in another way. How a participant is categorized indeed
has an impact on that participant's role and on the standard-setting process.

   In this chapter, we aim at three things. First, we elaborate on the
establishment of stakeholder categories within ISO, the FSC, and the MSC –
a discussion we began in Chapters 3 to 5. Second, we discuss the
fragmentation or integration within stakeholder categories through six
examples found in our three cases, each illustrative of homogeneity or
heterogeneity, depending on the stakeholder category we observe. The degree
of homogeneity and heterogeneity is, in turn, important, as it affects the way
participants of each category are able to perform collective action and make a
powerful impact on the standards and policies established. This leads us to
our third point about consequences – both advantageous and disadvantageous
– that follow the use of a chosen categorization. Not all people perceive the
same advantages or disadvantages in a specific categorization.

CATEGORIZATION AND REPRESENTATION IN THE FSC, MSC, AND ISO

ISO would usually classify all participants of a standard-writing committee as 'experts' (or 'observers'). This terminology, according to the ISO definition,[1] refers to individuals assumed to act in a personal capacity, and not as representatives of a specific interest group. As it entered this new field, which differed from its traditional work, ISO decided to broaden participation and increase representativeness (cf. Chapter 3). Organizations were still invited to participate as either experts or observers, but ISO categorized all the experts and observers into six additional stakeholder categories: government, NGO, consumer, labour, industry, and Others. Experts and observers without a specific national affiliation (e.g. international organizations) were given a liaison membership.

Some additional efforts, such as the guidance document stating clear definitions of each category, were needed to make the stakeholder categorization work – an issue that was described in Chapter 3. This document, defining the stakeholder categories, was merely a guidance document, however, communicated by the ISO 26000 Secretariat to the ISO members to be used when selecting participants for the national delegations. There were no additional control mechanisms to ensure that these definitions had been followed, which lead to variations in the composition of national delegations present at international work meetings of the ISO 26000 committee. Moreover, as we examined how the stakeholder categorization system handled representation, we observed that ISO had problems with unequal representation at the international level; it was clear that the six stakeholder groups were not equally represented in the actual work, partly due to variations in the financial situations of participants. The Others group and industry group were allotted the highest representation, followed in descending order by government, NGO, consumer, and labour.

Stakeholder representatives did not always remain with the stakeholder group to which they were originally appointed. An expert representing the financial sector (stakeholder category Others) complained about the unclear criteria set by ISO before the meeting:

> I talked to a person there from the Italian financial sector. Later, when we had the stakeholder discussion about the nomination of experts to the Chairman Advisory Group, which is an important group, I looked for her but she wasn't there. When we met afterwards, I asked her why she didn't join the discussion in our stakeholder group ... She said that she had been in the industry group and explained that they were the only three people from Italy, and that she had been asked to represent industry in this particular debate. To me, this is not good (interview with expert of the financial sector, April 2005).

This interviewee was questioning the functioning of the multi-stakeholder structure. There were other examples of participants that changed from one stakeholder category to another during the course of events, and examples of individuals with dual employment. Although representatives could not formally belong in two categories, we did observe representatives who, for example, belonged to the industry category by virtue of working part time for a corporation, while simultaneously belonging to the Others group, because they had their own consulting firms. We already mentioned changes of stakeholder affiliations in Chapter 7, in our discussion of the inner circle, but we observe similar changes and ambiguities regarding all participants – probably because stakeholders applying to participate at the international level of the ISO 26000 work complete their applications themselves, and indicate the stakeholder category to which they want to belong.

One possible motive for the switching strategy and other ambiguous representations is the gaining of power by disguising one's real interests. If the quota of experts allowed in one stakeholder category of a specific country is already filled by the time a new stakeholder wants to enter the process, for example, there could be other stakeholder positions still free. In some countries, an expert has been able to sign up as an expert for a stakeholder category that still had positions left over, while promoting the interests of the 'real' stakeholder group at the international work meetings – at least at the beginning of the process. Given such circumstances – with voluntary control of the nominations of experts delegated to the national members of ISO – we can expect that the task of creating a good multi-stakeholder structure that clearly defines and controls who belongs to each category is not an easy task for the international secretariat. And if many participants should use a switching strategy, there is a risk of the legitimacy of the multi-stakeholder structure being undermined in the long run because of power asymmetries evolving through a structure that does not function as it was meant to function.

The categorization of stakeholders into five (and later six) groups in the ISO setting largely reflects those people and organizations that attended the first meetings and that appeared to be easily separated. In the FSC, the categorization into three chambers was less ad hoc. As described in Chapter 4, there were intense controversies over tropical deforestation taking place between developing and developed countries before the FSC was established. The founders of the FSC felt a need to include southern and northern members equally, to help them attain legitimacy worldwide. Likewise, there was a strong need to balance the relationship among different types of stakeholders. The current tripartite structure with equal weight for the economic, environmental, and social chambers emerged gradually. The original organizational structure involved only two chambers: one with social and environmental interests, with 75% of the votes; and one with economic interests, with 25% of the votes. In 1996, after suffering criticism from trade and industry players, the FSC modified the arrangement to the current tripartite structure, supported by the increasingly dominating sustainability discourse.

The sorting of members into three chambers appeared more deliberate and less ad-hoc than is was in the ISO case. That is not to say, however, that the FSC managed to create a less problematic structure in its balance of homogeneity and heterogeneity (see later discussion in this chapter) or to have a well-balanced representation from various actor categories. It has been much more difficult to recruit members to the social chamber than to other chambers.

Membership in the economic chamber is open to actors with a financial interest in forest production, including employees, consultants, certification bodies, retailers, whole-sellers, and end users (Dingwerth, 2005). These members must demonstrate their commitment to FSC Principles and Criteria. Certification bodies must apply for the recognition of the FSC, producers must commit to having their forest property certified, and traders must commit to selling certified products. Consequently, all actors having an economic interest in relation to the FSC are lumped together within the same category. Making a distinction such as that between Industry and Others (which includes consultants and certification bodies), as in the ISO case, has apparently not been seen as a critical issue.

Membership in the social and environmental chambers is open to not-for-profit NGOs and assigned individuals with a demonstrated commitment to FSC goals. Members of the social chamber could be trade unions, academics, indigenous people, or people representing community-based forests. The boundaries between the chambers are relatively imprecise and the chambers relatively heterogeneous, with small and large actors. The economic chamber has a broad membership, ranging from the Swedish Church (as a forest owner) to large TNCs. In addition, the FSC has both organizations and individuals as members – thus an element that adds to heterogeneity. Each member has voting opportunities, and can use other informal channels to affect FSC standards and policies. Members can also participate in other organizational units, on the board, in various working groups and committees, and at meetings. We noted the same ambivalence over participation as was the case with the ISO.

The FSC is, in one sense, more transnational, as it does not have the tradition of national representation. Yet a board member should have a number of attributes and qualities, which creates some ambivalence. Similar to the ISO case, each participant or representative should be an expert in relation to forest practices. Furthermore, there are six types of board

members, reflecting a representational logic: economic/south, economic/
north, social/south, social/north, environmental/south, environmental/north.
Although the FSC created a decision-making structure that is 'unique in the
current system of global governance in its balance between Northern and
Southern interests' (Dingwerth, 2005, p. 201), the delimitation of northern
and southern countries could be seen as arbitrary. These labels have a
geographical connotation; yet the north/south distinction is based on the
national order of things, according the UN criteria of high-income countries
(northern) versus low-, middle-, and upper-middle-income countries
(southern). This means that Estonia, for example, was defined as a southern
country. Above that lies the differentiation into chambers, which is implicitly
associated with the idea of different interests and values.

Several interviewees from the FSC case talked about the ambivalence of
representing both a particular expertise and a particular interest. We received
diverse responses from interviewees who had served as board members.
Although they all stressed their expert role, they differed in their view of the
category they represented and should be accountable to. As a previous board
member representing economic/north said, 'Everybody knows what we are
doing. We are representing a chamber. So my role there is to look at things
from an economic chamber perspective'. Yet another previous board member
representing economic/north stressed the following:

> You represent all members equally, because the members elect you. Yes, you can
> say that I represent the economic/north. What happened was that people contacted
> me and asked me to forward certain views. But during my time as a board
> member, I was also contacted by other groups, by the environment chamber, and
> by the social chamber. So one shouldn't look at borders in that way.

These ambiguities over representational loyalties, and whether to follow an
expert or representational logic, not only create ambivalences and dilemmas
for the individuals holding these positions; they create tensions within and
between organizational units. One source of tension mentioned by several
interviewees – including those from the secretariat – is that the board was
'too involved' in technical details. Board members felt pressures from 'their'
constituencies locally and regionally. In order to fulfil their responsibilities –
being accountable to the body they were supposed to represent – they felt a
need to 'make a difference' on the board. This pressure created repeated
tensions between board members and the secretariat, and the distribution of
roles was unclear. The confusion was an incentive for a revision of the
relationship between these organizational units, as mentioned in Chapter 7.
The organizational reform that followed contributed, as we have noted, to
increase the autonomy of the secretariat.

Turning to the MSC case, we see both similarities and differences in the way participants have been classified. The MSC is not a membership organization, but a foundation. Yet like the examples from the two other standard setters, it is organized as a multi-stakeholder arrangement, and has sorted its 'members' into categories, which like the FSC categories, did not occur merely because of who attended the first meeting. The MSC was started by two organizations: Unilever from the market sphere and the WWF representing the global civil society. And although the MSC developed as an organization independent of these two, it has always sought to balance carefully the involvement of organizations from different societal spheres.

One significant feature in the MSC arrangement is its division into a unit for science and standard-setting expertise (the Technical Advisory Board) and a unit for interest representation (the Stakeholder Council) (see also Chapter 5).[2] In the MSC arrangement, the differentiation of roles was not blended, at least on paper. We also noted from our interview material that interviewees tended to speak of the Technical Advisory Board as a unit for experts and the Stakeholder Council as a body for interest representation. Those who were supposed to give objective and neutral expert advice would appear in the Technical Advisory Board and those who were supposed to push their views, values, and concerns in relation to sustainable fishery were more likely to appear in the Stakeholder Council. We asked several interviewees about this distinction, and received diverse answers. Some believed that this distinction correctly reflected a distinction between technical and political issues, whereas others tended to question this view:

Q: The division between a technical advisory board and a stakeholder council gives the impression that you can separate technical and political issues. Should it be seen in this way or have I misinterpreted it?

R: No, I think your interpretation is right, and I think you're hitting on an important point (MSC Board member, industry stakeholder).

Like the respondent, we believe this to be an important point, and that there are power differentials involved in the separation between these units, a situation that we discuss later in this chapter. When we asked interviewees about key topics discussed in their forum, those representing these two units mentioned similar things: whether the MSC should stay in wild catch or diversify into aquaculture, for example; how to expand the MSC to the developing world and improve access for poor countries; what should be the MSC's view on controversial fishing methods such as bottom-trawling; and issues surrounding auditing, certification, and traceability. One possible difference may be that the Technical Advisory Board discussed various topics in greater detail.

Not everybody could be a participant within these organizational units of the MSC, in contrast to the situation in the ISO and the FSC. Whereas any individual or organization other than government actors with an interest in forestry practices could, in principle, become members of the FSC; it is up to the current members of the board, the Technical Advisory Board, and the Stakeholder Council of the MSC to propose and decide upon new participants in its units. Within the Stakeholder Council, it has been more difficult to recruit members from the public interest sector and to get representation from small-scale fisheries, developing countries, and consumer associations. There is a bias of representation from northern, developed countries. Dealing with heterogeneity at the general level has been a challenge for the MSC. Because of complex discussions in the Stakeholder Council among between 30 and 50 persons representing various interests, the council recommended the establishment of the Stakeholder Council Steering Group. Accordingly, a steering group of eight people (one for each subgroup) was established to facilitate regular interaction with the various organizational units. This group should then be able to send clear messages, preferably consensus-based messages, to the Board.

THE FRAGMENTATION OR INTEGRATION OF STAKEHOLDER GROUPS

We now turn to our second point – how these categories worked in practice. We have already touched upon some practical dilemmas in relation to representation, but there are other noteworthy aspects of these practices. One is the degree of homogeneity and heterogeneity in each category. In order to gain influence on the standard-setting activity in multi-stakeholder processes that involve many people and organizations, it is essential to develop collaboration and form alliances. If a particular stakeholder group appears to be internally fragmented, it is likely that it will, as a group and for each individual member, face difficulties in making an impact. In contrast, if the people and organizations within a particular stakeholder group manage to form and express a shared agenda in front of the other stakeholder groups, then the probability increases that it can have a significant impact on standards and policies. To understand how power plays out within multi-stakeholder standard-setting work, therefore, it is necessary to see how stakeholder groups manage to act and appear in an integrated manner. The homogeneity of an actor group relates partly to the possibility of such a group creating (at least an image of) common positions within the stakeholder group, even though the group comprises diverse and changing interests.

We now discuss six examples from our investigations of the FSC, MSC, and ISO. Each example illustrates how the degree of homogeneity or heterogeneity varied within various stakeholder categories. The cases vary, depending on the actual degree of homogeneity and heterogeneity of views within a group, contrasted to the way representatives of these groups managed (or did not manage) to produce an image of homogeneity, irrespective of the actual practice.

An Industry Group with One Voice in ISO

A common perception of the industry group in ISO was that of a strong, united group with consistent views. As discussed in Chapter 3, the points made by industry in the early phase (2003–2005) were directed primarily against the development of the standard (Tamm Hallström, 2006); and the image of the industry group, as perceived by other stakeholder representatives, was that it was a united group with converging views. Another example from 2006 shows how industry acted as a united group. In the debate (particularly intense in 2006) about the transparency of the ISO 26000 process, the industry stakeholder group managed to muster many of its representatives and to deploy 'sustained opposition' to exclude the media presence that had been proposed (see Chapter 9). An obvious strength of the industry group was the fact that there were already established networks and collaborations among industry players from earlier ISO standardization projects. In addition, most industry associations had long associations with ISO through the national standards bodies that constituted the organization's membership. Industry actors used their networks, with organizations like the International Chamber of Commerce and the International Organization of Employers having prominent positions at the global level, and national industry associations being active at the national level. Behind that surface, however, the industry group also contained divergent interests:

> A common perception is that industry is one group with one voice. But now you discover that there are as many voices as there are within the NGO group. There are those who are critical toward the industry group's way of engaging in specific issues. There are a few people who are seen everywhere and talk loudly, but the most extreme viewpoints are articulated by these people. Thus a few people manage to make it look like this is the common position of industry. And they are well-organized and well-represented (interview with NGO representative, April 2007).

During interviews with individual industry representatives, a similar picture of diversity evolved. There were those who were continuously resisting and trying to stop or delay the project, but there were also several companies that actually preferred a voluntary standard set by ISO instead of more mandatory legislation. Supporting the ISO process could be seen as the lesser of two evils. One industry representative talked about a growing influence and pressure from NGOs and the threat of governments imposing regulation. Another interviewee representing industry mentioned the 'business case' – that increased profits could actually be generated through SR.

One could infer that the view of a specific company might depend on the extent to which it was already involved in CSR activities. A progressive company with experience in CSR work would probably enjoy a certain competitive advantage linked to its CSR profile. One could imagine it assenting to the new standard requiring at least the same commitment to CSR as the company already maintained. A more conservative company with no CSR experience, on the other hand – a company that had representatives there to learn about how to get started – might be expected to prefer a weaker standard. Despite the fact there were diverse interests among industry representatives, the industry group often managed to present itself as a united group with homogenous interests. This, in turn, meant that the voice of this group became powerful (cf. Jutterström, 2004).

Looking at the written comments communicated to ISO when a new working draft of the standard was to be discussed, the image of industry as a group with one strong voice persisted. The industry group often presented a united view on documents that were sent out for comments. Written comments made by national industry representatives were often identical to the comments made by the International Chamber of Commerce, for example, or the International Organization of Employers. The opposition to include the concept of 'sustainable development' in the ambit of the standard was one such comment, as was the insistence that ISO should aim for a short and generic text for all types of organizations – not merely business practices. Moreover, as observed by a number of interviewees, some of the most progressive companies were not participating in the ISO 26000 work, whereas a few well-organized industry associations were articulating most of the views communicated by the industry group. Under these circumstances, it is reasonable to conclude that, even though there were diverse interests within this group, its leaders could still maintain its solidarity.

Unified Environmental and Economic Chambers in the FSC?

Within the FSC, we noted similar views of homogeneity in relation to both the economic and environmental chambers. On the one hand, the three-chamber structure 'suggests a homogeneity of interest that does not exist in practice. As an example, grouping forest owners, forest managers, wood traders, retailers, and certifiers into a single "economic" chamber has caused much concern, in particular with landowners and forest managers' (Dingwerth, 2005, pp. 199–200). Such concerns contributed to the establishment of the competing standard setter, the Programme for the Endorsement of Forest Certification (PEFC) schemes.[3] The image of 'one industry' was nonetheless apparent in the FSC case as well. In the view of several interviewees, the main split within the economic category, is, in the broader sense, between those who support and use the FSC and those who support and use PEFC, although many economic actors used both systems. In a sense, some degree of homogeneity was created because of differentiation into competing arrangements in the transnational regulatory space.

Interviewees from all three chambers talked especially about the integrated environmental chamber. They referred to the organizational and networking skills of global environmental NGOs – social power resources – which can assume a leadership role within the chamber. As a previous board member representing economic/north told us, '[T]hey have very good networks, indeed, and communicate internally and they ... have their meetings, networks and information channels that they have created'. She also argued that both the economic and social chamber should learn from their skills and experiences. Succeeding to create an image of homogeneity also implies another skill, as another interviewee from the economic chamber/north mentioned: 'You can talk with Greenpeace or WWF and they will give you global views.'

Although homogeneous interests and (global) framing skills, were important, as suggested by this quote, it should be emphasized that there were often many organized efforts behind images of homogenized interests, including the concealing of viewpoints and concerns that ran counter to the dominant one. According to an interviewee from environment/south, there was a wide array of viewpoints from various environmental organizations, and even varying viewpoints within subunits of such organizations as the Friends of the Earth. This interviewee also talked about the strong uniting role played by large environmental NGOs such as the WWF and Greenpeace, yet with a more critical tone. According to him, the FSC faced serious credibility challenges that these large environmental NGOs failed to address sufficient seriousness.

Organized Consensus: The Cases of Consumer and Labour in ISO

Two stakeholder groups in ISO – the labour group with their International Trade Union Confederation and the consumer group with Consumers International – enjoyed the advantage of having a single organization coordinating the interests of national member organizations and representing their interests globally. Each of these groups could advance a strong coherent view, as noted by a consumer representative from one of the national delegations:

> We are a more homogenous group than the others. There is only one global organization: Consumers International. Two or three consumer experts belong to an organization that is a member of Consumers International, and many of those remaining are governmental organizations. But we are used to working together, and now we are here to work for this. So it is easier for us to focus on strategic issues when we do not have to spend time disagreeing (interview with a consumer representative, May 2006).

The organized consensus among consumers was demonstrated by the written comments that ISO received on the first working draft of the standard. Reminiscent of the industry group, comments made by national consumer representatives often included exactly the same formulations as the comments made by Consumers International. The consumer group interviewee who spoke with us in Lisbon continued to specify the primary interests of consumers in the ISO 26000 work: that ISO standards are good tools to spread CSR among companies and that the ISO standards are well-known (compared to SA 8000 and AA 1000, for example), and have the potential to be widely used. Another consumer representative, whom we interviewed in 2006, talked about consumers in general supporting certification to standards: 'We are pro-certification, really. We are concerned about credible information; that is really the main issue for consumers.'

The labour group was generally not pro-certification. It tended, instead, to be pro-legislation, promoting compulsory frameworks and democratic rule-setting processes. It was similar to the consumer group in its small number representatives; at center of both groups was a strong global organization representing their main interests globally, and both were seen as having strong expert status. Another characteristic specific to the labour group was its emphasis on the representative character of the standard-setting work, and thus the importance of the stakeholder categorization.

Disorganized Others, NGOs, and Governments in ISO

In contrast to the consumer and labour groups, the NGO group and the group called Others had several interests that were represented by a large number of organizations. When we asked an NGO representative about the main points her group had in common with other NGOs, she said:

> There is no NGO-think. It's difficult to put all NGOs in one group. Their interests are very different. There are small NGOs, very local, and there are huge, global organizations ... Do we have a good common language? No! I feel it is impossible

for me as an NGO expert to be representative for all NGOs. These are artificial distinctions really (interview with NGO representative, May 2006).

There was probably no 'Others-think' either, yet the Others group did seem to agree on the importance of including practical guidance on the implementation of the standard, preferably using a management systems approach that included certification. A representative of the Others group believed that members of this group shared two goals: to improve the world and get the standard published as soon as possible.

Representatives of both the Others and NGO groups mentioned during interviews that they perceived that members of their specific groups were not considered by some of the other stakeholders to have either high expert status (compared to industry expert representatives, for example) or as high status as stakeholder representatives (compared to labour expert representatives, for example). We thus see how prototype effects evolved among the group of experts, with some experts being regarded (at least by some) as less prototypical, whereas others were considered more 'real' or prototypical in their expert role.

The government group, at least at the beginning of the process, comprised organizations that were not used to communicating or working together: 'I don't think that we in the government group will ever create alliances and develop common views', a government representative told us. This is understandable, given the enormous economic, political, and cultural differences among states around the world. Some government representatives of developing countries aired their concerns about national differences, making the ISO 26000 work difficult. As one government representative from a developing country said about the proposal to include restrictions on working hours:

SR is really too complex; it's not easy to standardize ... differences between countries are too big ... We have very different problems that can't be handled by one standard. For example, in regions where you can work only parts of the year, the workers want to work longer days in order to get enough money to support their families. Then it becomes a problem if there is a standard restricting the hours they are allowed to work (interview with developing country/government representative, May 2006).

There were other such debates that concerned differences in the viewpoint of delegates from developed versus developing countries. One issue revolved around the age limit defining child labour. Another issue concerned whether the ISO 26000 could become a trade barrier for small and mid-sized companies in developing countries. A solution to these types of worries that was proposed by many was to allow for differences in the application of the standard. Other stakeholders held, however, that international law (e.g. UN conventions and norms) would always enjoy precedence when national laws conflicted with them.

The Fragmented Social 'Leg' in the FSC

All interviewees from the FSC spoke in different ways about the fragmented feature of the social 'leg'. The social chamber included a diverse cluster of groups and individuals representing indigenous people, local communities, labour interests, small landowners, and individual academics. Such groups often have an antagonist relationship with each other. An interviewee from the FSC Secretariat maintained that it was more difficult consulting with social constituencies than with members of the other chambers, because they are often completely unorganized and have difficulty expressing what they want. Another interviewee with experiences from both the 'environmental' and 'social' sides, discussed how to mobilize support for specific motions in the general assemblies. He maintained that people from the social chamber are far less skilled and integrated in their ability to mobilize alliances both within and across chambers than are people from the environmental chamber. Furthermore, all interviewees representing social groups from the north or the south maintain that differences in concerns and opportunities for participation differed enormously among social groups in various parts of the world. Such differences added to the heterogeneity and to the difficulties creating unified views within the FSC.

Interviewees talked about the difficulty for indigenous and local groups to have someone representing their view in the global organization. And how could each local view in all corners of the world be generalized and aggregated into one global view? An interviewee from the economic/north talked about fragmentation in relation to the global/local divide: '[N]ormally, social interests are local, and don't extend across borders. So in the end most of the social organizations are local and based upon local interests.' The important thing, then, is not if there are local versus global interests; the important thing is whether or not there are organizational structures within which to aggregate and unite local groups with various views and to create a common frame. Trade unions are seen as the strongest group in the social chamber in this regard, yet they are clearly lagging behind environmental NGOs.

An Integrated MSC and the Distinction between the Technical Advisory Board and the Stakeholder Council

Interviewees described the MSC as 'a very large organization', reflecting a 'diverse mix' with a 'huge variety of interests'. In general, however, the

MSC's participating stakeholders appeared to be far more homogeneous than the stakeholders of either the ISO or the FSC. This pattern has nothing to do with the contextual factors in the sector. The fishing industry is extremely diverse, with individual coastline fishermen on the one hand, and large-scale industry vessels on the other (Hoel, 2004), and as these groups compete over access to the fishing resource, it is likely that they have different views on the issue of sustainable fishery.

Despite this heterogeneity of interests, however, our material suggests that stakeholders within the MSC appear far less fragmented than do the other two cases. MSC is a tighter organization, with fewer participants, mainly from the Anglo-Saxon world; it enjoys the legal form of a foundation rather than a membership organization, and its formative agenda-setting phase was controlled by only two organizations. Moreover, the MSC deliberately excluded the social sustainability factor from its beginnings, and concentrated merely on economic and ecological aspects. The implication was that a large group – the social actor categories – was excluded, by definition, from the start. To be sure, the MSC had to face strong criticism from organizations of fishing workers, and social sustainability may be an issue that the MSC needs to address more carefully in the future, in order to maintain legitimacy. Yet the MSC has not needed to organize such a heterogeneous actor category of social players as seen in the case of the FSC. Moreover, the MSC does not have the global structure of national initiatives that adds to the heterogeneity found in the FSC.

The homogeneity has one specific implication, as some of our interviewees mention (and criticize): the representation in the MSC tends to be biased toward large-scale industrial-country fisheries (notwithstanding the fact that the MSC is struggling to improve representation from small-scale fisheries). As an interviewee from Greenpeace said, with a clearly critical tone, 'MSC is very, very industry-friendly'.

Interviewees from the MSC context generally speak of two groups: the commercial sector and the environmental NGOs. The Stakeholder Council comprises two chambers, both of which had four subgroups; it is mainly the two-chamber structure to which interviewees refer. When we asked which stakeholder groups are best-organized and have the capability of forming a unified view on various matters, several interviewees mentioned the NGOs. One interviewee, who has been involved in the MSC right from the start, said there are 'marginal differences. Look, the NGOs are well-organized. The industry is well-organized'. He also mentioned, as did other interviewees with positions in the Stakeholder Council, that there is a good balance between these two groups, and that there is a constructive and friendly discussion climate. It is interesting to note how the NGO category can appear homogeneous (despite heterogeneity under the surface) in one standard-setting organization (the MSC) and extremely fragmented in another (the ISO). We return to this topic later in this chapter.

Perhaps the most interesting distinction within the MSC is the one between the Stakeholder Council and the Technical Advisory Board. If we compare these units in terms of relative weight, it is obvious from the interviews that the Technical Advisory Board, comprising scientific and technical experts, is the most influential. To be sure, the Stakeholder Council is not without influence, as interviewees can report about concrete, significant policy changes that stem from discussions within the Stakeholder Council. There is an asymmetry, however, which relates in part to a strong trust in expertise in the MSC. Moreover, the asymmetry relates to the different abilities among the bodies to digest and channeling *homogenous* viewpoints. Both aspects are indicated in the following quote from a member of the MSC Board:

> I think the TAB [Technical Advisory Board], as a body, has been more successful [than the Stakeholder Council] within the MSC because it has a very clear task. It's providing an expertise that no other body can do. The Stakeholder Group is almost like an extended board; it's much more about debate than about decision or recommendations, and it has been less successful as a result. It's a way you can bring not just the 14 people sitting around the Board table, but you can bring another 30 plus people ... But it's almost like an extended board, so some of the debates tend to be similar to the ones we had around the board table. And clearly, you couldn't operate any board with 30 plus people; it just would be ineffective (interview with member of the MSC Board).

The interviewee also mentioned that the board interacts more closely with the Technical Advisory Board. A number of facts strengthen the impression that this advisory board is closer to the inner circle of the standards work within the MSC. It gives the impression of being an expert organ, has less people involved, and meets more often – two or three times a year – whereas the Stakeholder Council meets once a year. 'People can talk forever without agreeing [laughter]', said one interviewee who had a position in the Stakeholder Council. The Technical Advisory Board was established early in the history of the MSC, although with a different name (Standards Council), whereas the Stakeholder Council was created much later as a response to accumulating criticism about the MSC not being sufficiently transparent and having weak stakeholder representation. The advisory board is consequently more institutionalized and well-rooted. Although it is an advisory unit, it even has the last word on some issues: the fishery certification methodology, for instance.

STAKEHOLDER CATEGORIES AND POWER

How can the variation in these examples be explained? Why are some groups perceived as strong and united, whereas others are extremely heterogeneous and perceived as weak? How can we explain the prototype effects that evolve among experts in the three cases? Why are some participants regarded with high and others with low expert status? In the final section of this chapter, we offer two explanations for this puzzle. One is based on a power resource perspective, emphasizing such dimensions as access to technical and financial resources, including the capability of organizing and communicating within the group, as well as the capability of framing an argument as a global issue – a crucial factor in the creation of homogeneity within a stakeholder group. The second explanation reveals a structural and less visible power dimension in standard-setting practices: the power of actor categories. In this discussion, we analyze how categorization of participants has consequences for participants' perceptions of the preferences and capabilities of themselves and others.

Power Resources to Create Common Positions through Organized Activities

One obvious explanation for the power variations we observed relates to the fact that positions can be shaped through organized activities. As a general rule, we see social power resources – networking skills and leadership experience – as well as material resources to arrange meetings, seminars, and workshops as being crucial for enabling organization and communication within stakeholder groups. Material resources facilitated organizing activities such as pre-meetings held before important decisions were made, which in turn helped to create homogeneity within a group. The size of the organization affiliated with the stakeholder typically determined its resource base (large organization – more resources), and the funding logic of such organizations was another determinant (commercial actors – more resources).

In the FSC case, interviewees representing the economic and social categories mentioned the organizational and networking skills of global environmental NGOs (see also Kekk and Sikkink, 1998; Smith, 2005; Scholte, 2005). In the ISO case, such capabilities were linked to the size of the stakeholder group (small group – good communication) and to the habit of working within representative structures (e.g. trade unions and consumer organizations, both of which enjoy the advantage of having a single organization coordinating the interests of national member organizations and representing their interests globally). Other important characteristics were the capability and skill to develop arguments using frame-bridging techniques (cf. Boström and Klintman, 2008) – cognitive power resources. Such framing requires some degree of a compromising attitude: preparedness for negotiation; awareness of others' viewpoints, concerns, and ideologies; and, not least, willingness to offer or bracket some of one's own viewpoints and concerns. Strong organizational and cognitive platforms facilitate such characteristics.

Another significant characteristic of our cases was the extent to which an interest in participating in standard-setting activities has strong local connections. Do organizations with such interests lack the discursive or organizational capability of generalizing from diverse local interests and establish a global frame? Ulrich Beck (2005) relates power 'in the global age' with the capability of moving from a national outlook toward a global – what Beck calls a 'cosmopolitan' – view. The cosmopolitan outlook, according to Beck, involves a transnational frame of reference, which includes knowledge about global interdependencies and an understanding of the interaction between national and global risks and crises. This outlook is not confined to national boundaries; it simultaneously acknowledges equality and difference, and is committed to the planet as a whole. Actors that are not confined to a national outlook have an advantage here. According to Beck, organizations such as Greenpeace:

> ... receive their mandate from their commitment to the key issues facing humanity: environmental destruction, global financial risks, human rights violations, civil rights, the struggle against increasing global poverty and flagrant violations of the unwritten rules of a "global justice". These "global problems" do not constitute the "domestic affairs" of nation-states or international corporations. This is why it is legitimate for these movements to become involved (Beck, 2005, p. 76).

Such organizations may be seen, from a national viewpoint, as illegitimate, because they have no electoral mandate within their nation state to speak for universal interests. They are granted legitimacy or moral authority, however, precisely because the transnational political scene lacks representative democratic structures. And they are granted legitimacy because the public does not usually suspect that organizations such as the WWF, the Red Cross, and Amnesty International speak merely for some specific national interests. They are credible because their orientation is primarily, or exclusively, global (or cosmopolitan, to use Beck's terminology).

In contrast, many labour unions can be more easily targeted for merely addressing a national viewpoint. The wealth of workers in one country is often framed as being related to the poverty of workers in other countries. In practice, it has been much more difficult for representatives of national labour unions to think beyond their national borders in their political struggles and solidarity thinking. The environmental movement has been less fettered with a national outlook, and frames a global crisis that calls for global action and solidarity. Moreover, global environmental risks are risks for all – no one on the planet can escape them – whereas local social risks concern only 'them', despite the fact that similar 'local' social risks are seen everywhere on the planet. One key exception, as seen in the ISO case, is, of course, the International Labour Organization (ILO), which is difficult to categorize in terms of either an international governmental organization (IGO) or an NGO. The ILO is strongly linked to labour (social) interests, which can explain the organizational strength of the labour stakeholder group in the ISO 26000 process. We may interpret the ILO's presence in the ISO 26000 process and its lack of presence in the FSC process as being rooted in the sector-specific standards of the FSC, which are not regarded as being equally competitive. The generic ISO standards may be valued more highly as possible 'carriers' of the ILO's core values.

Those who speak of the global risks have a strong risk-defining power, according to Beck (2005). We could therefore expect greater strength from local groups, including groups representing indigenous people, local community-based forestry, local fisheries in developing countries, or labour unions, should they search for alliances with globalized social and environmental NGOs that operate more freely on the transnational regulatory scene with strong risk-defining power.

To conclude, we see that organizations with certain power resources are more favoured and influential in these non-state standard-writing settings, as such resources can affect their *capability of addressing and visualizing common viewpoints*, and their *capability of building coalitions and organizing pressures* in the first place. As we discuss in the last section of this chapter, however, there is yet another power dimension to be found in the discursive construction and use of stakeholder categories.

The Power of an Advantageous Categorization

In order to analyze further the consequences of stakeholder categories within ISO, we should remind ourselves of the way ISO has defined the core subjects of SR: human rights, labour practices, environment, consumer issues, organizational governance, fair operating practices, and community involvement and development (cf. Chapter 7). Then it becomes clear that a few stakeholder definitions used in the ISO process correspond to such core subjects, while others do not. Labour and consumer groups, the two groups with the smallest membership had the advantage of being monopolists of two clearly defined areas of expertise: labour practices and consumer issues, both of which were core subjects of SR according to the standard. The labour group also had an advantage in the fact that the ILO core labour standards were generally perceived as being highly authoritative rules and crucial reference documents in the ISO 26000 process.

As it turned out, the industry group was separated from the consultants by the creation of another group, labeled 'Others', thereby limiting the industry group to non-consulting corporations and industry associations. The industry group could then appear as a large homogenous group enjoying high expert status; corporations were usually perceived as the obvious and proper experts (or stakeholders, really) for ISO settings in general, as ISO is traditionally an arena that attracts corporations to agree on standards:

> ISO's interests are within industry, for the most part ... So it's natural that industry has more influence in this process. It's understandable. Industry trusts ISO and that is a fundamental reason for this process; they are the ones who will implement it, so you don't want to ruin this trust that industry has in ISO (interview with NGO representative, June 2008).

The NGO and Others groups did not hold such positions of trust, nor did a definition of these groups correspond to a core competence. Instead they had a broad and inclusive definition of those who were welcome and needed for their expertise. They became heterogeneous, and difficulties arose from their lack of common points of view. The NGO group failed to attract authoritative organizations for human rights (e.g. Amnesty International) or environment (e.g. the WWF), which were core subjects of SR. Accordingly, these groups were questioned both for their expert status and status as proper representatives of a stakeholder interest.

If we turn instead to the FSC case, we can draw yet more conclusions. In the FSC – with its environment, economic, and social categories – the environmental stakeholder group, which included many environmental NGOs, was actually perceived as homogeneous and strong. The social group, however, which included a diversity of interests, was perceived as heterogeneous and weak. Thus we observe a view of people representing both labour and environmental interests that evolved within the FSC structure differently than it evolved in the ISO (see Table 8.1).

As noted by Bowker and Star (1999), any given classification provides surfaces of resistance as they block against certain agendas while they create smooth roads for others. Even though classifications have real consequences, however, they are not always clearly visible. The NGO group (including environmental NGOs) was not characterized as a strong and homogeneous group within the ISO setting, partly because of its definition; NGOs is not an area of expertise, per se, but a type of organization, and that reality left the group open to a wide range of organizations seeking membership. In contrast, within the FSC setting, environmental NGOs were affiliated with the

Table 8.1 Stakeholder categories and their status in ISO and the FSC

ISO – 6 categories 'Those who happened to turn up'	Status of category*	FSC – 3 categories Based on sustainable development thinking	Status of category
NGO	-	Environment	+
Industry	+	Economic	+
Labour	+	Social	-
Consumer	+		
Government	+/-		
'Others'	-		

Note: * (+) perceived homogenous as a group, having a strong voice and high expert status; (-) perceived heterogeneous as a group, having a weak voice and a low expert status.

Environment chamber – a clearly defined area of competence – and it was therefore regarded as a strong and homogeneous group with the advantage of being familiar with a global dimension. The labour group within ISO, on the other hand, was regarded as a strong and homogeneous group, having the advantage of familiarity with a global dimension through the International Trade Union Confederation and the ILO. Furthermore, the definition of the group corresponded to a crucial and clearly defined area of expertise. In contrast, the social chamber (including labour issues) within the FSC – with its narrow scope on forest – may not have been relevant for the ILO to engage in or be threatened by. Consequently, the social chamber was regarded as a weak heterogeneous group, comprehending several issues and interests, and unfamiliar with work in the area of global issues.

In the case of the MSC, it was not even relevant to speak of social constituencies, because they were excluded from the outset, because of the MSC's narrower focus on environmental and economic sustainability. Thus the MSC did not have to face problems of fragmentation faced by the FSC. The NGO group within the MSC could appear homogenous. Whereas several participants within ISO saw NGO-think as unthinkable, this actor category appeared powerful, and was seen as reflecting something distinctive within the MSC. Because the prefix 'environmental' can be inserted before 'NGO', as it was in the environmental chamber within the FSC, a smaller group of NGOs sharing a particular competence and worldview could appear to be well-integrated.

CONCLUSION

In summary, as the power-resource-based explanation to homogeneity within a stakeholder group is complemented by the analysis of structural and more invisible power embedded in actor categories, we reach a better understanding of the practices and dynamics of multi-stakeholder standardization. We see that preferences are shaped largely through organized activities, and that the advantage goes to organizations with access to cognitive, economic, social, and symbolic power resources that can facilitate their organized activities. We can also conclude that there is power embedded in the way actor categories are constructed, as such categories affect a group's creation of its preferences, how its members can act, and the perceptions of its representatives. The way actors and actor categories are constructed does indeed matter for the organizing, maneuverability, and self-awareness of the stakeholders involved, and eventually for the outcome and authority of the standard-setting process. As categories quickly become reified, our study suggests, the type of power that is embedded in discourses and organizational structures does not typically lead to open conflicts or resistance. Nor does a single actor, however powerful, typically decide such structures. An interviewee who had been active and influential from the beginning – in 2003 – was asked if these six groups were the right ones. He hesitated a few seconds before responding: 'I have no idea ... I don't know how they were created.'

We see structural power as a key power dimension to consider in our search for increased knowledge about organizing and legitimizing activities of standard setters. As we further discuss in Chapter 9, the way people are classified is also a crucial part of the effort to create legitimacy for a transnational multi-stakeholder standard-setting activity.

NOTES

1. The experts act in a personal capacity, and not as the official representative of the P-member [i.e. the country they come from; authors' remark] or A- or D-liaison organizations (see 1.17) that have appointed them. However, it is recommended that they keep close contact with that P-member or organization, in order to inform them at the earliest possible stage about the progress of the work and of the various opinions in the working group (ISO/IEC Directives – Part 1: Procedures 2008).
2. We can see a similar division in standard-setting work within the former International Accounting Standards Committee, with a smaller board consisting of chartered accountants (experts) responsible for technical decisions, and a widely based Advisory Council for stakeholder representation (Tamm Hallström, 2004).
3. This competing organization comprised three 'legs', as did the FSC, but two of these legs consisted of business interests. The economic category was divided into the forestry

industry (forest owners and forest companies) and processing industries (e.g. sawmills and paper producers). The third leg consisted of other interests, which could be either social (e.g. trade unions) or environmental. According to the proponents, business interests obtained a majority position in this arrangement, and the division better reflected real differences in business interests.

9. Legitimacy in the Making

The types of standardization that we discuss in this book – social and environmental responsibility – cannot be characterized as having an obvious technical character, like the traditional standard setting in areas dominated by engineers. They do have a political dimension, however, which is reflected in the multi-stakeholder structures established for these standard-setting activities. Yet these multi-stakeholder standard setters do not constitute political arenas in the traditional sense. They are non-state organizations lacking government as a center of authority, and they have no access to the means of enforcement that governments enjoy. Given their hybrid nature, their ability to legitimize their rule-setting activities is of academic interest. How do they convince various audiences that their standards are good and useful, and that they will assist in the development of more socially and environmentally responsible management? And how can they claim that their rules are better, trustworthier, or at least complementary to existing rules?

Like governments, standard-setting organizations are faced with the fact that 'legitimacy ... requires creating systems of accountability and effective governance mechanisms' (Waddell and Khagram, 2007, p. 281). These governance mechanisms must be established and institutionalized, and systems of accountability must be based on a creative and flexible approach, if they are to handle the various requirements that constantly confront a standard-setting activity organized within a multi-stakeholder logic.

As proposed in Chapter 2, our analysis is based upon the concepts of *input legitimacy*, *procedural legitimacy*, and *output legitimacy*, to distinguish among the various types of legitimizing strategies used in the establishment of authority. Input legitimacy refers to the people and organizations appointed and tasked to write the standards – a number of experts, for example, or a widely based set of stakeholders representing various interests. Procedural issues refer to the way standard-setting activities are organized and conducted, based on values such as transparent work procedures, decision making, and effective means for participation. Thus to establish authority through procedural legitimacy is to ensure that procedures are perceived as well-organized, transparent, effective, and efficient. Output legitimacy is the problem-solving capability or the assurance that standards are useful and valuable on a market. In the next section, we present seven legitimacy strategies that transnational standard setters can or must adopt. It is not an exhaustive list, to be sure, but it represents some of the central strategies utilized in our cases, and taken together they should provide a good overview of the continuous and often cumbersome struggles that confront transnational standard setters in their effort to establish legitimacy and authority.

SEVEN LEGITIMACY STRATEGIES

Standard-setting organizations must consider several sources of legitimacy (input, procedural, output), although they may not use the same strategies or necessarily combine them in exactly the same way. Whereas input and procedural legitimacy are the most relevant sources or strategies to be used during the initial standard-setting process, standard-setting organizations with standards that are applied to a market will gradually have greater expectations thrust upon them to achieve output legitimacy. Table 9.1 lists the seven legitimacy strategies and the type of legitimacy they address, and the following sections explore these strategies in greater detail.

Table 9.1 Seven legitimacy strategies of transnational multi-stakeholder standard setters: input, procedural, and output legitimacy

Legitimacy strategy	Type of legitimacy
Creating stakeholder categories and balanced representation	input
Including high-profile actors	input
Using and referring to expertise	input
Enabling transparency	procedural
Facilitating effective participation through sufficient language skills and the right vocabulary	procedural
Practicing consensus as a decision-making principle	procedural
Balancing market impact versus stringent standards and auditing	output

Creating Stakeholder Categories and Balanced Representation

The very multi-stakeholder arrangement that enables broad inclusion and representativeness is a basic legitimizing strategy for an increasing number of standard setters, including our three examples. Related to the idea of broad inclusion is the notion of a proper balance and equal opportunities to participate. These ideals were difficult to translate into practice, however, and created power problems that in turn challenged legitimacy.

In the early stages of this standard-setting process, ISO created of a number of stakeholder categories to be represented in various task groups. In Chapters 3 and 8, we discussed some of the problems that arose as this multi-stakeholder structure was put into practice. But we also noted that several interviewees appreciated the achievements. As a liaison member expert representing an international governmental organization (IGO) said: 'I think the division into six stakeholder categories is very, very good. It's a tremendous achievement.'

One consumer representative commented that this ISO process differed from ISO's previous activities – the ISO 14000 standards, for example. She noted that all stakeholder groups were not equally interested in this ISO 26000 process, even though ISO needed all of them to establish legitimacy. ISO needed to assure participation from a broad set of stakeholders, yet it had problems attracting all of them; there were stakeholders who were said that they were willing to participate but had to be pushed to move forward. Commercial actors such as large corporations (the industry group) and management consulting firms (the Others group) were typically well-represented, whereas consumer groups, trade unions, and NGOs, did not seem to have strong motives to participate; nor did they possess the same resources – financial or otherwise (cf. Chapter 6).

The ISO Secretariat responsible for the ISO 26000 work responded to criticism about unbalanced representation by launching a series of activities aimed at securing a multi-stakeholder approach – new rules stating limits on the number of stakeholders allowed from each stakeholder group and country, for instance.[1] Establishment of new funding solutions to empower weaker groups was another way of improving stakeholder balance. The specific problem of involving developing countries, while attracting labour, consumer, and environmental organizations, was an issue of debate early in the ISO 26000 process. According to the representatives of the poorer countries, ISO's encouragement to member bodies to seek autonomous funds from national governments and other organizations was not realistic for them. The idea of twinning arrangements for leadership positions that theoretically enabled developing countries to assume leadership positions was often impossible to realize in practice, because of their weak financial situation. In addition to the work of the strategic task force responsible for funding issues, the ISO Secretariat responded to these concerns by creating an ISO SR Trust Fund as a mechanism to raise and provide funding for under-resourced stakeholders and to support a limited number of awareness-raising and competence- and capability-building events in the ISO SR process. A number of times – usually in connection with international work meetings – ISO, sponsored by aid organizations, arranged workshops for developing countries only. The purpose of such workshops was to encourage and prepare participants to engage actively in the ISO 26000 process, and to prevent a few strong actors from becoming too powerful.

The problems of unbalanced representation were present at the national level as well, in the so-called *mirror groups* established by the ISO members participating in the ISO 26000 process. It is from these mirror groups that national experts are selected for participation in the international working group, and it is in these groups that national comments are prepared to feed into the international work process. Not all participating members managed to organize and run mirror groups, however. In the countries in which they did exist, they typically had an imbalance in the stakeholder division, with weak representation of labour stakeholders, for example. It is not surprising then, that participation in various task groups of the international ISO 26000 committee was not balanced either.

Most interviewees within our three cases appeared to endorse the value of 'inclusiveness' and 'multi-stakeholder dialogue'. What is seen as 'proper' or 'balanced representation' were subjects for debate, however. In his discussion of multi-sectoral 'partnerships', Glasbergen maintains that: 'the right balance might be different for each partner. The balance will also have to be convincing to the constituencies of the partners' (Glasbergen 2007, p. 8–9; see also Bäckstrand, 2006). Although several stakeholders within the FSC argued that social stakeholders were underrepresented in such areas as membership and capability for participating, others claimed that these stakeholders were not underrepresented because, in any case, they had one-third of the voting power. An interviewee representing the economic chamber had a contrasting view:

> Even if your organization is representing a community of 100 people, they are one member of FSC. And even if WWF represents hundreds of thousands – millions of people – they are also one member. So from that perspective, the social organizations have much greater power because they can be as influential as WWF or Greenpeace – even if they are representing a small community or a small group of people.

One environmental scientist interviewee from the MSC said that 'persons with an eco background or with a strong interest in sustainable fishery' were overrepresented, and argued that that was just as it should be: 'This can't be balanced, because it serves a certain purpose.' Other interviewees presented a different picture of the balancing of representation within the MSC, and talked about the overrepresentation of big business, including retailers and large-scale fisheries. There is a striking difference between some of the MSC interviewees and the FSC interviewees. The latter strongly emphasized the need to balance social, environmental, and economic interests, whereas the MSC interviewees were more likely to question the inclusion of social actors. This naturally relates to the MSC's narrower, exclusive focus on economic and environmental sustainability. Yet both the FSC and MSC experience imbalances in representation, and must make efforts similar to those we described in the ISO case. Although the actors participating in the MSC tend to be relatively resourceful, some of the stakeholders from developing countries receive economic compensation to travel to international meetings.

To achieve a more balanced representation, the standard setters need to do more than merely offer formal opportunities for many types of stakeholders to participate. They are pressured to assist weaker groups in ways that may relate to various power resources. The standard-setting organization can empower under-resourced stakeholders with:

- *financial resources* (for travel);
- *cognitive resources* (e.g. training, education or information, or assisting with translation; see further discussion in this chapter);
- *symbolic resources* (e.g. visualizing and recognizing the name and activities of NGOs that have difficulty presenting themselves to global audiences); and
- *social resources* (such as opening up informal channels – special workshops for specific stakeholders, for example to provide them with the opportunity to communicate internally and voice their concerns).

A few interviewees, commenting on the FSC activities, take the argument one step further, saying that the standard-setting organizations actually must *discriminate formally* to the advantage of weak stakeholders.

Unfortunately, the various legitimacy strategies used by standard setters do not necessarily go hand in hand. Even as they are facing pressures to balance participation, which require measures to empower the weaker stakeholders, they are simultaneously confronted by a need to mobilize the stronger ones.

Including High-Profile Actors

Standard setters trying to establish legitimacy for their own organizations and processes need to borrow legitimacy from others by inviting stakeholders with strong legitimacy in the eyes of a broad audience (cf. discussion about cooperation with 'reference organizations' in Tamm Hallström, 2004, p. 152–154). First, the standard setter may include *categories* (cf. Chapter 8) that are generally legitimized and part of the vocabulary of transnational governance. It should surprise no one to learn that ISO included an NGO category, despite all the ambiguities inherent in the term. Second, the standard-setting organization must look for *specific actors* within such categories that are highly legitimate. Few standard setters would say no to the inclusion of such organizations as the WWF, Amnesty International, and the Red Cross. In the words of Hall and Biersteker (2002), they can confer 'moral authority' to standard-setting processes.

High-profile actors may be so important to the legitimacy of the standard-setting organization that it is inclined to develop special arrangements in order to secure their participation. It is difficult to talk about global labour standards, for instance, without considering the role of the International Labour Organization (ILO) and its standards in this area. If the ILO were to decide not to participate, key stakeholders such as trade unions could be lost. The ILO raised a number of critical concerns regarding the ISO initiative and was not overly enthusiastic about becoming involved in the process. As discussed in Chapter 7, however, the ILO changed its participation strategy with the signing of the memorandum of understanding (MoU), through which this high-profile actor obtained special status. In 2006, the UN Global Compact managed to negotiate a similar MoU, and in 2007–2008, discussion took place about yet another MoU between ISO and the Organization for Economic Co-operation and Development (OECD).

The ILO, OECD, and UN Global Compact are all enjoying some degree of democratic legitimacy linked to their representative work structures and status as governmental or quasi-governmental organizations. Several interviewees questioned the MoU between ISO and the UN Global Compact, as well as the possible inclusion of the UN Global Compact as one of the core references in the ISO 26000 standard. They did not find it appropriate to compare the Global Compact and its principles with the (representative and authoritative) UN Declaration of Human Rights or the core labour standards of the ILO. The choice of high-profile actors was not a simple one and stakeholders debated about who would be counted as appropriate and authoritative in this respect.

In both the FSC and MSC, the inclusion of governments or IGOs was somewhat less pronounced. This was true especially during the initial agenda-setting stage, because these organizations were established as an explicit critical response to the perceived failures of governmental and intergovernmental regulatory efforts. Yet these organizations gradually sought a rapprochement to other actors in the transnational regulatory space. One of the noticeable developments was the MSC's effort to comply fully with the UN Food and Agriculture Organization's (FAO) guidelines, issued in March 2005, with a minimum requirement for credible marine ecolabeling certification programs (see Chapter 5). To date (June, 2009) only the MSC has managed to reach these guidelines, albeit through interaction with the FAO after making a few key changes in the MSC governance structure in order to achieve '100% FAO compliance'. One of these changes was the separation of the accrediting function from the MSC to an independent body (the FSC owned Accreditation International Services), which necessarily implied loss of some control over certification bodies. The interviewees from the MSC appeared to be concerned about this step and about other changes, but strongly argued that '100% FAO compliance' was a critical achievement worthy of the cost – simply, as we see it, because of the FAO's strong legitimacy.

As we noted in Chapter 5, Greenpeace decided to quit its engagement in the MSC. As a response, the MSC's executive engaged in a dialogue with Greenpeace and offered the organization 'a standing invitation to sit on our stakeholder council, even to attend as observers', probably fearing what Greenpeace might have done otherwise. If Greenpeace did not choose collaboration as an insider, it might have been important, nevertheless, to ensure that an antagonist relationship was not emerging and to prevent negative public campaigning that could hurt the legitimacy and authority of the MSC.

We have also observed that the involvement of so many high-profile actors creates certain risks to legitimacy. Unilever may have strong market authority, and WWF may have strong moral authority, which is good for the MSC, but overly strong involvement of Unilever and the MSC could also trigger criticism among a number of stakeholders – a common experience for the MSC. Again, we observe how power imbalances can lead to legitimacy problems. Although there were situations in which the role and impact of high-profile actors had been almost overemphasized, it is noteworthy that the role and impact of Unilever on the MSC process was also toned down by several interviewees. As a board member of the MSC told us, MSC continued to be challenged by the incorrect perception that Unilever and WWF still dominate it.

Establishing legitimacy requires the inclusion of stakeholders in the environment, including a number of strong, high-profile actors that grant *moral* legitimacy, *market* legitimacy, *democratic* legitimacy, or *cognitive* legitimacy and authority to the standard setting. Yet it is crucial to keep them at some distance, as too much involvement can also create risks. They cannot become too powerful, as that would run counter to the idea of a balanced multi-stakeholder logic. Yet there is another type of high-profile actor that can be invited to grant legitimacy to a standard-setting process: *experts* representing relevant knowledge.

Using and Referring to Expertise

Although some of the high-profile actors discussed so far can also be characterized as representing relevant expertise, we have chosen to discuss expertise separately. The use of expertise is a fundamental legitimacy strategy found in regulatory practices in general (Dahl, 2007), and specifically among standard setters in various fields of standardization (Schmidt and Werle, 1998; Boli, 1999; Tamm Hallström, 2004; Kerwer, 2005; Botzem and Quack, 2006; Boström and Klintman, 2008; Higgins and Tamm Hallström, 2007, 2008). More explicitly, this type of legitimacy rests on the argument that standards are developed by experts who reach consensus on the optimal solution to a recurring technical problem (Jacobsson, 2000; Higgins and Tamm Hallström, 2008). Some scholars would argue that expertise, together with rationalizing effects anticipated from the use of standards (output legitimacy), often provides the main source of legitimacy for standard setters:

> The logic of the sector is quite simple: the character of the standards and the nature of the processes by which they are generated – universal, consensually derived standards of unimpeachable technical merit – are themselves sufficient rationale for their adoption (Loya and Boli, 1999, p. 181).

Expertise can be gained through practical experience; the participants who serve as experts are not necessarily professional experts in their regular employment, in the sense that they are certified or authorized professionals. Preferably, experts should have some status as an expert in a specific field, however, and are probably affiliated with a professional association (cf. Dahl, 2007). More precisely, experts are those who rely on a professionally compiled set of rules and a particular conceptual framework, and who base their decisions on relevant knowledge (cf. Abbott, 1988). According to this perception of experts, their modus operandi are important characteristics: expert work is supposedly conducted systematically – preferably scientifically – and with disinterest. An expert works methodically, the story goes, making judgments based purely on technical grounds, and identifies the best technical solution to a given problem (Tamm Hallström, 2004). By virtue of their expertise, then, experts can provide sound advice – advice that does not rest on a political decision-making process or on opinions and the received wisdom of old traditions (Sikka and Willmott, 1995).

In all the cases we examined, a mix of expert and stakeholder representation was used, but the mix differed by case. In the ISO 26000 case, participants were labeled experts (or observers), but as they were sorted into stakeholder categories, they were expected to be representatives of a specific stakeholder interest. The ISO 26000 standard is to be regarded, therefore, as both 'a distillation of international expertise on social responsibility' (ISO and Social Responsibility, 2006, p. 3) and the product of a multi-stakeholder process. Thus participants of the ISO 26000 committee have multiple identities. We observed the same ambiguity and mixing of roles in the boards of the FSC and MSC, in which the members were expected to be experts on forest issues while representing a specific actor category, such as the economic/north. We noted from the interviewees that they differ in their interpretation of this role (see Chapter 8). In the MSC, a balance was obtained by placing technical and standard-setting experts within the Technical Advisory Board, whereas stakeholder representation was seen as belonging in the Stakeholder Council – an organizational decoupling (Meyer and Rowan, 1977). We noticed in Chapter 8 that the Technical Advisory Board, with its pronounced expert representation, appeared to be the most influential of these two units. Among our three cases, the MSC appears to be the one that provides the most enthusiastic communication about its scientific orientation. Perhaps the MSC's more exclusive focus on the ecological/biological and its exclusion of SR and sustainability issues enables it to uphold its naive view that technical and political issues are easily separated.

There was variation in the ISO 26000 case in stakeholders' perceptions of expertise, following this combination of participants simultaneously serving as experts, stakeholder representatives, and national representatives. Interviewees from NGOs mentioned how people from other stakeholder groups tend to hold a negative view of NGO expertise:

> NGOs are not seen as a real expert group. But industry sees itself as composed of experts contributing with their experiences … that "real" experts come from industry. The contributions of the NGO group are charged in a negative way. We are a heterogeneous group with low expert status (interviewee representing an NGO in the ISO 26000 process, April 2007).

Some stakeholders considered the Others group as odd in this context, not being a proper expert category, and not having representatives. One Others representative, when interviewed in November 2007, held the opposite view on legitimate participants and how they should act: 'Others is the only group with objective experts. We don't have any hidden agendas; we aren't steered in a certain direction; we are independent of pressure from above, from outside this group.'

In Chapter 8, we tried to explain this variation by looking at the status or prototypical character of an expert as determined by the expert's categorization as a stakeholder. Some stakeholder groups corresponded to an area of expertise (e.g. labour, consumer) and were thereby perceived as more prototypical among the whole group of experts. Other stakeholder groups corresponded to a type of organization (e.g. NGO, government), implying that the experts belonging to those categories were perceived as less prototypical. In this chapter, we can add a further explanation: The confusion and tension between participants being experts or representatives, and between participants being 'real experts' or 'inappropriate experts' can be further explained by the fact that the standard setters mix two legitimacy strategies that collide: the strategy of balanced representation and the strategy of reliance on expertise. The problem, as we see it, comes from incompatibilities between, on the one hand, expertise linked to *individuals* trying to reach consensus around a technically optimal solution: and, on the other hand, stakeholder representation linked to interests of *organizations* that demand anchoring and are often (legitimately) conflicting with the interests of other organizations, making consensus decisions more difficult to reach.

Enabling Transparency

We now proceed to discuss the creating of transparency, which is the first of our three examples of procedural legitimacy. We have used illustrations primarily from the ISO case in the section on procedural legitimacy. We do use references to the other cases, however, when we analyze our last legitimacy strategy, which is an example of output legitimacy. It should be noted, however, that procedural legitimacy is equally important in the other two cases.

In all three cases, we observed how the word 'transparency' was among the most frequently used and debated when describing the processes; thus a strong rhetoric emerges around the value of transparency. But again, it is a concept that allows for interpretative flexibility (e.g. Garsten and Lindh de Montoya, 2008). Does the concept refer to open access through a web page to the many documents produced and referenced in the work process? What should be transparent and what should remain hidden? To whom should something be revealed? Is it possible to comprehend in any meaningful way the information that is made public?

Transparency is both a key principle for organizations to consider in their efforts to be socially responsible and a democratic value that appeared to be critical for ISO during this process. The issue of transparency arose as early as 2005, at the first international work meeting of the ISO 26000 committee, and the topic of transparency was discussed there in relation to accessibility to all relevant stakeholders. One aspect was with regard to the availability of working documents produced within the committee. One suggestion realized shortly after the 2005 meeting was to open the so-called ISO Livelink Area to the public on the ISO website, in which all internal working documents were posted.[2] Another transparency issue concerned media presence during international work meetings. One week before the committee's third international meeting in Lisbon, Consumers International circulated a press release with the heading 'Consumer groups outraged as business lobby seeks to silence media on corporate social responsibility'. It included the following statement about the inappropriateness of keeping the ISO process closed, especially given that the issue of standardization was about being socially responsible:

> Consumers International and other ISO stakeholder groups are outraged that the business lobby is forcing the ISO to block press access to the main debates. The situation is all the more shocking because the weeklong talks are aimed at creating the first global standard on Social Responsibility. Accessible, transparent information is an essential part of this principle, as well as a core consumer right (Consumers International press release, 8 May 2006).

The message of the press release continued:

> [I]f the creation of the ISO Social Responsibility standard itself is not transparent, industry will continue to hold transparency in poor regard. Transparency begins at home and the ISO must resist pressure from the business lobby and allow full media access to the debate on Social Responsibility in Lisbon (Consumers International press release, 8 May 2006).

At the international work meeting the following week, Consumers International invited media to come to the conference center for a press release. The action did not succeed the way it was planned, however, as the few journalists who showed up were thrown out by security guards, and the pre-printed T-shirts that Consumers International had prepared could not be handed out at the press release as planned. During the following day, however, a number of consumer and NGO representatives were walking around the conference building with white T-shirts labeled LET THE PRESS IN, on the front side; on the back was a the logo of Consumers International followed by the words: Access = transparency. Consumers Seeking Responsibility.

A number of members of the NGO group decided at the Lisbon meeting to cooperate with a group of consumer representatives around this issue. As a representative of an environmental NGO told us:

> Industry has taken a very hard line and used its veto power through sustained objections as a whole stakeholder category. Industry has tried to block the process in this way. What is emerging is lack of consensus about the media issue. It is the first issue to bring the question of transparency ahead. The openness toward media is not satisfactory to industry, just as it is not satisfactory to NGOs and consumers to have it closed rather than transparent (interview with NGO representative, May 2006).

There were mixed feelings among the participants of the Lisbon meeting about the press release initiative. An ILO representative commented on the Consumers International action in the following way:

> The CI press release the other day was not a very constructive action. We didn't appreciate it. It mostly created a lot of distress, which isn't needed in a multi-stakeholder work like this. You know, transparency has a purpose, but open and frank dialogues [among representatives] also have a purpose. There's serious horse trading taking place, and you need to be able to speak frankly about your positions. This is what negotiations are all about! I would give primacy to that in order to get somewhere. You just have to decide what are the important moments for openness and when it's important to close (interview with ILO representative, May 2006).

Many stakeholders endorsed the value of transparency, but this person (representing the ILO that, given its special position in the ISO 26000 process, was part of the inner circle) argues that there is such a thing as too much transparency. Another interviewee, who was also part of the inner circle, believed that the transparency was, in fact, acceptable, but that people sometimes got the wrong impression of 'talks behind the curtains'. This interviewee explained that some discussions are held behind closed doors because the issues are delicate – informal and unexpected questions or details that need to be handled separately, for example (Tamm Hallström, 2009) – yet this does not mean that the whole work process is nontransparent.

In response to the 2007 debate about transparency problems impeding legitimacy, yet another step was taken by the ISO Secretariat. A new media policy was launched, allowing the media to be present and able to talk to experts during coffee breaks of the international work meetings, given that a written request was communicated to the secretariat in advance.[3] According to an interviewee, there was a risk involved in allowing media into work meeting sessions: the wrong impression could be obtained if a journalist or researcher attended a single meeting in which only a fraction of a debate happened to occur. Because of the new media policy, the secretariat decided to come up with a compromise on the level of openness allowed. Our interpretation of these legitimacy efforts is that they satisfied at least the stakeholders who were part of the inner circle, which already possessed powerful positions and had good insight into the process.

Facilitating Effective Participation through Sufficient Language Skills and the Right Vocabulary

If there is a good balance of stakeholder representatives participating at international meetings, and most working documents are available through ISO's website, but only half of all participants can speak the language that is used in the documents and during debates and standard-writing sessions, a legitimacy problem still exists. Again the problem is linked to power. If only a few representatives can understand and exercise their influence on the standard-setting work, the multi-stakeholder process will be imbalanced. In all three cases we studied, there were debates about unequal opportunity to participate effectively, whether because of a lack of resources to prepare for decisions, necessary language skills, or some other factor. Again the ISO case is illustrative.

A representative of a small NGO working on human rights was asked about people or groups who had weak influence, and this interviewee named Hispanics, who tended not to have a good command of English. She knew this, because she could speak Spanish herself and had heard Hispanics continuously asking each other, 'What did they say?' The concern was raised before the standard-setting work ever started, and they came from stakeholders who were not fluent in ISO's official language: English. As the standards development work began, the discussion about language problems continued. In 2005, the ISO established the Spanish Translation Task Force, as well as a group called Official French Language Experts, and later the Arabic and Russian Translation Task Forces. There were also plans in 2007 to start a German-speaking task group. In 2007, the question of simultaneous translation was raised at a plenary meeting, but consensus was not reached on this proposal. An NGO representative was critical toward the attitude that English was the only language within the ISO standardization, as opposed to the EU and the UN, for example, where simultaneous translations in a number of languages were taken for granted:

> I have tried to argue about the need for direct translations, but when you propose this, others claim that you are stupid. It would be too costly, they argue. And within the ISO, English is the norm, whereas within, for example, the UN, there are direct translations into seven languages. And of course there is a reason behind that. But I don't think that the secretariat has handled the issue of language problems properly, even though they are flexible about procedural issues otherwise. I think they haven't thought everything through, and sometimes they

avoid taking responsibility by referring to the ISO directives ... (interview with NGO representative, April 2007).

Similar problems were lack of experience of the standardization work and lack of familiarity with the correct standard-setting vocabulary. The ISO worked to overcome such criticism through educational solutions, to enable weaker stakeholders to participate effectively. Problems of lack of transparency in the process – often related to language barriers – were still evident. A consumer representative from a developing country was interviewed in 2007. He spoke little English, was attending his first international work meeting of the ISO 26000 committee as an observer, and was concerned about the legitimacy of the process, especially regarding the language issue:

> It's only in English. It should be in French, English, and Spanish – that is, the big languages. Documents summarizing what happened every day should be distributed, and that's not the case. Each day all discussion points for the following day should be announced. There should be a list of participants for each day, and the names of the convenors of various group meetings should be announced. It's a question of information, transparency, and historic record (interview with French-speaking consumer representative from a developing country, November 2007).

This person thus argues that transparency requires written documents describing the process, and a condition for effective participation. An NGO representative in 2006 suggested that language barriers could be used as a resource and power strategy, and that there may, indeed, be a sincere concern behind the ironic comment:

> A conclusion that I start to see now is that it might be a good strategy to keep the language barriers, ha ha ... if you want consensus you just let people talk "bad" English – people with strong accents that demand special attention – because people stop listening and then it is easy to get consensus (interview with NGO representative, May 2006).

Although the problems of language barriers were difficult to solve, ISO made efforts to find solutions, and several stakeholders believed that the situation improved, at least in some ways. The specific language groups were greatly appreciated. A French-speaking representative from the Others group explained that he attended every meeting of the French-speaking group because it offered opportunities to discuss both the process – what is actually happening – and possible interpretations of various concepts and wordings that were proposed in the standard drafts. During plenary meetings, on the other hand, such discussions about details and interpretations could not be held, and it was crucial to be prepared to make final decisions.

Practicing Consensus as a Decision-Making Principle

The last strategy linked to procedural legitimacy that we discuss is the ideal of consensus as a decision-making principle. The idea of consensus decisions fits well with the principle of expertise discussed earlier, as it implies that it is possible to reach consensus about a best solution to a technical problem. Experts are capable of doing this (although, in practice, they generally disagree). In a resolution taken at the first international work meeting of the ISO 26000 committee, it was decided that: 'there will be no voting in the WG [Working Group] or in any of its subsidiary bodies. All decisions will be made on the basis of consensus' (ISO/TMB/WG SR N16, 17 March 2005, p. 6). According to ISO's work directives, consensus is defined in the following way:

> Consensus: general agreement, characterized by the absence of sustained opposition to substantial issues by any important part of the concerned interests and by a process that involves seeking to take into account the views of all parties concerned and to reconcile any conflicting arguments. NOTE: Consensus need not imply unanimity (ISO/IEC Directives–Part 1: Procedures, 2008).

When the drafting work began, in 2005, several stakeholders commented that, according to them, this definition of consensus was specific to ISO. It was not what they were used to by the notion of consensus, they contended, because everyone did not need to agree on every point. The ISO definition, by which majority acceptance of a proposed decision constituted consensus, was confusing to these commentators. The ISO Secretariat responded to these concerns by issuing a clarification of how the views of all relevant stakeholders should be considered. The secretariat pointed out that the positions of all stakeholder groups 'should be treated equally, regardless of the number of individuals included in the respective group', and that 'the criteria for assessing consensus should be based on the number of stakeholder groups in favour or opposed, not the absolute number of individuals in favour or opposed' ISO/TMB/WG SR N 131, 9 November 2007, p. 2). In this way, it was assumed, a stakeholder group should be able to raise opposition at a work meeting, even if the absolute number of experts representing that group was low.

One of our interviewees who acknowledged the consensus principle believed that there was sometimes a high price to pay in trying hard to reach consensus on every point during the drafting process. The ISO 26000 Secretariat encouraged its members to work with national consensus for the comments made on various drafts of the standard, but this interviewee perceived that there were situations in which stakeholders should not be forced to agree on national consensus comments. According to her, there were cases in which the specific views of stakeholders were particularly important to a particular stakeholder group – cases that should be made visible, and not toned down in favour of consensus. Her reasoning is linked to the fragility embedded in the use of expertise (including consensus decision making) as a main legitimacy strategy, as it suppresses stakeholder interests and thus the political character of the standard-setting activity. Instead of assuming objectivity of expertise, one could speak, instead, of the 'politics of expertise'. It is reasonable to expect experts participating in multi-stakeholder standard setting to represent diverse knowledge claims, and that the standard-setting process will therefore include struggles and competition between these claims. In these struggles, the power resources of individual experts, including the way the experts are categorized as stakeholders, are crucial factors for the outcome. Organizational design may affect the extent to which consensus is used as a decision-making principle in multi-stakeholder organizations. We have found that the notion of consensus has been much more pronounced within ISO and the MSC, compared with the FSC. The FSC has less of an expert rhetoric. Moreover, the FSC's three-chamber structure naturally fosters a culture of voting and the forming of majorities. In contrast, as expressed by our interviewees, the MSC is often perceived as comprising two general types of stakeholder – industry and NGOs – despite the fact that a number of other actors, including scientists, participate as well. This dualistic view, however, is organizationally materialized in the two general chambers of the Stakeholder Council (see Chapter 5), which implies, our interviewees stress, that they must necessarily come to an agreement. One chamber alone cannot form a majority.

There were other concerns regarding the consensus principle, centering on the distrust that evolved around the way consensus was interpreted. According to the ISO procedures, the chair of a working group or task group decides if consensus is obtained on a specific decision. If all experts could agree on a proposed decision (as some participants would say was needed for consensus, according to their perception of the principle), the situation is clear. If there are those who object, however, the chair must decide if the objecting stakeholders constitute a 'sustained opposition' and if the opposition regards the issue as being 'substantial'.

According to an interviewee who chaired one of the task groups, the estimate of sustained opposition is linked to an analysis of the number of opposing experts originating from one or several stakeholder group(s). The interviewee also mentioned that if some experts oppose a decision, the chair should determine if the they belong to a developed or developing country, to ensure that that the opposition is not sustained.[4] The interviewee continued to explain that chairs are often required to make technically sound judgments and decisions, with support from a sufficient number of experts, and that they are expected not to delay what is a time-consuming process unnecessarily. This interviewee was arguing that the organizing of the standard-setting activity includes a tension between efficiency and legitimacy:

> If a representative of a liaison organization turns up at a meeting, for example, and there are 400 people there who have been at every meeting for several years, then that single liaison organization could raise sustained opposition. It's the responsibility of the chair to interpret whether or not there is consensus, if the voice of that liaison organization should be regarded as sustained opposition on a substantial issue (interview with a chair of a task group, June 2008).

Thus the procedure for consensus decisions used within the ISO offers the chairs flexibility to interpret whether issues of debate are substantial or not. It is therefore crucial for legitimacy that the judgment of chairs be perceived as trustworthy. 'The process lives and dies on the credibility of the chairs', as one interviewee explained. During our interviews, some chairpersons were singled out as not being good at handling their positions, and were accused of not being completely neutral, whereas others were seen as being highly competent and trustworthy. Yet during the period investigated, there were never any formal appeals communicated to the ISO 26000 Secretariat regarding consensus decisions, even though an appeals process was in place.

Balancing Market Impact versus Stringent Standards and Auditing

Efforts to increase input and procedural legitimacy, as reflected in the six legitimacy strategies elaborated upon so far, are made with the assumption that increased output legitimacy will follow. Good procedures will lead to good outcomes and problem-solving capabilities. Yet after the standards have been set and are introduced into a market, the standard setters will face the challenge of demonstrating their uses, and will again learn that a number of stakeholders assess output and outcome very differently. Output legitimacy does not come automatically.

In the area of standard setting for socially and environmentally responsible conduct, we may refer to output legitimacy in relation to both economic and noneconomic goals. Naturally, many stakeholders involved in negotiating criteria for the ISO 26000 process share a hope for more socially responsible organizations in the future. Others express a hope that the systems will have a visible market impact, and argue that the standards must be 'feasible' and of positive economic value for direct users. Social or environmental advocates agree that some degree of market impact is necessary; otherwise, the standards serve no useful purpose. Yet economic and noneconomic goals do not always go hand in hand.

The stakeholders' first concern about output legitimacy is what effects should be subjected to measurement and assessment. Another is to determine if specific standards and certification schemes have made any difference in the effects that stakeholders have anticipated and desired. It is usually extremely difficult to assess the effectiveness of a specific standard because of the complex causal relationships between standard criteria and industry practices, including multiple direct, indirect, unintended, and mutually counteracting effects (cf. Stokke, Gulbrandsen, Hoel, and Braathen, 2005), 'given the "background noise" of other factors' (Biermann, Chan, Mert, and Pattberg, 2007, p. 291). It may be easy to count numbers of users and growth in the number of users as the FSC and MSC do and (proudly) report about, and that ISO does about its previous management system standards ISO 9001 and ISO 14001. It is much more difficult to assess the social and environmental benefits or drawbacks of using the standards. Observable positive effects could be due to other factors that would have occurred without the intervention of the standard.

Despite such complexity and indeterminacy, the FSC and MSC – both with their standards up and running – face numerous expectations to report positive outcomes. What they can do, and do, is to provide anecdotal evidence. The standard-setting bodies must rely on persuasion by using specific good examples placed in their broader context (cf. Henning, 2000), and by highlighting key factors as they report on the effectiveness of certification (see also May, Leadbitter, Sutton, and Weber, 2003).[5] The FSC's *News and Notes* is filled with concrete success stories from various parts of the world. The FSC is clearly less eager to report failures or discuss controversial certification. Such biases in reporting can itself fuel criticism, however. The FSC Watch has, among other things, criticized FSC's inclination to report only its success stories.[6]

Stakeholders also debate what should be counted as a legitimate outcome. Is growing market impact necessarily good? In labeling and certification in general, there is a continuous tension between the goals of a market pragmatist and the goals surrounding stringent social and environmental values (cf. Boström and Klintman, 2008). In both the MSC and FSC, there is an ongoing debate around *fast-growth, mainstreaming* versus *top, high-profile, small-growth* approaches. Should only the top companies – the 'real' forerunners – be able to certify their production or their products, or should the schemes include a much larger number of producers? In both the FSC and MSC, economic stakeholders tend to stress the need for fast growth and mainstreaming, whereas social and environmental stakeholders pressure for the opposite – or at least for moderating between these two goals. In the view of the latter stakeholder categories, it is critically important that the FSC and MSC monitor and ensure high quality in certified practices. Industry actors tend to favour inclusive standards, because it is important, they argue, that more than a minority of market players has a realistic chance of certifying their production and products and gaining the many business advantages that certification may offer.

In the ISO case, the issues of the target group of transnational corporations (TNCs) only versus all types of organizations, including small and medium-sized enterprises (SMEs) and the requirements of the standard were intensely debated (see Chapter 7). This debate indicated that the topic of fast-growth mainstreaming versus top, high-profile, small growth was present and controversial during the process of setting the ISO 26000 standard. The position of many consumer organizations – that a management system standard approach is desirable for the ISO 26000 standard – is also linked to this topic. The argument is that a management system standard is not perfect, that it would not include precise assessable requirements, but that it is good enough. It has the potential of being accepted and used by a large number of organizations, and can help consumers to distinguish between good and bad producers. This bears resemblance to a fast-growth, mainstreaming approach that includes the idea that all organizations should be able to start wherever possible, as long as they work for continuous improvements, which is a central idea of a management system standard. Like the FSC and the MSC, industry associations tended to favour inclusive standards, in that all types of organizations should be targeted, but did not agree that this goal should be reached through a management system approach. NGOs, on the other hand, at least at the beginning of the process, preferred to stick to the CSR agenda, targeting mainly TNCs.

There are legitimacy motives speaking for and against the fast-growth, mainstreaming approach. Large volumes can be important for symbolic reasons, particularly in relation to economic stakeholders. The MSC label, for example, gains legitimacy by having many fisheries committed, particularly major fisheries, as well as major retailers such as the Wal-Mart. Whereas low product volume is a risk, however, a high volume of products that attracts controversy could be equally disadvantageous (May et al., 2003; Kuntzsch, 2003). Granting a certificate to organizations with controversial economic practices, and advertising them as 'sustainable', could undermine the legitimacy of the standard-setting organization. One of our Greenpeace interviewees worried about the MSC's fast-growth strategy: 'I think there is a very dangerous trend coming up, that Wal-Mart and others are making big commitments to selling only certified fish within three years.' Indeed, a member from the industry side of the MSC Board expressed similar worries in discussing the role played by competitors:

As it [MSC] grows, ... the temptation will be, I think, to weaken the standard. Generally I think the competitors' standards are weaker in this area, and it will be much easier and much more convenient for other people to adopt some of the other standards. And I think that is a big challenge for the MSC to maintain its long-term credibility and its authority in this area.

In various FSC documents, we found many expressions indicating a strong hope to grow and to grow fast. Such hopes are often framed with the argument that the achievement of a more sustainable forestry worldwide requires fast growth. Another serious concern is that the hugely under-financed MSC and FSC require it (see Chapters 4 and 5). There is a constant need to increase the percentage of income coming from license fees from certified business. Both these organizations rely heavily upon various donations, which give rise to a financial risk in the longer term and set certain limits on the working capability of the secretariats. We see a clear preference for the growth strategy among the staff of the secretariats and other inner circle stakeholders.

There is, furthermore, a mismatch between the demand and supply. Unless the FSC manages to meet the growing demand, competing certification schemes will stand ready and able to overtake the FSC (FSC, 2002). It is not self-evident, in the view of many observers and debaters, however, that a growing FSC is the most legitimate strategy for achieving the vision of sustainable forestry worldwide. Counsell and Loraas of the UK environmental NGO Rainforest Foundation made a strong argument in their well-known critical report, *Trading in Credibility*, that the fast-growth strategy should be formally abandoned, because too many deeply questionable practices have been certified according to the FSC system.

Similar concerns were expressed in a letter signed by a long list of environmental NGOs, addressed to the FSC Board and Secretariat in October 2006. 'We, the undersigned, are writing to you to express our serious concern about FSC increasingly losing credibility, both in the market place as well as among NGOs.' Among the signatories were representatives of WWF International and Greenpeace International and several of their national sections; Fern; Sierra Club; Friends of the Earth in UK, Australia, Austria, and Germany; the Rainforest Foundation; Rainforest Action Network; and a number of others. Some of them are FSC members and others are not. Their concern related in part to output legitimacy issues, and they raised particular worries over the performance of certification bodies, including the economic link between certification bodies and their clients in the forestry, and the uneven performance of the FSC.

Of course, this letter was a heavyweight, which could in itself significantly undermine the legitimacy of the FSC. Thus the Executive Director of the FSC had to respond. One of his responses related to the debate over fast versus slow growth, and there was no doubt that as representative of the secretariat, he tended to speak for the fast-growth approach when he said, 'it is without question that FSC needs to grow its base of commercial clients (e.g. certificate holders, trademark users)'.

The MSC and FSC, and probably the ISO 26000 face huge expectations in the future to demonstrate successful outcomes in order to gain output legitimacy. Yet as is the case with input and procedural legitimacy, stakeholders have radically different expectations and yardsticks, and it is ultimately impossible to satisfy all stakeholders. They must choose some expectations and yardsticks upon which to focus.

ESTABLISHING LEGITIMACY – A NEVER-ENDING STORY

Through the accounts of legitimizing activities that the three standard setters engaged in during the periods investigated, we can conclude that these processes had a *trial-and-error character*, with continuous demands to meet criticism about the legitimacy of the organizing process.[7] One reason for the high level of stakeholder criticism and continuous efforts to respond to such criticism is the character of the subject matter of standardization. The subject included a global dimension and touched upon various kinds of politicized problems – not merely, or even primarily, technical ones. A related reason is the fact that the standard setting occurs in a multi-stakeholder context. The logical consequence is that the standard setter must endorse such values as 'broad representation' and 'transparency', even as the very inclusiveness of the processes leads to the inclusion of distinctly divergent ideas about the meaning and interpretation of these values in practice (cf. Boström, 2006a, 2006b). Standard setters typically experience contradictory demands raised by a number of stakeholders.

It is thus clear – as a general assertion – that legitimacy cannot be a stable condition. Legitimacy is something fluid that *must be repeatedly created, recreated*, and *conquered*. Establishing legitimacy can therefore be characterized as a *continuous* and *intensive* negotiation and framing struggle among stakeholders that do not necessarily share the same perceptions and interpretations.

The continuous efforts to establish legitimacy involve a *combination of several legitimacy strategies*. In the ISO 26000 case, we observed a move from a traditional ISO strategy of expertise combined with output legitimacy, toward many efforts linked to input and procedural legitimacy. ISO still used expertise as a central strategy, together with the consensus principle for decision making, but added the multi-stakeholder organization with procedural claims on proper stakeholder categories, balanced representation, transparency, and effective participation, together with the inclusion of a number of high-profile actors, mainly from the public sphere. *Inconsistencies between the strategies* led to tension – those between a balanced representation and the inclusion of high-profile actors on the one hand, and the use of individual, objective expertise and representation of stakeholder interests on the other.

In both the MSC and FSC, the movement was the other way around, with *increasing attention being paid to output legitimacy.* A standard-setting organization such as the MSC or FSC that has been in operation for a number of years will, in addition to input and procedural legitimacy, face increasing expectations to demonstrate positive outcomes. The dilemma is that such expectations escalate, even though it is extremely difficult to provide clear evidence of positive outcomes. We have demonstrated in this chapter that merely focusing on fast growth, such as numbers of certificates issued, is insufficient means for self-legitimization.

The process of legitimizing standard-setting activities depends, therefore, on the degree of institutionalization of the standards, but also on who is involved in these processes, why they are there, and what they want. It also depends on how they act and react during the course of work – which depends partly on the way in which the process is organized. By comparing the three cases, we see that there were diverse decisions taken about the stakeholder categories to establish, to whom the standard should be targeted, its level of requirement, and how various legitimacy strategies should be interpreted and combined, to mention a few dimensions that differed, depending on the participants involved and their actions during the processes.

In this chapter, we have also demonstrated that standard setters face expectations to 'walk the talk'. They must practice the same standard-setting principles and criteria that they articulate through their legitimizing efforts and expect other actors to follow – when ISO speaks about transparency, for instance. When actors become engaged in efforts to formalize accountability tools and arrangements, their very engagement in this work may boomerang (Boström and Garsten, 2008).

It is noteworthy how the demands for and efforts to increase legitimacy often collide with the ways in which the standard-setting activity can be performed efficiently. In the examples of transparency, effective participation, and consensus decisions in the ISO 26000 process, we observed how participants perceived that *trade-offs between legitimacy and efficiency* existed in various ways.

A consequence of these conditions – that the standard setter in a multi-stakeholder context continuously faces huge challenges in establishing legitimacy – is that the authority that comes from various legitimizing efforts becomes fragile. In Chapter 10, our concluding chapter, we elaborate on the notion of a fragile non-state authority.

NOTES

1.   The ISO 26000 secretariat started to schedule some time at work meetings for stakeholder debate within each stakeholder category. The secretariat encouraged specific stakeholder comments (not merely national comments, as elicited in other ISO committees and working groups), and started to keep track of statistics about stakeholder representation in meetings, working groups, and the secretariat itself, as well as in chairperson positions. A special strategic task force was established to develop procedural rules for the work. One of its decisions was to restrict the number of experts and observers from each country, stakeholder group, and liaison member participating in international work meetings, in order to set limits on financially stronger stakeholder groups that could afford to field a disproportionately large representation.

2.   The Livelink system was initiated in the late 1990s in all ISO committees, but was open only to those experts formally participating in a specific group or committee. People had access to documents produced within their committee only if they were registered as experts of that committee and had received a password to enter. For this ISO process, however, the ISO Livelink Area was made more accessible to the public without the need for membership registration or a password.

3.   It was decided that the same policy would apply for researchers who had not been nominated as an expert or an observer (document ISO/TMB/WG SR N 102).

4.   See also the document with clarifications about consensus-making issued by the ISO 26000 Secretariat (ISO/TMB/WG SR N16, 17 March 2005, p. 6–7).

5.   For an example, see http://www.msc.org/about-us/credibility/measuring-environmental-impacts, information accessed 12 August 2008.

6.   The FSC Watch (www.fsc-watch.org), is an independent observer of the FSC, and was developed by FSC supporters, members, and nonmembers who are concerned about what they perceive as 'the constant and serious erosion of the FSC's reliability and thus credibility'. The group critically examines several FSC certifications in a number of countries, and reports these results on its website. Its members argue that the FSC is increasingly captured by vested commercial interest in the form of the economic chamber, and criticize the FSC's inability to address the problem, as well as its disposition to report only success stories.

7.   Similar observations about dynamics in the establishment of legitimacy, or 'legitimacy in the making' as suggested by the title of this chapter, have been made in other investigations of standardization work, such as investigations of the ISO 9000 committee and the International Accounting Standards Committee (Tamm Hallström, 2004; Botzem and Quack, 2006), and a number of green labeling processes (Boström, 2006a, 2006b; Boström and Klintman, 2008).

10. Fragile Non-State Authority: The Long and Winding Road to Legitimate Power

A starting point for the research discussed in this book was the key global and historical shifts that occurred at the macro level: economic, political, and cultural globalization. These processes have fueled and conditioned such concrete activities as transnational multi-stakeholder standardization. Some scholars even write of a virtual explosion of regulatory innovation and new rules in all areas of political and social life (Rosenau, 2003; Brunsson and Jacobsson, 2000; Hall and Biersteker, 2002; Ahrne and Brunsson, 2004; Mörth, 2004; Djelic and Sahlin-Andersson, 2006; Power, 2007; Pattberg, 2007; Boström and Garsten, 2008; Graz and Nölke, 2008). Such developments have been discussed in much of the current literature on transnational governance and private authority, and we agree with these scholars that 'governance is in the making', that we are living in a globalizing world undergoing dramatic historical shifts. We are witnessing the creation and early institutionalization of a variety of new transnational organizational and regulatory arrangements. As we researched this topic, we felt the need to complement these general historical descriptions, with more precise analyses of the processes of establishing and maintaining non-state authority in a multi-stakeholder setting – and the mechanisms at play in these processes – particularly at the organizational level.

In our introductory chapter, we presented two points of departure, which we considered crucial for understanding the establishment of non-state authority. First, we applied a *contextual approach* to the study of organizing and legitimizing processes of transnational multi-stakeholder standardization. We did that by introducing the concept of *regulatory space*, and stressed a relational, interorganizational, and contextual perspective. Second, we acknowledged the need for an *organizational process approach*, which accounts for such aspects as time, organizing, legitimacy, and power. We combine these approaches as we synthesize our key findings about the ways in which non-state authority is established in transnational, multi-stakeholder standard-setting organizations. Our purpose is to highlight what we find to be a significant conclusion about non-state authority: its fragile, unstable, and

163

temporary nature. Our emphasis on fragility fits well with the view of a changing world. One could easily argue that the authority of many old and new state and non-state authorities in transnational politics and regulation could be described as fragile in this changing globalizing context. The cases of multi-stakeholder standard setting we have investigated in this book, however, are particularly fragile, and in this synthesizing chapter, we conclude that that their fragility is caused by the destabilizing tendencies to be found in transnational non-state authorities using a multi-stakeholder logic.

The fragility of authority must be seen in relation to challenges in establishing *legitimate power* – in relation to both the components of power and legitimacy and their intersection. We begin by discussing five aspects of the problematic establishment and maintenance of legitimacy, and proceed to discuss five aspects that relate to the challenge of maintaining a power balance within the multi-stakeholder organization. Although we focus on destabilizing tendencies, the chapter also addresses the glue that holds the organizations together. Indeed, to claim that authority is fragile is not the same thing as claiming that these organizations are necessarily fading away.

CUMBERSOME LEGITIMACY-MAKING

Legitimacy as 'Incessantly Preliminary'

Standard-setting organizations try to establish and maintain legitimacy by employing a number of legitimacy strategies (Chapter 9). What are perceived as a desired structure and appropriate work procedures from an efficiency perspective may not be the best solutions for the legitimacy of the standard-setting activity (cf. Werle and Iversen, 2006). This situation creates the classic dilemma that Weber discussed in his analyses of state bureaucracy and democracy in the early 20th century. The broad inclusion of stakeholders in transparent decision-making fora often leads to time-consuming and bureaucratic processes. It does, however, create a better opportunity for a closed, small expertise-based group to reach consensus within relatively short time frames.

As we demonstrated in Chapter 9, there is no one best solution for this type of decision around legitimate structures and procedures. The unstable nature of the institutional setting includes a lack of dominant frames or sources of legitimacy for transnational multi-stakeholder standardization. Moreover, such decisions are not made by a single party. Rather, legitimacy should be understood as a relational – as well as variable – concept that is established through constant negotiations within a network of stakeholders.

In the three cases we have examined in this book, the establishment of legitimacy had a trial-and-error character and the outcome for legitimacy strategies often constituted a combination of several sources of legitimacy. In general terms, negotiating about a legitimate organization, various stakeholder representatives tried to push for their specific interests and views about legitimate standard setting. The standard setter, in turn, had to prove that the process is open and fair, assuring that all stakeholders can make their voices heard and assuring that their inconsistent interests are balanced in a proper way. And different stakeholders will judge and interpret the notion of 'balanced in a proper way' differently, because each stakeholder has its own view about who actually are the legitimate stakeholders. By hosting such as process, the standard setter (including its secretariat and its advisory units), being a stakeholder itself, acquires a special power to choose exactly how legitimacy values should be interpreted and translated into the practice of the standard-setting activity.

The Contested Construction of a Problem and Legitimate Solution

In order for an organization to be considered a possible and legitimate rule setter, there must be a perception of a certain problem that needs to be handled through rules, and about a certain solution that could constitute the remedy to the problem. This dimension can be thought of as the process of establishing a mandate or a clearly specified jurisdictional area for the rule-setting activity (cf. Weber, 1948). The mandate we have in mind is not clearly specified, however; it is not one that can be obtained once and for all. There is no hierarchical center that can delegate the rule-setting task through a specified mandate in the way that nation states do at the national level. Rather the issues must be argued for, over and over again. Problems and solutions must be shaped and defined through the efforts of players in the regulatory space. In the ISO 26000 case, for example, we observed actions by a number of stakeholders, aimed at framing the need for the new standard as a management system standard – a problem suitable for solving through an ISO standard.

Among these stakeholders was ISO itself, as the host of the process; the UN; consumer organizations; and service providers such as management consultants, certification bodies, and publishers of literature linked to the use of ISO management system standards (classified within the ISO process as Others). Such actors became allies in the regulatory space in their efforts to reframe the need for a new standard into the need for a new ISO management system standard (cf. Rose and Miller, 1992; Young, 1994; Higgins and

Tamm Hallström, 2007). In parallel, as we have demonstrated throughout our analysis, there were several opponents and continuous efforts against a management system approach, which, in turn, challenged the authority of ISO as a rule setter in this area. Accordingly, through a transnational regulatory space approach, we have systematically attended to existing regulatory frameworks and rule-setting organizations that entrepreneurs and newcomers to a specific space are essentially compelled to consider as they try to enter and create a position. Our approach highlights tension and competition in such legitimizing efforts (cf. Botzem and Quack, 2006), thereby underlining the fragile character of rule-setting authority.

A Balancing Act of Distance and Proximity to State Actors and IGOs

The transnational standard setters that we studied have a double relationship with other transnational and national rules (and rule setters and rule enforcers). On the one hand, the vagueness and ambiguity of existing regulations is a fertile context for various framing efforts. We have seen, for example, that the FSC and MSC identified and framed many shortcomings and failures of existing regulations, which functioned as a motivation for their alternative regulatory initiatives. On the other hand, they picked arguments from and related their own standards to broad policies and regulations (see also Boström and Klintman, 2008). Their total rejection of previous regulatory efforts is likely to boomerang and give rise to strong criticism. In the FSC case, it was unthinkable, at least during the agenda-setting phase, to invite state organizations into the standard-setting activities, as the FSC initiative was a response to existing state initiatives that were perceived as severe failures. Yet the FSC has experienced the need to develop a rapprochement to government actors, without making them formal members.

Existing regulation may provide indirect support and legitimacy. When non-state actors assume responsibility for societal goals, policy actors may argue that they are accountable only to their own constituencies, and not to the public (Rhodes, 1997, 2000; Pierre and Peters, 2000). They are framed simply as private, and such framings may have a negative resonance in certain policy circles. State authority is, in contrast, rendered legitimate, as it serves as an agent of representative democracy, through an appeal to popular will. To the extent that state actors frame non-state initiatives as welcome, relevant, and important, therefore, a perception of such private initiatives as public, democratic, and accountable may develop (Boström, 2003, 2006a; Wälti, Küjbler, and Papadopoulos, 2004). The MSC has sought legitimization, particularly from the FAO, the FSC, and the International Labour Organization (ILO). In the case of the ISO 26000 process, we also noted that ISO collaborated with such organizations as the ILO and the UN Global Compact, making use of their symbolic and cognitive power resources. Consequently, the ILO and the Global Compact managed over time to become authoritative in the ISO 26000 setting.

An officer at the UN Global Compact Office talked about the operational capacity that ISO could offer, whereas the Global Compact, lacking such capacity, could offer legitimacy instead. The interviewee also mentioned the risks of 'bluewashing',[1] there were still legitimacy risks for the (blue) UN, should the ISO 26000 process not prove to be sufficiently legitimate. To handle the balance between benefits and risks was indeed a difficult task, according to this interviewee.

Existing national and international rule setters are, simultaneously, significant targets of criticism and sources of legitimacy. Standard setters feel compelled to relate to and approach consistency with existing regulatory frameworks. Otherwise, their standards may prove to become politically infeasible. Non-state authority is actually created by a complex interaction between state and non-state regulatory efforts. Distinctions such as *public versus private*, even *non-state versus state* run the risk of missing this critical point.

The non-state authorities – in their efforts to legitimize their standard setting – face a balancing act between distance and proximity in relation to state actors. They cannot become too close, because of the varied criticism that non-state actors (both business and NGOs) address toward state-led policy and regulatory processes. And they cannot become too distant, because of the risk of being accused of sidestepping the public will and representative democracy.

Gradually More Complex Decision Making and Administration

Through our organizational process approach, we have systematically investigated the way in which the FSC, MSC, and ISO have developed over time. We have found that during the organizational development – or institutionalization – of standard setting and certification, the organization tends to become increasingly bureaucratic and complex. Such a trend, which clearly exists in all three cases, can have a strong impact on both legitimacy and the power game in the arrangement. The work does not necessarily become more hierarchical, at least not in a single-directional way. Rather, it simultaneously expands in all directions: centrally, de-centrally, and horizontally. In the FSC, for example, we notice the growth of members in all three chambers and the gradual expansion and integration of National

Initiatives. At the same time the international secretariat is strengthened, including its networking activities with such external actors as other transnational rule setters, certification bodies, and government actors in a large number of countries. The governance and interaction structures and processes become increasingly complex with fora for decision making, stakeholder consultation (for both members and nonmembers), expert advice, ad hoc groups, and regional and national structures. In the cases of the MSC and FSC, which have been operating since the 1990s, we observe a rapid growth of additional standards, policies, guidelines, documents, and methodologies, some of which are written merely to clarify or help interpret others. The situation resembles a treadmill (Boström and Garsten, 2008); the imperfections of existing standards and governance arrangements lead to new attempts at refining standards and arrangements, leading in turn to new problems, and so on, and so on.

It is unlikely that this situation develops by chance. In all our three cases, the increased complexity has to do with operating in a multi-sectoral (hybrid) area on highly controversial matters. The standard setters experience a *need to develop complex structures* because of all the contradictory expectations that are placed upon them.

According to Glasbergen (2007, p. 14), 'Partnerships that establish new standards will *take on more of a traditional regime character*. In other words, they will resemble government regulation. In that light, they will come to be judged in the same manner as government policy'. With the MSC, FSC, and ISO, we have seen a need to establish mechanisms and structures that resemble state structures. They are far from identical to state representative democratic structures, yet they share similarities. They refer to input, procedures, output, forms for representation, representativeness, and division of power: dividing, standard setting, accreditation, and certification, for instance. The increasing complexity of these governance arrangements relates, at least partially, to legitimacy aspirations – to aspirations to achieve various democratic ideals around deliberation, participation, and representation in the eyes of a plurality of stakeholders. The increasing complexity may have unintended consequences and counter-effects, however, such as making it more difficult for participants to be effective and to comprehend the entire process – which creates a legitimacy challenge in itself (see the section on the shaky power balance later in this chapter).

Illegitimate Participation and Power

Here we emphasize the intersection of power and legitimacy. Broad participation (or inclusiveness) and the mobilization and use of participants' power resources are seen as ideals in themselves, legitimizing the standard-setting process. The standard-setting organization must therefore make room for all stakeholders to participate, whether formally or informally. The challenge for the standard setter is to establish an organizational arrangement that allows stakeholders both to provide and to use their own power resources, and to see that all stakeholders mutually accept the power strategies that are developed and used by the organizations involved. It is not obvious, for instance, that all participation strategies employed by stakeholders are perceived as equally legitimate. Do all the participation strategies serve the legitimizing aspirations of the standard-setting organization?

In Chapter 7, we described eight strategies of participation that we observed in our material, some of which were aimed at influencing the contents or the future status of the standard; others were aimed at influencing the status of the participating organization/stakeholder. Some of the participation strategies have a relatively problematic relationship to a standard-setting organization's effort to establish legitimacy, including delaying strategies, monitoring of others, status-enhancing techniques, stakeholders' protection of their own standards – and even, in the case of high-profile actors, nonparticipation. Some participation strategies are openly manifested, whereas others, such as delaying tactics, are covert. The existence of hidden strategies can be problematic from the point of view of legitimacy: mutual (mis)trust among stakeholders, for instance (cf. Boström and Klintman, 2008). Moreover, interests and strategies of participation are not always given and stable, but are shaped and changed during the process. Learning occurs; actions are taken in response to the actions of other actors; and new, sometimes unexpected, alliances are formed as the work proceeds. This, in turn, makes the organizing and legitimizing efforts of the standard setters even more complex, and their authority more fragile and in need of constant adjustment.

In Chapter 8, we took our analysis yet further by examining how actor categories established for a standard-setting activity contribute to the shaping of preferences and strategies of participation. Some of the stakeholder groups we examined managed to appear relatively homogeneous and strong in their views and positions, whereas others were perceived as heterogeneous and weak. Asymmetries resulting from this categorization may affect the way various actors legitimize the process, and can ultimately affect the authority of the standard-setting body. Actors that are disadvantaged by a particular categorization may ultimately look for participation in a competing rule-setting process program – choosing the Programme for the Endorsement of Forest Certification (PEFC) schemes, in favour of FSC, for instance – thereby de-legitimizing the standard-setting activity.

The issue of illegitimate participation and power connects to our general discussion about power, which we address in the next section in our discussion of five destabilizing mechanisms – centrifugal factors – of power imbalances. We argue that these factors are of key importance for understanding the fragility of multi-stakeholder rule setters. We should emphasize, however, that although authority is fragile, it is possible to maintain a degree of power balance in such arrangements. The very fact that an organization such as the FSC still exists and grows, and continues to operate as a multi-stakeholder standard setter, is sufficient evidence. In our last section of this chapter, we elaborate on this issue.

THE SHAKY POWER BALANCE

Pre-Existing Asymmetric Power Relations Shape the Power Balance within the Multi-Stakeholder Arrangement

Among all the actors that are active in a regulatory space, *organizational status* and *resources* constitute key conditions governing access to and impact on regulatory space (Hancher and Moran, 1989; Young 1994). We have, for example, discussed this topic in relation to high-profile actors, which may have the ability to negotiate special arrangements for their participation. We demonstrated in Chapter 6 that the capacities and resources of various actors are highly differentiated globally – something that will necessarily affect the establishment and outcome of a standard-setting process. Pre-existing power asymmetries, which in turn can be analyzed as asymmetries in access to different types of power resources – material, symbolic, cognitive, and social – can help us to understand some of the prerequisites and capacities for participation, as well as the complexities involved in transnational multi-stakeholder standard setting.

By combining our regulatory space and organizational process approaches, we have been able to analyze the way in which the existing order and power balance can be challenged by new entries, depending on the existence of and actions by both dominant actors and 'pretenders' – candidates for the power to define that which is good, right, or correct (cf. Bourdieu, 1986). At the time of ISO's entry in the field of SR, it was not obvious that this standard setter would obtain a position at all. Dominant standard setters such as the ILO and the UN Global Compact had been long established, together with numerous non-state standard setters such as the Global Reporting Initiative (GRI) and the Social Accountability International (SAI). It appeared that the space for such standard setters had been filled. Yet through successful alliances, the use of other power resources, and adjustments of its working structures, ISO managed to enter that space and create a position for itself.

The Ambiguous Role of Power Resources

The power resources held by stakeholders play double, ambiguous roles (Boström, 2006a). On the one hand, standard-setting organizations want to mobilize and make use of the individual material, symbolic, cognitive, and social power resources of each participant. The strength and legitimacy of the hybrid organizational arrangement depend on the sum and combination of these power resources. On the other hand, each individual stakeholder may use its own power resources to argue and push for its own concerns. There may also be a power game being played between an individual stakeholder and the multi-stakeholder organization (cf. Ahrne and Brunsson, 2008), such as the one between ISO and the ILO.

Acknowledgement of this ambiguity of power resources helps us to explain why power imbalances may increase over time, thereby rendering the authority fragile. We believe that it is necessary to analyze such tendencies in greater detail, by examining varying conditions for participation among stakeholders within the multi-stakeholder arrangement.

Different Conditions for Participation among Stakeholders within the Multi-Stakeholder Arrangement

Varying conditions for participation can be explained in several ways. In this section, we discuss four possible explanations: the sorting of stakeholders into categories, the transnational scale, the durability of the arrangement, and the increasing level of complexity.

The sorting of actors into stakeholder categories. As we noted earlier in this chapter, our analysis in Chapter 8 showed that some stakeholder groups managed to create an image of homogeneity and strength in offering their views and positions, whereas others were perceived as heterogeneous and weak. We explained these differences from a power resource perspective, arguing that organizations with access to certain power resources can create at least an image of homogeneity (and thereby a strong position) through various organizing activities. We also demonstrated how a specific categorization – such as 'experts' and 'stakeholders' in both the ISO and the MSC cases – lead to asymmetries and prototype effects within such groups. A few stakeholder groups were perceived by some participants as 'best examples' (and authoritative) among the whole group of experts, whereas other stakeholder groups were perceived as more peripheral. Our analysis of the social and discursive construction of the definitions of stakeholder groups helped to explain this variation. It seemed more advantageous for a participant to be labeled 'environmental expert' (in the FSC and MSC cases) rather than 'NGO representative' (in the ISO case). The first label alludes to some type of relevant and specific expertise, whereas the second merely signals that the person originates from a nongovernmental organization.

This analysis reveals, then, that the way of categorizing participants into specific actor categories – NGOs, government, industry – that are commonly used within multi-stakeholder processes includes a critical power dimension. Although such categories may be perceived as representing reality and dismissed as issues of debate, they are social constructions that can indeed affect they way participants of individual categories are perceived by themselves and others (or the asymmetries and prototype effects that are likely to evolve). And they affect how participants of various categories are able to perform collective action.

The transnational scale. Although it requires considerable resources for any stakeholder to participate in transnational standard setting, the difficulties for the weakest ones are multiplied when considering the transnational scale. Not only do they have to contend with traveling expenses and language barriers; there are also such organizational and cognitive aspects as the difficulties of framing and representing a 'global view' or a universal interest in a problem (see Chapter 8).

Durability. The fact that the standard-setting projects have become a relatively permanent, regular activity creates both material and ideological obstacles for participation, particularly for some value-driven organizations such as NGOs. If a transnational standard-setting process is stretched in time, or even has a permanent feature, it creates certain material difficulties for all (but particularly some) stakeholders to participate. Long-term commitment may also conflict with core activities, ideologies, or the 'movement-identity' of particular value-driven stakeholders (see also Boström, 2004, 2006a). Campaign-oriented organizations may focus each year an a few salient topics, and it is in the nature of such an organization to address new topics every year and to engage in public awareness raising and campaigning, which our interviewees from Greenpeace stressed. Being committed to a regular activity may appear odd in the view of many social movement activists. Particularly if the organization has elements of a radical, uncompromising, or confrontational identity, some members may expect that it should not expend too many resources on cooperative activities within multi-stakeholder standard-setting arrangements, because they do not want to embrace the cooperative spirit by compromising with big business. Other stakeholders, in contrast, may have a clear economic interest in relation to a permanent standardization activity, and it may appear more natural for them to participate regularly. Retailers (in the FSC case) and service-providing companies (in the ISO case) can be understood in this way. Compared with NGOs, it is less problematic for such commercial actors, for ideological reasons and for their identities, to become permanently committed. Several TNCs proudly announce that they have become part of such arrangements; and in Chapter 7, we discussed how some participants engaged in standard setting in order to learn about CSR, to develop their social networks, or to increase their professional status. NGOs and IGOs, on the other hand, may place their symbolic capital and credibility at risk when doing so.

Complexity. We noted in the section on legitimacy in this chapter, that the standard-setting organization tends to become increasingly bureaucratic and complex during its organizational development. This trend affects conditions for participation, and in the long run it affects legitimacy. Several of our interviewees commented on the increasing complexity of the standard-setting organizations. It is noteworthy that interviewees from such a relatively strong NGO as Greenpeace addressed this problem. During our interviews, they returned repeatedly to the topic of complex procedures and all time-consuming efforts that need to be made in order to create an impact in the standard-setting work. Accordingly, it becomes difficult for any stakeholder – including the stronger ones – to obtain an overview and to know where to focus attention, resources, and strategies. *Inter alias*, this task is even more difficult for actors with few material, cognitive, and social power resources.

Asymmetries of Power as Created by the Organizational Process – Challenging the Multi-Stakeholder Logic?

The diverse criteria for participating in the standard-setting process, analyzed in the previous section, serve to increase power imbalances. Some stakeholders may increase and gain power resources, whereas others need to use their resources in order to participate. Some (such as service providers using the standards) benefit economically, whereas others find that their lack of material resources makes it impossible for them to participate. Yet others benefit symbolically through participation in multi-stakeholder standard setting, and still other stakeholders may place their symbolic capital at risk. Stakeholders may also be able to strengthen their social and cognitive power resources through participation.

We can see, therefore, how the process can create asymmetries of power. In a similar vein, Cutler, Haufler, and Porter (1999) discuss two distinct roles played by power within private authority. First, there is an *ex ante* consideration: the role of power makes it possible for actors to establish authority. Second, there is an *ex post* consideration: power produced by private authority once it is established. According to Cutler et al. (1999),

'Actors with power create private authority, and private authority creates power' (p. 345). Unfortunately, such power imbalances can have implications for the long-term stability and viability of private authority. Actors with good opportunities to participate – by having an overview of the entire bureaucratic complexity, for instance, are those who host the standard-setting process and those in the inner circle (Chapters 6 and 7). There is a growing need for a relatively autonomous organization with financial resources, professionally trained staff, and time to conduct the day-to-day work and monitor what is happening with the standard-setting activity, while engaging in networking and moderating among the stakeholders.

This bureaucratic authority (Barnett and Finnemore, 2004) presents itself as neutral, objective, disinterested, and expert-oriented. Arguably, one should not see it as neutral in relation to all stakeholders. We observed that the standard setter hosting the process and allied service-providing companies – can be expected to be positive toward new standard-setting initiatives. Barnett and Finnemore (2004) argue that there is a tendency toward expansion in the secretariats of international organizations, or we may speak of a tendency toward a fast-growing accountability industry (Tamm Hallström, 2008; Boström and Garsten, 2008). In line with the analysis in this book, we may argue that the inner circle, and particularly the secretariats, is disposed to favour the fast-growth mainstreaming rather than top, high-profile, small-growth approaches (see Chapter 9).

Although such tendencies could challenge the multi-stakeholder logic of the multi-stakeholder organization, we do not believe that they must necessarily do so. Yet we argue that it is relevant to problematize notions around the stakeholder (seeing the secretariat as a stakeholder) and representation (participants within the inner circle may, over time, lose their connection with the stakeholders they are assumed to represent, for example). One could also discuss whether it is more relevant to speak of bureaucratic authority rather than multi-stakeholder authority. Such issues are relevant topics for further research on durable multi-stakeholder work.

Power Moving Away?

A few of our interviewees have been concerned about the fact that in practice standard-setting bodies lack effective means of controlling the operation of industries, and that the real power is to be found outside these standard-setting arrangements. Several interviewees mentioned issues relating to certification and certification practices, including the power of certification firms and the lack of control over poor certification practices. They worry about increasing power asymmetry between certification bodies and the standard-setting body, to the advantage of the certifiers. In the cases of the

FSC and MSC, it is possible to argue that such an increasing power asymmetry relates to these standard setters losing some control over the accreditation. There is an increasingly hegemonic norm in transnational standard setting surrounding the division of power among accreditation, certification, and standardization, as expressed in ISO standards (Reinecke 2009). Although interviewees from the secretariats of these organizations acknowledge this norm around the division of power, they also express some worries. Several interviewees argue that the most critical challenge of the FSC is to increase its budget to improve the capability of monitoring certification bodies.

A CSR standard, inevitably comprising compromises and generalizations about disputed issues, offers flexibility of interpretation and room for action for the actors involved in its application. These actors are the auditors, the audited, and stakeholders involved in a certification process, all of which have various economic, political, and ideological interests. The opportunity for various actors to influence what is measured and prioritized in a local context means that we can expect some degree of interpretative flexibility and decoupling to occur between the aims of the standard and how it is used for certification (cf. Meyer and Rowan, 1977; Powell and DiMaggio, 1991). It is intriguing not only to monitor and examine the corporations being certified, but also to examine the practices of certification, including the role of certification auditors (cf. Power, 1997, 2005; Courville, 2003).

EPILOGUE: ANTIDOTES TO FRAGILITY?

Although we have emphasized fragility in this chapter, there are fundamental stabilizing mechanisms in multi-stakeholder arrangements as well. The broadly perceived need to maintain multi-stakeholder logic is one such example. The very differences of stakeholders – some being strong on symbolic capital, whereas others have material resources and relevant expertise, for example – is itself a stabilizing factor. Scholars of interorganizational collaboration in various forms usually talk about the interdependence of actors as a fundamental stabilizing mechanism (Streeck and Schmitter, 1985; Young, 1994; Cutler et al., 1999). Actors are bound together in relationships of exchange and interdependence. In our cases, there are organizations performing standard setting, intergovernmental rule setting as binding agreements, standard following, and certification and auditing, all of which are interconnected in various ways. The interdependence between such actors as TNCs and value-based organizations, including NGOs, is not immediately apparent, but NGOs can significantly influence TNCs, for instance, through bad publicity (e.g. Beck, 2005). In order to avoid such threats, it can be a good strategy for a company to participate in a multi-stakeholder CSR program. According to Ahrne and Brunsson (2008), the authority of a meta-organization is destabilized by its dependence on specific high-status members. However, in a multi-stakeholder organization, the mutual dependency among *different types* of member organizations may be an antidote for such centrifugal tendencies. When the members are of different types, the differentiation of roles may function as glue. It would be virtually impossible for FSC to reaffirm its authority if, for example, all environmental NGOs were to leave. Such massive use of the exit option could actually happen, if too much criticism were to occur.

The ultimate antidote to a fragile authority would be to create a more robust authority, but it would be contradictory to argue there are avenues for such a pathway. The type of rule setters we have analyzed in this book need to face challenges, including centrifugal forces and a changing context, as summarized in this chapter, in order to maintain their authority. We believe we can generalize our results, as we expect these tendencies to appear in any such arrangement, not merely in the three cases investigated. Accordingly, the multi-stakeholder organization is inherently fragile.

Although we do not believe fragility can be eliminated, we do believe it can be handled. What the multi-stakeholder standard setter can do – and from a normative point of view one could argue, should do – is to incessantly engage with the topic of trying to maintain a power balance that is seen to be legitimate. Such measures could involve empowerment of the weakest stakeholders by various means, and by reflecting and debating the consequences of stakeholder categorizations. Many such measures have been taken: improving the conditions for balanced and effective participation, for example (Chapter 9). One problem with this solution is that the standard-setting organizations, being meta-organizations, which are typically weaker than many of their members (Ahrne and Brunsson, 2008), face scarcity of resources and cannot empower every stakeholder. One board member, representing economic/north, in the FSC concludes:

> It is not possible to believe that FSC should be able to solve within 10 years what the UN has not solved within 40 years. The differences that exist between poor and rich countries exist within the FSC precisely as they do in the rest of the society. The FSC is only part of the society.

Still, we think that empowerment issues are essential for the practitioners of a multi-stakeholder arrangement to engage in, and that they are particularly intriguing for further research. Standard setters may either try to empower weak stakeholders themselves, or encourage stronger stakeholders to empower weaker ones. As standard setters typically have scarce resources, they must rely on the donations and activities of other organizations. Interviewees from the FSC and ISO 26000 secretariats speak warmly about the role of some international NGOs, such as the WWF, and governmental development organizations for their help in many forms and for competence-building services, for example. Such organizations can empower under-resourced stakeholders with financial resources for traveling to meetings and workshops; cognitive resources such as training, education, or information; assistance with translation; symbolic resources such as visualizing and recognizing the name and activities of particular NGOs; and social resources such as enabling stakeholders to meet, thereby strengthening their networking abilities. The topic of empowerment does raise issues, however. The empowerment of weaker stakeholders does not come without associated dilemmas. As one interviewee from the FSC Secretariat says:

> What we wouldn't want to is to create elites; I don't think the FSC would like to be associated with creating elites within the, let's say indigenous peoples – people who can get funding to attend big international meetings but lose their representatively. So I think that's a real problem.

One could also problematize the fact that northern-based environmental NGOs tend to speak on behalf of southern-based social constituencies. Is it really self-evident that the former know what the latter need and want? Is there a risk that the northern NGOs focus too much on environmental sustainability and miss important aspects of social sustainability? On the other hand, one could also argue that no one would speak on behalf of these communities if these northern-based environmental NGOs did not do so. We believe that such topics of empowerment, including representativity, should be an important area of further research in transnational multi-stakeholder rule-setting activities, including how such empowerment may be linked to the maintenance of legitimacy and authority.

We may also look at the role of 'outsiders', and how this type of actor can indirectly challenge or reaffirm the authority of a standard setter. One example of an outsider effort is the monitoring activities conducted by civil society groups regarding rule-setting activities and certification. Indeed, as soon as transnational corporations (TNCs) commit to the principles of human rights, democracy, or healthy environment – values that social movements struggle for – civil society organizations immediately receive a weapon they can use: assessing performance against promises and exposing the distance between rhetoric and practice (cf. Kekk and Sikkink, 1998; Scholte, 2005). Stakeholders that participate in the standard setting of the MSC, FSC, and ISO can actually gain insight, experience, and knowledge about standards, policies, viewpoints, strategies, and framings. They develop expectations, learn what is behind standard criteria and principles, what the compromises were about, and what they should look for when evaluating practices that are certified according to these standards. As a side effect of their participation, then, they develop skills for the monitoring of future processes (both standard-setting and certification processes); as well as for the re-opening (re-politization) of the issues that once were the core concerns behind the very establishment of the standard-setting project.

To the extent that insiders or outsiders, service providers or civil society watchdogs actually refer to the norms, frames, principles, and criteria that emanate from non-state authority, they simultaneously reaffirm its legitimate power. And organizations enjoying non-state authority can proceed with – and expand – their standard-setting operations for some time to come.

NOTE

1.   Bluewashing is a negative term used to describe a relationship between the UN and a company that has agreed to the terms of the UN Global Compact.

Appendix 1

REFLECTIONS ON THE COLLECTION OF MATERIAL IN THE ISO 26000 STUDY

The analysis of the ISO 26000 case builds on the research of Kristina Tamm Hallström, beginning with her 2004 study of the investigative work conducted by ISO in 2003–2004. Her examination of the three following years, during which ISO wrote its standard draft, was undertaken during the period 2005–2007. The ISO 26000 committee had yet to undertake another year of drafting before the standard text was turned into a committee draft, in which only minor amendments could be made. The first three years of the process, together with the period of investigation preceding the drafting work constitutes a crucial period in which several major issues were debated and decided upon.

During the investigative phase, more than 30 interviews were conducted with stakeholders from different countries and stakeholder categories. Documents and reports produced and discussed within the ISO process during 2003–2007 (e.g. various issues papers, the design specification, the first working draft of the standard, and comments on these documents) were analyzed. From the beginning of 2004 to the beginning of 2008, Kristina Tamm Hallström participated as a permanent observer at work meetings of the Swedish mirror group that follows and works in parallel with the international work process (usually one six-hour working day, four to six times a year). Between 2006 and 2008, she participated in five public seminars held to inform the public about the ISO 26000 process. These events took place in Stockholm, and were organized by the Swedish Standards Institute in collaboration with the Swedish Foreign Ministry. Direct observations were also made during a two-day pre-conference on social responsibility (SR) held for developing countries in Sweden in June 2004, during the two days following the main ISO conference on SR. In 2005, interviews lasting 60 to 90 minutes were conducted with five experts active at the international level and two experts active at the national level. During the Swedish mirror committee meetings in 2004–2008, the pre-conference for developing countries and the main ISO conference in 2004, observations of actual work sessions were conducted, including dialogues among stakeholders.

In May 2006, Kristina Tamm Hallström spent one week in Lisbon, Portugal, to follow the ISO work. She spent two days at a workshop for developing countries participating in the ISO work, followed by ISO's third five-day international working group meeting. She was not allowed to observe any meetings (e.g. task group meetings, stakeholder group meetings, plenary sessions). She stayed in the conference building and the lobby of the main conference hotel during six of the seven workdays, however, and was able to conduct 22 15-to-60-minute interviews with experts and observers during their breaks. In 2007, she conducted 15 15-to-60-minute interviews with experts in Vienna and four 60-to-90-minute interviews with experts in other countries. The Vienna interviews were made during the fifth international work meeting that Kristina Tamm Hallström attended for three days as a special guest with observer status. Again, she was not allowed to participate in work sessions to observe actual debates, but allowed to talk to and conduct interviews with experts during breaks and after work sessions. In total the study of the ISO 26000 process included:

* observations of actual debates at 20 Swedish mirror committee meetings in 2004–2008,
* attendance at five public seminars in Sweden in 2006–2008,
* 30 interviews and an observation of one pre-conference and one international meeting in 2004,
* seven interviews in 2005,
* 22 interviews and an observation of one international meeting in 2006, and
* 19 interviews and one international meeting in 2007.

Altogether, 77 interviews of various lengths were conducted, along with observations of three international meetings (one as observer of actual debates) and two workshops for developing countries (one as observer of actual debates). Most of the interviews were conducted in English; Scandinavian interviewees were interviewed in Swedish, and a number of the interviews were in French. Kristina Tamm Hallström translated all the non-English interviews.

All the meetings observed were not of actual debates, which were restricted for outsiders, including researchers. Yet many important activities took place during coffee and lunch breaks, at breakfast or in the bar or restaurant after the working day. By staying in the same hotel as registered meeting participants were staying, it was possible to talk to participants during breaks, and shorter interviews and talks with interviewees were possible before and after the working days during international meetings. On such occasions, it was possible to gather information about ongoing debates and activities that had just occurred or were planned for the coming day.

Observations could also be made as participants communicated with each other, and such observations could be used to help form questions for later interviews.

One obvious weakness in this method was the fact that it was sometimes necessary to chase interviewees in order to obtain their attention; many participants wanted to use the time outside of the formal program to network, have informal conversations, and anchor their ideas. Some people were reluctant to open up for an interview. Others seemed more than happy, and in some cases even eager, to take time for an interview. It was not easy to know the reaction of a potential interviewee in advance, which made the interview process demanding. Between international meetings, the situation was different however, and several interviews were conducted then, in the regular offices of international participants. On two occasions, telephone interviews were conducted.

It is impossible to know, of course, about the content of the telephone calls, e-mail conversations, and private stakeholders' meetings that occurred between formal gatherings, although we have tried to get a picture of such activities through direct questions to interviewees. Together with our examination of a large number of documents, however, we do believe that the interview data collected for the ISO 26000 investigation provide a clear picture of the dynamics of the standard-setting activities that occurred during the period examined.

For all three cases – MSC, FSC and ISO – each quote is referenced with the role of the person being interviewed, and this information has been enhanced for the ISO 26000 case. The fact that the examination of the ISO 26000 process was conducted over a period of four years has enabled the analysis of the dynamics. Each time we use interview quotes from the ISO 26000 study, we have therefore referenced not only the role of the person quoted but also the time of the interview.

REFLECTIONS ON THE COLLECTION OF MATERIAL IN THE FSC AND MSC STUDIES

Magnus Boström assumed primary responsibility for selecting and reading the academic literature and other information on the FSC and MSC cases. In these cases, particularly the FSC case, there were many more secondary sources available than there were for the ISO study. Much had already been written on the background and the initial processes of the establishment of FSC and MSC and their standards. This literature was used for our study of the FSC and MSC, and for our comparisons with the ISO case.

We decided early in our research process there was no need to conduct as many interviews and participant observations in the FSC and MSC cases as had been conducted in the ISO case. Yet we understood the need to gather relatively extensive primary data on our research topic and our novel analytical approach. For this purpose, we conducted a series of interviews, read various documents, and, in the case of the FSC, participated as an observer in a General Assembly (see below).

Magnus Boström and Kristina Tamm Hallström planned the FSC interviews together. Between the spring of 2006 and the spring of 2009, 29 of these interviews were conducted by Magnus Boström and two research assistants: Ida Seing and Sara Söderström. We strived to select interviewees that could be assumed to represent the most central actor categories – interviewees from each of the three chambers within the FSC (social, environmental, and economic). We also selected nonmembers that were related in some way to the FSC at the transnational level, although some were concerned mainly with their local level. For some of the interviewees, transnational experience consisted of activity in the initial development of the FSC; four others held positions on the FSC board; others were current or previous members of the FSC, participants in the FSC General Assembly or in various working committees, or critical external observers of the FSC. Three of our interviewees, one of whom was interviewed twice, were on the staff of the FSC Secretariat.

As we focussed at the transnational level in this project, it was necessary to select interviewees from various parts of the world, including developed and developing countries. Most of the interviews in distant countries were conducted by telephone. Because of the comprehension and technical difficulties that ensued in this more cost-effective interview option, we conducted a number of additional, face-to-face interviews, including some with members of the FSC Secretariat at FSC headquarters in Bonn, in the spring of 2006. And in spite of the difficulties in finding relevant interviewees, particularly from the developing world, and in spite of some language barriers we sometimes encountered, we were pleased to be able to acquire a relatively balanced group, representing geographical coverage and stakeholder category.

We conducted 19 interviewees for the MSC case with actors from various categories and countries. One person was interviewed twice, and one interview was conducted with two interviewees. In contrast to the FSC case, the MSC interviewees came only from the developed world and generally spoke good English, an imbalance that reflects the MSC's lesser concern with the balancing of northern and southern participation.

It was necessary in this process to select people with the MSC Board, Technical Advisory Board, or Stakeholder Council experience, in order to reflect the varied interests in MSC standardization. We also conducted face-to-face interviews with two people from the international secretariat in London in the spring of 2007; and we interviewed a few people who had experiences with the MSC, while not being part of any of its organizational units – people engaged in assessment processes or as critical observers. In addition, we are grateful to Lars Gulbrandsen, who provided us with two interviews with three people from the MSC Secretariat (or executive).

The interviewers followed a common interview guide, with specific questions that reflected the key topics of the book. Our approach was flexible, however, and based on a key criterion that we could adjust questions in accordance with the interviewee's particular experience and expertise. Questions were also adjusted in line with the type of actor category represented by the interviewee.

Again, we relied heavily upon various documents: scholarly literature; reports, press releases or other documents issued by stakeholders; information and reports accessed from the MSC and FSC websites; reports, minutes, and memory notes given to us by interviewees; newspapers issued by the FSC and MSC (*FSC News and Notes*, for example), and others.

Finally, our research assistant, Sara Söderström, visited the FSC General Assembly (GA) in Cape Town, South Africa, in November 2008, to participate in the GA and in various side meetings and field trips that were arranged in parallel to the GA. This participant observation provided us with a valuable contribution for obtaining direct insight into the discussions and debates among FSC stakeholders and an understanding of the complexity of the preparation and decision-making process. Söderström took the opportunity to engage in informal conversations with many people representing diverse interests that spoke directly to some of the key topics addressed in this book, all of which provided a valuable complement to formal interviews.

Appendix 2

List of organizations represented in the ISO Advisory Group on Social Responsibility active in 2003–2004, including clarification of the interest represented. Source: ISO Central Secretariat.

Organization	Representing
International Chamber of Commerce (ICC)	International Chamber of Commerce (ICC)
Instituto Mexaicano de Normalización y Certificación, Mexico	Americas Region
Service de Normalisation Industrielle Marocaine, Morocco *	African Region
Trinidad and Tobago Bureau of Standards	ISO Committee on Developing Country Matters (DEVCO)
Danish Consumer Council	Consumers International (CI)
Alcan Inc	Chairperson of the Advisory Group (neutral position)
Business and Human Rights *	Human Rights Watch
Daimler Chrysler AG	International Federation of Standards Users (IFAN)
US Council for International Business	International Organization of Employers
Siemens AG, Germany	European Region
ISO Central Secretariat	Secretary of the Advisory Group
International Labour Office (ILO)	International Labour Office (ILO)
Global Reporting Initiative (GRI)	Global Reporting Initiative (GRI)
Motorola Inc, USA	Americas Region

International Confederation of Free Trade Unions (ICFTU)	International Confederation of Free Trade Unions (ICFTU)
Global Compact Office of the Secretary-General, United Nations	Global Compact
Business-Humanitarian Forum	International Chamber of Commerce (ICC)
Australian Competition and Consumer Commission (ACCC), Australia	Asia/Oceania Region
Ecofuturo Institute, Brazil	Americas Region
Ministry of Health, Botswana *	African Region
Swedish Industry Association, Sweden	European Region
Industry Standards Committee for Petroleum and Gas, Malaysia	Asia/Oceania Region
International Institute for Sustainable Development (IISD)	International Institute for Sustainable Development (IISD)
WWF-International *	WWF-International
ISO Central Secretariat	ISO Central Secretariat
Reitaku University, Japan	Asia/Oceania Region
Observatoire sur la Responsabilité Sociétale des Entreprises (ORSE), France	European Region
International Labour Office (ILO)	International Labour Office (ILO)
Canadian Office of Consumer Affairs	ISO/Committee on Consumer Policy (COPOLCO)
International Organization of Employers (IOE)	International Organization of Employers (IOE)
Global Compact Office of the Secretary-General, United Nations	The UN Global compact

*Organizations that were added to the list after the establishment of the group.

Appendix 3

FSC'S PRINCIPLES AND CRITERIA

The ten principles:

Principle #1: Compliance with laws and FSC Principles
Forest management shall respect all applicable laws of the country in which they occur, and international treaties and agreements to which the country is a signatory, and comply with all FSC Principles and Criteria

Principle #2: Tenure and use rights and responsibilities
Long-term tenure and use rights to the land and forest resources shall be clearly defined, documented and legally established.

Principle #3: Indigenous peoples' rights
The legal and customary rights of indigenous peoples to own, use and manage their lands, territories, and resources shall be recognized and respected.

Principle #4: Community relations and worker's rights
Forest management operations shall maintain or enhance the long-term social and economic well-being of forest workers and local communities.

Principle #5: Benefits from the forest
Forest management operations shall encourage the efficient use of the forest's multiple products and services to ensure economic viability and a wide range of environmental and social benefits.

Principle #6: Environmental impact
Forest management shall conserve biological diversity and its associated values, water resources, soils, and unique and fragile ecosystems and landscapes, and, by so doing, maintain the ecological functions and the integrity of the forest.

Principle #7: Management plan
A management plan – appropriate to the scale and intensity of the operations – shall be written, implemented, and kept up to date. The long term objectives of management, and the means of achieving them, shall be clearly stated.

Principle #8: Monitoring and assessment
Monitoring shall be conducted – appropriate to the scale and intensity of forest management –too assess the condition of the forest, yields of forest products, chain of custody, management activities and their social and environmental impacts.

Principle #9: Maintenance of high conservation value forests
Management activities in high conservation value forests shall maintain or enhance the attributes which define such forests. Decisions regarding high conservation value forests shall always be considered in the context of a precautionary approach.

Principle #10: Plantations
Plantations shall be planned and managed according with Principles and Criteria 1-9, and Principle 10 and its Criteria. While plantations can provide an array of social and economic benefits, and can contribute to satisfying the world's needs for forest products, they should complement the management of, reduce pressures on, and promote the restoration and conservation of natural forests.

Source: FSC International Standard. FSC Principles and Criteria for Forest Stewardship. FSC-STD-01-001-(version 4-0) EN (2008). Electronically available at http://www.fsc.org/fileadmin/web-data/public/document_center/international_FSC_ policies/standards/FSC_STD_01_001_V4_0_EN_FSC_Principles_and_Criteria.pdf

References

Abbott, Andrew (1988). *The system of professions – an essay on the division of expert labor*. Chicago: The University of Chicago Press.

AG Report 2004, Working Report on Social Responsibility prepared by the ISO Advisory Group on Social Responsibility, April 30 2004, for submission to the ISO Technical Management Board.

Ahrne, Göran (1994). *Social Organizations. Interaction inside, outside and between organizations*. London: Sage.

Ahrne, Göran, and Brunsson, Nils (Eds.) (2004). *Regelexplosionen*. Stockholm, Sweden: EFI, Ekonomiska Forskningsinstitutet at Stockholm School of Economics.

Ahrne, Göran, and Brunsson, Nils (2008). *Meta-organizations*. Cheltenham, UK and Northampton, MA, USA: Edward Elgar.

Ahrne, Göran, and Papakostas, Apostolis (2002). *Organisationer, samhälle och globalisering*. Lund, Sweden: Studentlitteratur.

Alexius, Susanna (2007). *Regelmotståndarna – om konsten att undkomma regler*. Doctoral dissertation in management. Stockholm, Sweden: EFI, Ekonomiska Forskningsinstitutet at Stockholm School of Economics.

Bachrach, Peter, and Baratz, Morton S. (1970). *Power and poverty: Theory and practice*. New

Bäckstrand, Karin (2006), Multi-stakeholder partnerships for sustainable development: Rethinking legitimacy, accountability and effectiveness. *European Environment*, 16, 290–306.

Barnett, Michael, and Finnemore, Marta (2004). *Rules for the world. International organizations in global politics*. London: Cornell University Press.

Bass, Stephen (2003). Certification in the forest political landscape. In Errol Meidinger, Chris Elliot, and Gerhard Oesten (Eds.), *Social and political dimensions of forest certification* (pp. 27–50). Remagen-Oberwinter: Forstbuch.

Beck, Ulrich (1992). *Risk Society. Towards a new modernity*. London: Sage.

Beck, Ulrich (2005). *Power in the global age*. Cambridge: Polity Press.

Bendell, Jem (Ed.). (2000). *Terms for endearment. Business, NGOs and sustainable development*. Sheffield, UK: Greenleaf Publishing.

Bendell, Jem, and Murphy, David (2000). Planting the seeds of change. Business-NGO relations on tropical deforestation. In Jem Bendell (Ed.), *Terms for endearment. Business, NGOs and sustainable development* (pp. 65–78). Sheffield, UK: Greenleaf Publishing.

Bernstein, Steven, and Cashore, Benjamin (2004). Non-state global governance: Is forest certification a legitimate alternative to a global forest convention? In John J. Kirton, and Michael J. Trebilcock (Eds.), *Hard choices, soft law: Combining trade, environment, and social cohesion in global governance* (pp. 33–65) Aldershot, UK: Ashgate Press.

Biermann, Frank; Chan, Man-san; Mert, Avsem, and Pattberg, Philipp (2007). Multi-stakeholder partnerships for sustainable development: Does the promise hold?. In Pieter Glasbergen, Frank Biermann, and Arthur P.J. Mol (Eds.), *Partnerships, governance and sustainable development reflections on theory and practice* (pp. 239–260). Cheltenham, UK: Edward Elgar.

Boli, John (1999). Conclusion: World authority structures and legitimations. In John Boli, and George Thomas (Eds.), *Constructing World Culture – International Non-governmental Organizations Since 1875* (pp. 267–300). Stanford, USA: Stanford University Press.

Boli, John, and Thomas, George (1999). INGOs and the organization of world culture. In John Boli, and George Thomas (Eds.), *Constructing World Culture – International Non-governmental Organizations Since 1875* (pp. 13–49). Stanford, USA: Stanford University Press.

Boström, Magnus (2003). Environmental organizations in new forms of political participation. Ecological modernization and the making of voluntary rules. *Environmental Values*, 12, 175–193.

Boström, Magnus (2004). Cognitive practices and collective identities within a heterogeneous social movement: The Swedish environmental movement. *Social Movement Studies*, 3, 73–88.

Boström, Magnus (2006a). Regulatory credibility and authority through inclusiveness: Standardization organizations in cases of eco-labelling. *Organization*, *13*(3), 345–367.

Boström, Magnus (2006b). Establishing credibility: Practising standard-setting ideals in a Swedish seafood-labelling case. *Journal of Environmental Policy & Planning*, 8, 135–158.

Boström, Magnus, and Garsten, Christina (Eds.). (2008). *Organizing transnational accountability. mobilization, tools, challenges*. Cheltenham, UK and Northampton, MA, USA: Edward Elgar.

Boström, Magnus, and Klintman, Mikael (2008). *Eco-standards, product labelling, and green consumerism*. Basingstoke: Palgrave Macmillan.

Botzem, Sebastian, and Quack, Sigrid (2006). Contested rules and shifting boundaries: International standard-setting in accounting. In Marie-Laure

Djelic, and Kerstin Sahlin-Andersson (Eds.), *Transnational governance. Institutional dynamics of regulation* (pp. 266–286). Cambridge, UK: Cambridge University Press.

Bourdieu, Pierre (1986). Modeskaparen och hans märke. *In Kultursociologiska texter, i urval av Donald Broady och Mikael Palme* (pp. 77–146). Stockholm, Sweden: Salamander.

Bowker, C. Geoffrey, and Star, Susan Leigh (1999). *Sorting things out.* Cambridge, Massachusetts: MIT Press.

Braithwaite, John, and Drahos, Peter (2000). *Global business regulation.* Cambridge: Cambridge University Press.

Brunsson, Nils; Jacobsson, Bengt, and Associates (2000). *A world of standards.* Oxford, UK: Oxford University Press.

Cashore, Benjamin; Auld, Graeme, and Newsom, Deanna (2004). *Governing through markets: Forest certification and the emergence of non-state authority.* New Haven, CT: Yale University Press.

Chaffee, Chet; Leadbitter, Duncan, and Aalders, Edwin (2003). Seafood evaluation, certification and consumer information. In Bruce Phillips; Trevor Ward, and Chet Chaffee (Eds.). *Eco-labelling in fisheries. What is it all about?* (pp. 4–13). Oxford: Blackwell Science.

Clapp, Jennifer (2005). Transnational corporations and global environmental governance. In Dauvergne, Peter (Ed.), *Handbook of global environmental politics* (pp. 284–297). Northampton: Edward Elgar.

Clegg, Stewart; Courpesson, David, and Phillips, Nelson (2006). *Power and organizations.* London: Sage.

Cochoy, Franck (2004). The industrial roots of contemporary political consumerism: The case of the French standardization movement. In Michele Micheletti, Andreas Follesdal, and Dietlind Stolle (Eds.), *Politics, Products, and Markets. Exploring Political Consumerism Past and Present* (pp. 145–160). New Brunswick, London: Transaction Publishers.

Constance, Douglas H., and Bonanno, Alessandro. (2000). Regulating the global fisheries: The World Wildlife Fund, Unilever, and the Marine Stewardship Council. *Agriculture and Human Values, 17* (2), 125–139.

Consumers International press release of 8 May 2006, title: *Consumer groups outraged as business lobby seeks to silence media on corporate social responsibility.*

Cooney, Kate (2006). The institutional and technical structuring of nonprofit ventures: Case study of a U.S. hybrid organization caught between two fields. *Voluntas: International Journal of Voluntary and Non-Profit Organizations, 17,* 143–161.

COPOLCO Report (2002). Report prepared by the ISO Consumer Policy Committee, published in 2002.

Counsell, Simon, and Loraas, Kim Terje (2002). *Trading in credibility. The myth and reality of the Forest Stewardship Council*. The Rainforest Foundation, UK, available at http://www.rainforestfoundationuk.org/ files/Trading%20in%20Credibility%20full%20report.pdf#search='Counse ll%20and%20Loraas, (accessed 28 October 2005).

Courville, Sasha (2003), Social accountability audits: Challenging or defending democratic governance?. *Law & Policy, 25*(3), 269–297.

Cummins, Alexia (2004). The Marine Stewardship Council: A multi-stakeholder approach to sustainable fishing. *Corporate Social Responsibility and Environmental Management, 11*, 85–94.

Cutler, Claire; Haufler, Virginia, and Porter, Tony (Eds.) (1999). *Private authority and international affairs*. Albany: State University of New York Press.

Dahl, Matilda (2007). *States under scrutiny*. Doctoral dissertation in business administration. Stockholm, Sweden: Stockholm University.

Dingwerth, Klaus (2005). *The democratic legitimacy of transnational rule-making: Normative theory and democratic practice*. Doctoral dissertation. Berlin: Freie Universität, Berlin.

Djelic, Marie-Laure, and Sahlin-Andersson, Kerstin (Eds.) (2006). *Transnational governance: Institutional dynamics of regulation*. Cambridge: Cambridge University Press.

Domask, Joseph (2003). From boycotts to global partnership: NGOs, the private sector, and the struggle to protect the world's forests. In Jonathan Doh, and Hildy Teegen (Eds.), *Globalization and NGOs. Transforming business, government, and society* (pp. 157–186). London: Praeger.

Elliot, Christopher (1999). *Forest certification: Analysis from a policy network perspective*. Doctoral dissertation. Lausanne: Ecole Polytechnique Federale de Lausanne.

Fern (2001). *Behind the logo. An environmental and social assessment of forest certification schemes*. Fern: Gloucestershire.

Fischer, Frank (2003). *Reframing public policy*. Oxford: Oxford University Press.

Fowler, Penny, and Heap, Simon (2000). Bridging troubled waters: The Marine Stewardship Council. In Jem Bendell (Ed.), *Terms for endearment. Business, NGOs and sustainable development* (pp. 135–149). Sheffield: Greanleaf Publishing.

Fransen, Luc W., and Kolk, Ans (2007). Global rule-setting for business: A critical analysis of multi-stakeholder standards. *Organization, 14*(5), 667–684.

FSC (2002). Synopsis of the Report of The Change Management Team. Bonn: FSC.

FSC (2003). FSC Social Strategy: Building and implementing a social agenda. Version 2.1. Bonn: FSC, available at http://www.fsc.org/fileadmin/web-data/public/document_center/institutional_documents/FSC_Social_Strateg y_version_2_1.pdf, (accessed 21 May 2009).

FSC (2005). FSC Strategy. Institutional, organizational and operational development of the global network of the Forest Stewardship Council. Bonn: FSC

FSC (2007). Strengthening forest conservation, communities and markets. The global strategy of the forest stewardship council, available at http://www.fsc.org/fileadmin/web-data/public/document_center/institutional_documents/FSC_Global_Strate gy-EN.pdf, (accessed 15 May 2009).

FSC (2008). FSC governance review process, available at http://www.fsc.org/fileadmin/webdata/public/document_center/institutiona l_ documents/FSC_Governance_Paper_2008.pdf, (accessed 15 May 2009).

Garsten, Christina, and Lindh de Montoya, Monica (Eds.). (2008). *Transparency in a new global order. Unveiling organizational visions.* Cheltenham: Edward Elgar.

Glasbergen, Pieter (2007). Setting the scene: The partnership paradigm in the making. In Pieter Glasbergen, Frank Biermann, and Arthur P. J. Mol (Eds.), *Partnerships, governance and sustainable development reflections on theory and practice* (pp. 1–25). Cheltenham: Edward Elgar.

Glasbergen, Pieter; Biermann, Frank, and Mol, Arthur P.J. (Eds.). (2007). *Partnerships, governance and sustainable development reflections on theory and practice.* Cheltenham: Edward Elgar.

Graz, Jean-Christophe, and Nölke, Andreas (Eds.). (2008). *Transnational private governance and its limits.* London: Routledge.

Green, Ken; Morton, Barbara, and New, Steve (2000). Greening organizations, purchasing, consumption, and innovation. *Organization and Environment,* 13, 206–225.

Guertler, Guido (2005). E-mail of 24 March 2005 by Guido Guertler/ICSCA Advisor, to ISO Secretary General Alan Bryden on the subject ISO/TMB WG on Social Responsibility, first meeting, observations and proposals.

Gulbrandsen, Lars H. (2004). Overlapping public and private governance: Can forest certification fill the gaps in the global forest regime?. *Global Environmental Politics,* 4(2), 75–99.

Gulbrandsen, Lars H. (2005). Mark of sustainability? Challenges for fishery and forestry eco-labeling. *Environment,* 47(5), 8–23.

Gulbrandsen, Lars H. (2008). Organizing accountability in transnational standards organizations: The Forest Stewardship Council as a good governance model. In Magnus Boström, and Christina Garsten (Eds.), *Organizing transnational accountability* (pp. 61–79). Cheltenham: Edward Elgar.

Gulbrandsen, Lars H. (2009). *Non-state global environmental governance. The emergence and effectiveness of forest and fisheries certification schemes.* Doctoral dissertation. Department of Political Science, Faculty of Social Sciences, University of Oslo.

Hacking, Ian (1999). *The social construction of what?.* Cambridge, MA and London, England: Harvard University Press.

Hall, Rodney Bruce, and Biersteker, Thomas (Eds.) (2002). *The emergence of private authority in global governance.* Cambridge: Cambridge University Press.

Hancher, Leigh, and Moran, Michael J. (1989). Organizing regulatory space. In Leigh Hancher, and Michael J. Moran (Eds.), *Capitalism, culture, and economic regulation* (pp. 271–300) Oxford, UK: Clarendon Press.

Hardin, Garrett (1968). The tragedy of the commons. *Science,* 162, 1243–1248.

Henning, Roger (2000). Selling standards. In Nils Brunsson, Bengt Jacobsson, and Associates. *A World of Standards* (pp. 114–124). New York: Oxford University Press.

Higgins, Winton, and Tamm Hallström, Kristina (2007). Standardization, globalization and rationalities of government. *Organization, 14*(5), 685–704.

Higgins, Winton, and Tamm Hallström, Kristina (2008). Technical standardization. In Akira Iriye and Pierre-Yves Saunier (Eds.), *The Palgrave Dictionary of Transnational History* (pp. 990–997). London: Palgrave Macmillan.

Higgott Richard, Underhill, Geoffrey, and Bieler, Andreas (Eds.) (2000). *Non-state actors and authority in the global system.* London: Routledge.

Hoel, Alf Håkon (2004). Ecolabelling in fisheries: An effective conservation tool? Tromsø, Norut Samfunnsforskning as Rapport nr 13/2004.

Howes, Rupert (2005). Reversing the decline in global fish stocks: Eco-labelling and the Marine Stewardship Council, Sustainable Development International 13 (spring edition) available at http://www.sustdev.org/index.php?option=com_content&task=view&id=365&Itemid=34, accessed 18 August 2005.

Huckel, Carmen (2005). Legitimacy and global governance in managing global public health, paper presented at the Score conference Organizing the world – rules and rule-setting among organizations, Stockholm, Sweden, 13–15 October 2005.

ISO and Social Responsibility (2006). Document issued by ISO in 2006.

ISO/IEC Directives — Part 1: Procedures (2008).

ISO/TMB resolution L/2004 of 25 June 2004.

ISO/TMB/WG SR N 102 (2007). Document issued by the ISO 26000 Secretariat in 2007, clarifying its media policy.

ISO/TMB/WG SR N 131 (2007). Document issued by ISO dated 9 November 2007.

ISO/TMB/WG SR N 132 (2007). Resolution 2 of November 2007.

ISO/TMB/WG SR N 72 (2006). Document issued by ISO dated 11 May 2006.

ISO/TMB/WG SR N131 (2007). Document issued by the ISO 26000 Secretariat 9 November 2007, with clarification regarding balance among stakeholders during consensus processes.

ISO/TMB/WG SR N16 (2005). Resolutions taken at the first meeting of the ISO 26000 committee, dated 17 March 2005.

ISO/TMB/WG SR N48 rev. 1 (2005). Guidance on stakeholder categories in the ISO/TMB/WG SR, dated 30 September 2005.

Jacobsson, Bengt (2000). Standardization and expert knowledge. In Nils Brunsson, Bengt Jacobsson and Associates, *A world of standards* (pp. 40–49). New York: Oxford University Press.

Jutterström, Mats (2004). *Att påverka beslut – företag i EUs regelsättande* [To influence decisions – Business firms' participation in the rule-setting of the European Union]. Doctoral dissertation in management. Stockholm: EFI, Ekonomiska Forskningsinstitutet, Handelshögskolan i Stockholm.

Kekk, Margaret, and Sikkink, Kathryn (1998). *Activist beyond borders: Advocacy networks in international politcs.* London: Cornell University Press.

Kerwer, Dieter (2005). Rules that many use: Standards and global regulation. *Governance, 18*(4), 611–632.

Klintman, Mikael, and Boström, Magnus (2008). Transparency through labelling? Layers of visibility in environmental risk management. In Christina Garsten, and Monica Lindh de Montoya (Eds.), *Transparency in a new global order: Unveiling organizational visions* (pp. 178–197). Cheltenham: Edward Elgar.

Kuntzsch, Volker (2003). Is eco-labelling working? An overview. In Bruce Phillips, Trevor Ward, and Chet Chaffee (Eds.), *Eco-labelling in fisheries. What is it all about?* (pp. 176–185). Oxford: Blackwell Science.

Lafferty, William M., and Meadowcroft, James (1996). *Democracy and the environment: Problems and prospects.* Cheltenham: Edward Elgar.

Lakoff, George (1987). *Women, fire, and dangerous things.* Chicago: The University of Chicago Press.

Lindblom, Charles (1977). *Politics and markets. The world's political-economic systems.* New York: Basics books.

Lovan, W. Robert; Murray, Michael, and Shaffer, Ron (Eds.) (2004). *Participatory Governance: Planning, Conflict Mediation and Public Decision-Making in Civil Society.* Aldershot: Ashgate.

Loya, Thomas, and Boli, John (1999). Standardization in the world polity: Technical rationality over power. In John Boli, and George Thomas (Eds.), *Constructing World Culture – International Non-governmental Organizations Since 1875* (pp. 169–197). Stanford, USA: Stanford University Press.

Lukes, Steven (1974). *Power: A radical view.* London and Basingstoke: The Macmillan Press Ltd.

Lukes, Steven (2005). *Power: A radical view.* Basingstoke: Palgrave Macmillan.

Mason, Michael (2005). *The new accountability. Environmental responsibility across borders.* London: Earthscan.

May, Brendan; Leadbitter, Duncan; Sutton, Mike, and Weber, Michael (2003). The Marine Stewardship Council (MSC). In Bruce Phillips, Trevor Ward, and Chet Chaffee (Eds.), *Eco-labelling in fisheries. What is it all about?* (pp. 14–33). Oxford: Blackwell Publishing.

McAdam, Doug, and Scott, W. Richard (2005). Organizations and movements. In Gerald F. Davis, Doug McAdam, Richard W. Scott, and Mayer N. Zald (Eds.), *Social movements and organization theory* (pp. 4–40). Cambridge University Press.

McNichol, Jason (2003). International NGO certification programs as new para-regulatory forms? Lessons from a frontrunner. Paper prepared for conference on The Multiplicity of Regulatory Actors in the Transnational Space, Uppsala University, Department of Business Studies, 23–24 May 2003.

Meidinger, Errol; Elliot, Chris, and Oesten, Gerhard (Eds.) (2003). *Social and political dimensions of forest certification.* Remagen-Oberwinter: Forstbuch.

Memorandum of Understanding (2005). Memorandum of Understanding between the International Labour Organization and the International Organization for Standardization in the field of social responsibility, dated 4 March 2005.

Meyer, John, and Jepperson, Ronald L. (2000). The "actors" of modern society: The cultural construction of social agency. *Sociological Theory, 18*(1), 100–20.

Meyer, John, and Rowan, Brian (1977). Institutionalized organizations: Formal structure as myth and ceremony. *American Journal of Sociology, 83,* 340–363.

Mol, Arthur; Lauber, Volkmar, and Liefferink, Duncan (2000). *The voluntary approach to environmental policy: Joint environmental policy-making in Europe*. Oxford, UK: Oxford University Press.

Mörth, Ulrika (Ed.). (2004). *Soft law in governance and regulation. An interdisciplinary analysis*. Cheltenham: Edward Elgar.

MSC (2003) Lessons learned in fisheries certification. The first four years of the Independent Marine Stewardship Council. Electronically available at http://www.msc.org/html/content_460.htm, accessed 18 August 2005.

MSC (2007) MSC Stakeholder Council Meeting No. 6. Electronically available at http://www.msc.org/documents/institutional/public-stakehol der-council-meeting-minutes/StC_meeting_April_2007.pdf, accessed 16 July 2009.

Oliver, Christine (1991). Strategic Responses to Institutional Processes, *Academy of Management Review, 16*(1), 145–179.

Oosterver, Peter (2005). *Global food governance*. Doctoral dissertation. Wageningen: Wageningen University.

Pattberg, Philipp H. (2007). *Private institutions and global governance. The new politics of environmental sustainability*. Cheltenham: Edward Elgar.

Pellizzoni, Luigi (2004), Responsibility and environmental governance, *Environmental Politics, 13*(3), 541–565.

Pierre, Jon, and Peters, B. Guy (2000). *Governance, politics and the state*, London: Macmillan and New York: St. Martin's Press.

Ponte, Stefano (2008). Greener than thou: The political economy of fish ecolabeling and its local manifestations in south. *World Development, 36*, 159–175.

Porter, Gareth; Brown, Welsh Janet, and Chasek, Pamela S. (2000). *Global environmental politics*. Third edition. Boulder: Westview Press.

Powell, Walter, and DiMaggio, Paul (Eds.) (1991). *The new institutionalism in organizational analysis*. Chicago, USA: The University of Chicago Press.

Power, Michael (1997). *The audit society: Rituals of verification*. Oxford, UK: Oxford University Press.

Power, Michael (2005). Organizations and auditability: A theory. Paper presented at the Score conference Organizing the world – rules and rule-setting among organizations, Stockholm, Sweden, 13–15 October 2005.

Power, Michael (2007). *Organized uncertainty. Designing a world of risk management*. Oxford: Oxford University Press.

Rametsteiner, Ewald (2002). The role of governments in forest certification: A normative analysis based on new institutional economics theories. *Forest Policy and Economics*, 4, 163–173.

Reinecke, Juliene (2009). Standardisation and the struggle for social legitimacy – fairtrade labelling as a tightrope walk between human development and market acceptance. Paper presented at the 25rd EGOS Colloquium, sub-theme 13: The social dynamics of standardization, 2–4 July 2009, Barcelona, Spain.

Rhodes, Roderick Arthur William (1997). *Understanding governance: Policy networks, governance, reflexivity and accountability.* Maidenhead, UK: Open University Press.

Rhodes, Roderick Arthur William (2000). Governance and public administration. In Jon Pierre (Ed.), *Debating governance. Authority, steering, and democracy* (pp. 54–90). Oxford: Oxford University Press.

Rose, Nicolas, and Miller, Peter (1992). Political power beyond the state: Problematics of government. *British Journal of Sociology, 43*(2), 172–205.

Rosenau, James (2003). *Distant proximities. Dynamics beyond globalization.* Princeton: Princeton University Press.

Ruwet, Coline (2009). Towards the democratization of standards development? ISO 26000 as an experiment of democratizing ISO. Paper presented at the 25rd EGOS Colloquium, sub-theme 13: The social dynamics of standardization, 2–4 July 2009, Barcelona, Spain.

Ruwet, Coline, and Tamm Hallström, Kristina (2007). How are the contents of multi-stakeholder standards shaped? The danger of using stakeholder categories as analytical tools – the case of the ISO 26000 standard on social responsibility. Paper presented at the 23rd EGOS Colloquium, sub-theme 40 Organizing the shape and create markets, 5–7 July 2007, Vienna, Austria.

Ruwet, Coline, and Tamm Hallström, Kristina (2008). Should CSR's "C" be dropped? Lessons from the process of setting the ISO 26000 on social responsibility. Revised unpublished version of 2007 paper.

Schmidt, Susanne K., and Werle, Raymund (1998). *Coordinating technology – studies in the international standardization of telecommunications.* Cambridge, MA, USA: The MIT Press.

Scholte, Jaan A. (2005). Civil society and democratically accountable global governance. In David Held, and Mathias Koenig-Archibugi (Eds.), *Global governance and public accountability* (pp. 87 –109). Oxford: Blackwell Publishing.

Sikka, Prem, and Willmott, Hugh (1995). The power of "independence": Defending and extending the jurisdiction of accounting in the United Kingdom. *Accounting, Organizations and Society, 20*(6), 547–581.

Smith, Jackie (2005). Globalization and transnational social movement organizations. In Gerald F. Davis, Doug McAdam, Richard W. Scott, and Mayer N. Zald (Eds.), *Social movements and organization theory* (pp. 226–248). Cambridge University Press.

Smith, Jackie (2008). *Social Movements for Global Democracy*. Baltimore: John Hopkins University Press.

Stinchcombe, Arthur (1965). Social structure and organizations. In James March (Ed.), *Handbook of organizations* (pp. 142–193). Chicago: Rand McNally & Co.

Stokke, Olav Schram; Gulbrandsen, Lars H.; Hoel, Alf Håkon, and Braathen, Jonette (2005). Ecolabelling and sustainable management of forestry and fisheries: Does it work?. In Magnus Boström, Andreas Føllesdal, Mikael Klintman, Michele Micheletti, and Mads P. Sørensen (Eds.), *Political consumerism: Its motivations, power, and conditions in the Nordic countries and elsewhere* (pp. 291–317). Copenhagen: Nordic Council of Ministers, available at http://www.norden.org/pub/velfaerd/konsument/sk/TN2005517.pdf.

Streeck, Wolfgang, and Schmitter, Philippe (1985). Community, market, state – and associations? The prospective contribution of interest governance to social order. In Wolfgang Streeck, and Philippe Schmitter (Eds.), *Private interest government. Beyond market and state* (pp. 1–29). London: Sage.

Synnott, Timothy (2005). Some notes on the early years of FSC, available at http://www.fsc.org/fileadmin/webdata/public/document_center/publications/Notes_ on_the_early_years_of_FSC_by_Tim_Synnott.pdf (accessed 14 May 2009).

Tamm Hallström, Kristina (2004). *Organizing international standardization – ISO and the IASC in question of authority*. Cheltenham, UK and Northampton, MA, USA: Edward Elgar.

Tamm Hallström, Kristina (2006). ISO enters the field of social responsibility (SR) – construction and tension of global governance. In Folke Schuppert (Ed.), Vol. 4 *Contributions to governance – global governance and the role of non-state actors* (pp. 117–156). Berlin, Germany: Nomos Publisher.

Tamm Hallström, Kristina (2008). ISO expands its business into social responsibility. In Magnus Boström, and Christina Garsten (Eds.), *Organizing transnational accountability. mobilization, tools, challenges* (pp. 46–60). Cheltenham, UK and Northampton, MA, USA: Edward Elgar.

Tamm Hallström, Kristina (2009). Forthcoming. The use of democratic values in the ISO 26000 process on social responsibility. In Göran Sundström, Linda Soneryd, and Staffan Furusten (Eds.), *Organizing Democracy. The construction of agency in practice*. Cheltenham, UK and Northampton, MA, USA: Edward Elgar.

Thedvall, Renita (2006). *Eurocrats at work. Negotiating transparency in postnational employment policy.* Stockholm Studies in Social Anthropology, 58, Stockholm, Sweden: Almqvist & Wiksell International.

van Rooy, Alison (2004). *The global legitimacy game. Civil society, globalization, and protest.* Basingstoke: Palgrave Macmillan.

van Tatenhove, Jan; Arts, Bas, and Leroy, Pieter (2000). *Political modernisation and the environment: The renewal of environmental policy arrangement.* London: Kluwer Academic Publishers.

Vifell, Åsa (2006). *Enklaver i stater. Internationalisering, demokrati och den svenska statsförvaltningen* [Enclaves of States. Internationalisation, democracy and the Swedish administration]. Doctoral dissertation in political science. Stockholm: Stockholm University, department of Political Science.

Waddell, Steve, and Khagram, Sanjeev (2007). Multi-stakeholder global networks: Emerging systems for the global common good. In Pieter Glasbergen, Frank Biermann, and Arthur P.J. Mol (Eds.), *Partnerships, Governance and Sustainable Development* (pp. 261–287). Cheltenham: Edward Elgar.

Wälti, Sonja; Küjbler, Daniel, and Papadopoulos, Yannis (2004). How democractic is governance? *Governance, 17*(1), 83–113.

Ward, Trevor; Phillips, Bruce and Chaffee, Chet (2003). Conclusions. In Bruce Phillips, Trevor Ward, and Chet Chaffee (Eds.), *Eco-labelling in Fisheries. What is it all about?* (pp. 186–191). Oxford: Blackwell Science.

Weber, Max (1919/1977). *Vetenskap och politik.* Gothenburg, Sweden: Korpen.

Weber, Max (1948). *Ekonomi och samhälle – förståelsesociologins grunder.* Volumes 1 and 3. Lund, Sweden: Argos.

Weir, Anne (2000). Meeting social and environmental objectives through partnership: The experience of unilever. In Jem Bendell (Ed.), *Terms for endearment. Business, NGOs and sustainable development* (pp. 118–124). Sheffield: Greanleaf Publishing.

Werle, Raymund, and Iversen, Eric (2006). Promoting legitimacy in technical standardization. *Science, Technology & Innovation Studies*, 2, 19–39.York: Oxford University Press.

Young, Joni J. (1994). Outlining regulatory space: Agenda issues and the FASB. *Accounting, Organizations and Society, 19*(1), 83–109.

http://www.fsc.org
http://www.fsc-watch.org
http://www.msc.org
http://www.iso.org

Index